THE SPIRAL OF TIME SERIES

RAV DOVBER PINSON

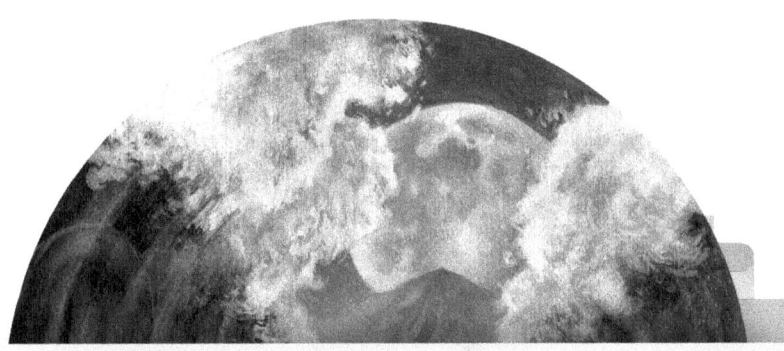

THE MONTH of NISAN

vol **1**

MIRACULOUS AWAKENINGS
◆ FROM ABOVE ◆

IYYUN PUBLISHING

THE MONTH OF NISAN © 2021 DovBer Pinson. All rights reserved. No part of this book may be used or reproduced in any manner whatsoever without written permission except in the case of brief quotations embodied in critical articles and reviews.

>Published by IYYUN Publishing
>232 Bergen Street
>Brooklyn, NY 11217

http://www.iyyun.com

Iyyun Publishing books may be purchased for educational, business or sales promotional use. For information please contact: contact@IYYUN.com

Editor: Reb Matisyahu Brown

Developmental Editor: Reb Eden Pearlstein

Proofreading / Editing: Reb Levi Robin

Cover and book design: RP Design and Development

Cover image:
"Nisan" by Dario Mekler from The Misaviv Hebrew Circle Calendar 5777 by Deuteronomy Press. www.circlecalendar.com

pb ISBN 978-1-7367026-0-4

Pinson, DovBer 1971-
The Month of Nisan: Miraculous Awakenings from Above
1. Judaism 2. Jewish Spirituality 3. General Spirituality

vol 1

THE MONTH *of* NISAN

MIRACULOUS AWAKENINGS
FROM ABOVE

INCLUDING ESSAYS ON
THE HOLY DAYS OF PESACH

IYYUN PUBLISHING

ב"ה

THE MONTH OF NISAN

DEDICATIONS

THIS BOOK IS DEDICATED
IN LOVING MEMORY OF

⇥ CHANA ELKON ע״ה ⇤

by her loving family.

May the merit of the learning in this volume bring blessings upon them and their home, and the elevation of her soul.

THIS BOOK IS DEDICATED
BY

CHESTON & LARA MIZEL שיחי׳

In honor of their beautiful children.
May they be Zoche to raise them to Torah, Chuppah and Good Deeds and may they be a shining light for Klal Yisrael.

CONTENTS

2 | OPENING
5 | THE MONTH OF NISAN: An Overview
14 | PERMUTATION OF HASHEM'S NAME
15 | TORAH VERSE
19 | LETTER
22 | NAME OF THE MONTH
36 | SENSE
42 | SIGN
54 | TRIBE
58 | BODY PART
61 | ELEMENT
63 | TORAH PORTIONS
65 | SEASON OF THE YEAR
69 | THE HOLIDAYS OF THE MONTH
72 | SUMMARY OF NISAN
97 | PRACTICE & INTENTION

CONTENTS

PART TWO:

149 | Essays on Pesach as a Time of Awakening from Above.

150 | THE STATE OF KLAL YISRAEL / THE PEOPLE OF ISRAEL, WHEN THEY LEFT EGYPT:
49th Level of Impurity or the 49th Level of Purity?

168 | STAGES OF FREEDOM:
Redeeming our Name, Voice, Speech, Song, and Silence

OPENING

Each month of the year radiates distinct qualities and provides unique opportunities for personal growth and spiritual illumination. Accordingly, every month has a slightly different climate and represents a particular stage in the 'story of the year' as expressed through the annual cycles of nature. The winter months call for practices and pursuits that are intrinsically different than those of the summer months. Some months are filled with Holy Days, some have only one, and others none. Each month therefore has its own natural and spiritual 'signature.'

According to the deeper levels of Torah, each month's distinct qualities, opportunities, and natural phenomena correspond to a twelve-part symbolic structure; the spiritual nature of each month is articulated in 12 points of light, which include: 1) a permutation of Hashem's Four-Letter name, 2) a verse from the Torah, 3) a letter of the Aleph Beis, 4) the meaning of the name of the month, 5) an experiential sense, 6) a Zodiac sign, 7) a tribe of Israel, 8) a body part, 9) a natural element, 10) a unit of successive Torah portions that are read during the month, 11) a season of the year, and 12) the Holy Days that occur during the month.

By reflecting on these twelve aspects, an ever-ascending spiral of insight, understanding, and practical action is revealed. Learning to navigate and harness the nature of change by holistically engaging with the cycles of time, adds a deeper sense of purpose and heightened presence to our lives.

The present volume will delve into the spiritual nature of the first month of the monthly cycle, the month of Nisan, according to these 12 categories.

NOTE: For a more comprehensive treatment of this 12-part system and the overarching dynamics of the "story of the year", an in-depth introduction has been provided in Volume One of this series, The Spiral of Time: Unraveling the Yearly Cycle.

THE MONTH OF NISAN

THE MONTH OF NISAN
Miraculous Awakenings from Above

The month of Nisan is the first month of the spring and summer months; in the Gregorian calendar it arrives approximately around mid-March into April.

Every season brings about a distinct visceral sensation. There is a tangible energy in the air that most people sense when spring comes around, especially when it comes after a long, harsh and cold winter. It is the sensation of renewal, renewed hope, possibility, freshness.

Spring brings with it a feeling that there is life again; that the affliction, as it were, of the barren, cold winter is over. Empty pastures, leafless trees, flowerless branches begin to bloom. Warmer weather is upon us, and the lands become fertile again.

An overwhelming feeling of hope enters with the new season. When spring is in the air, people feel more optimistic, thankful and grateful. There is something about the light and the warmer air, the budding of the flowers that gives us a sense that life is a wonderful gift, and that it is not to be wasted or taken for granted. This was especially true in times gone by, when winter meant a scarcity of food, cold weather and harsh conditions meant a struggle for mere survival. When spring finally came along, it was eagerly anticipated and graciously welcomed as a gift from Above, a respite from the oppressive winter. Spring was and is a time when people instinctively let go of their anxieties, fears, and uncertainties, opening themselves up to feeling comforted, embraced and cherished.

As the world wakes up from its winter slumber, we too feel renewed, awakened and filled with a sense of renewal. There is a newness in the air. In the words of one of the Rishonim (10th to 16th century Rabbis) כל ציץ חדש, לזמן חדש, יצא שוחק, לקראת בואו / "Every new bud for a renewed time, comes forth with joy and laughter to greet its arrival" (Poem by Rav Moshe Even Ezra). All of nature is re-awakened during this precious time, and everything is filled with newness and joy.

Spring represents a time of plenty, abundance, sunshine, hope, and possibility. Redemption, on whatever level, feels palpable and accessible. In spring, the world is redeemed from the cold winter, the flower is redeemed from the tree, the grass from the earth, and we too feel that redemption is possible.

A whole complex of ideas, including newness, redemption, going out of Egypt, and being freed from slavery, is intricately bound with the idea of *Aviv* / spring. With the onset of winter, everything that had seemed so lively in the summer now seems lifeless and hopeless. Then spring arrives and everything comes alive; there is a rebirth of hope and possibility. This is the secret of *Yetzias Mitzrayim* / the Going Out of Egypt. We, along with the earth, are literally freed from all our constriction and lifelessness with the arrival of spring. Appropriately, there is a tradition from the Geonim that the ultimate Resurrection of the Dead will occur in the month of Nisan (*Tur*, Orach Chayim, 490, in the name of Rav Hai Gaon), as all of nature is 'resurrected' at the time following the proverbial death of winter.

For this reason, the overarching sensations in the spring are renewal, relief, and redemption, opening us up to experiences of gratitude and expressions of giving thanks.

THE BEGINNING OF THE LUNAR YEAR

According to our calendar, there are two cycles occurring simultaneously within a year. There is the lunar cycle, the 12 months of the year, which each begin on the New Moon, and there is the solar cycle, which serves to correlate the calendar with the seasons. The first month in the lunar cycle is Nisan, whereas the beginning of the solar cycle occurs on Rosh Hashanah in the month of Tishrei.

Speaking of Rosh Chodesh Nisan, the Torah says, ...החדש הזה / "*this month* shall mark for you the beginning of the months; it shall be the first of the months of the year for you" (*Shemos*, 12:2).

Rosh Chodesh Nisan is thus the beginning of the lunar year, as commanded by the Torah. It initiates a new cycle of lunations, representing a new beginning.

In fact, the whole idea of a month, in Hebrew חדש, is connected with the word חידוש / *Chidush* / novelty, newness. Each month, timed with the appearance of the new moon, epitomizes a fresh start, a blank canvas, filled with infinite potential.

The solar cycle is connected with the world of observable predictability. Unlike the moon, the sun does not change, other than its position, as it travels through the sky. "There is nothing new under the sun" (*Koheles*, 1:9), as the sun represents the world of constancy and rigid linear structure, it rises and sets in the same way each day. The moon, however, represents renewal. The light of the moon changes throughout the month; it waxes and wanes, sometimes observably and sometimes not, depending on the day of the month and the rotation of the sun and (or) planet. So, while there is nothing new under the sun, the Zohar adds appropriately, "but the moon is new" (*Zohar* 1, p. 123b). The moon represents a paradigm of renewal and the potential for novelty that breaks the monotony of linear time, represented by the sun. The moon exemplifies חדש, meaning both 'month' and 'newness'.

It is for this reason that the redemption from exile, the Exodus from Egypt, was a great חידוש / *Chidush* / novelty, as "no slave had ever escaped from Egypt," let alone be set free — and let alone an entire people. This monumental event, which we commemorate on Pesach, occurs in Nisan, the first month of the spring, and the first month of the lunar cycle. (In the words of the Maharal, כי ראוים להיות נגאלים בחודש ראשון במה שהוא ראשון / "It is worthy for them to be redeemed in the first month, as it is first" *Gevuras Hashem*, 35.) This ultimate redemption begins to occur on the Rosh Chodesh of this month, and finds its full expression in the middle of the month, on the full moon, when we enact the Pesach Seder. Therefore, in this month, the power of newness, of Chidush, is expressed on three different levels at once: Aviv / spring / seasonal, Nisan / the first of the months / annual, Rosh Chodesh / the new moon / lunar.

A MONTH OF GEULAH / REDEMPTION

On Pesach night, we recite in the Haggadah a quote from the Mechilta: יכול מראש חודש, תלמוד לומר ביום ההוא... / "One might think that (the telling the story of the Exodus) must begin from the first of the month of Nisan. The Torah therefore says, 'On that day,'...and when on that day? When Matzah and Maror are placed before you," i.e., on Seder Night. Why would one have thought that the story should be told as early as Rosh Chodesh Nisan, a few weeks before the date of the Exodus?

Speaking about the Exodus from Egypt, the Torah says, "Today you are leaving, in the month of Aviv" (*Shemos*, 13:4). The Torah seems to be stressing two things: you are leaving Egypt, and specifically during the month of Nisan (referred to in the Torah as Aviv). Then the Torah continues, "*Shamor* / remember the month of Aviv." We need to know and remember that we left Egypt in the month of Aviv. According to the Ramban, from here we can deduce that there is a Mitzvah of the Torah to remember the day and also the month we left Egypt. In other words, there is a Mitzvah to recall the month itself.

This is because the narrative of *Yetzias Mitzrayim* / the Going Out of Egypt is intimately intertwined with the *Aviv* / spring season. They are in a sense one and the same; the narrative of liberation is the concrete reality and context of the month, as expressed in the blossoming world. We were collectively freed from bondage, slavery and hopelessness, in a month that embodies the qualities of freedom, renewal and rejuvenation. Therefore, we need to know and remember the *entire* month of Nisan. Based on these correspondences, there was a *Sevara* / suggestion of the sages that we ought to honor the beginning of the spring by starting to speak about the Exodus from Egypt, on Rosh Chodesh, the beginning of the month; as the month itself contains the energy of liberation.

Being freed from Egypt, on all levels of reality — physically, environmentally, mentally, emotionally and spiritually — is the focus of the entire month. All of Nisan is connected with freedom, seeking release from constriction and barrenness. This process engenders a deep appreciation of life, hope, and the flowering of renewal. The verse cited above then continues: ועבדת את־העבדה הזאת בחדש הזה / "And you shall keep this service (the Mitzvos of Pesach) throughout this month" (*Shemos*, 13:5). The liberation and freedom of Pesach permeates the entire month of Nisan.

Nisan is called the *Chodesh haGeulah* / the month of Redemption: "When Hashem created and chose the world, Hashem established months and years. And when Hashem chose Yaakov and his children, the tribes of Israel, the children of Yaakov, קבע בו ראש חדשים של גאולה, שבו נגאלו ישראל ממצרים ובו עתידין ליגאל / He established the head (first) of the months for Redemption, for in it Klal Yisrael was redeemed from Egypt, and in it Klal Yisrael will be redeemed in the future" (*Medrash Rabbah*, Shemos, 15:11).

Nisan is a month of redemption. The entire month is infused with the power to implant within us, the seeds of *Emunah* / faith and the foundations of *Avodas Hashem* / service of Hashem (*Emek Davar*, Shemos, 34:18). It is a time of inner and personal development. This is because the very foundation of all movement in life, whether that movement is emotional, mental or spiritual, is the awareness that every moment offers us new possibilities, and our past is not inevitably a prediction of our future. We have a moment-to-moment choice to begin again. This is the power and message of Nisan.

There is a power of *Hischadshus* / renewal latent within the created world, as Creation rises up from *Ayin* / no-thing-ness into *Yesh* / existence every moment anew. From the perspective of Yesh, the created entity, the world exists in the present and was created in the past. Experientially, this means our present state is conditioned by our past, and what will become of us in the future is determined by our choices from our past. Our past choices, in turn, were determined by previous choices, going back to the moment of our conception. Yet, from the perspective of Ayin, Divine 'no-thing-ness', every Yesh is a *Chidush* / novelty, something entirely new, not a given or an inevitability. Experientially, this means that at any moment we have the ability to instantaneously refresh our lives, and unburden ourselves of past experiences and choices. We can be free of our past, liberated in the present to envision the future.

The חדש / *Chodesh* / month of *Geulah* / redemption implants within us a consciousness and awareness of חידוש *Chidush* / newness, novelty, and renewal. It gives us the power to enter the Ayin, the fluid, formless dimension of the moment. Like the budding rose emerges from amidst the thorns, after a long cold winter, and as Klal Yisrael emerges from slavery into freedom during this month, we too can be redeemed from our negative past, and enter Geulah in this time.

When speaking about the liberatory potential of חדש / *Chadash* / the new, and the experience of חידוש / the radical novelty residing within the Ayin moment, it is important to point out that while the redemption of Klal Yisrael from Egypt begins with החדש הזה / 'this month' — our descent into Egypt and the beginning of our slavery also began with a type of חדש / newness. The Torah begins to describe our descent into slavery as follows, "And a חדש / new king arose in Egypt, who did not know Yoseph" (*Shemos*, 1:8). He did not remember how, through the innovations of Yoseph, the entire Land of Egypt was spared of famine. Clearly, we need to distinguish between healthy, empowering and liberating Chadash, and Chadash that causes more disempowerment and leads to deeper enslavement.

There is a Chadash of redemption, in which the past is not "forgotten," but it does not have a choke hold on the present. This allows one to live freely in the present and start anew while still taking full responsibility for and learning from their past. There is also a Chadash of exile and disempowerment, characterized by forgetfulness or lack of responsibility. One can believe that they are truly living in the present, but they are merely avoiding the past, living 'for' the now, without regard to the lessons of history.

Nisan gives us the *Koach* / power to connect with the holy, positive, empowering and liberating potential of Chadash. And yet, paradoxically, we tap most deeply into this power when we remember our past.

SPRING AND NISAN: A TIME OF DIVINE *Chesed* / KINDNESS

In this month, we receive the gift of renewal and release from our inner places of affliction and constriction. Spring itself is an exodus from the 'affliction' of winter. Thus, the entire month of Nisan, and in particular the days of Pesach, are an expression of Divine *Chesed* / loving kindness. This is the character trait embodied by the patriarch Avraham. Nisan is Chesed and "light." (Whereas, for example, Iyyar is connected with Gevurah and 'darkness'. *Pesikta Rabsi*, Parsha 20:2, *Matan Torah*.)

As everything is blossoming with life, Nisan feels miraculous after the dead of winter. When spring arrives, we recognize the blessings of life more vividly. There is a palpable sense that our own existence is a gift; perhaps even an undeserved gift. For this reason, we may find bubbling up within us a deep sense of humility and gratitude, both on a physical, visceral level, and also on an inner spiritual level.

Enshrined within the month of Nisan, there is a Mitzvah to eat Matzah, the bread of humility and simplicity. While eating Matzah, we realize we did not actually 'deserve' to go up out of Egypt and become a holy people. As the angels on high argued, "They (the Egyptians) were idol worshipers and they (the Nation of Israel) were also idol worshipers," so why split the sea for them (*Medrash Tehilim*, 1:20. *Zohar* 2, 170b. We were stuck in the 49th level of Tumah: *Zohar Chadash*, Yisro. *Shaloh haKadosh*. Alshich. *Siddur Reb Shabtai*, Haggadah. *Chayei Adam* (in their respective Haggadahs, on *Matzah Zu*) *Chesed l'Avraham*, 2:56. The Ramdu, *Eis LaChenina*. *Ohr haChayim*, Shemos, 3:8. The *Beis haLevi*, Derush 2, and many others. Although see the Leshem, *Sefer haDeiah*, 2, Derush

5:2, 5, where he explains that Klal Yisrael was actually on a very high spiritual level). And yet, we were redeemed as a gift from Above, without regard to our 'deserving' it or not. Nisan and Pesach are a time of Hashem's infinite *Chesed* / Divine, unconditional loving-kindness.

THE META-REASONS FOR SPRING AND NISAN

Nisan offers us the gifts of spring and the possibility of renewal, miraculous redemption and humble gratitude. Yet, we need to go deeper, and explore the spiritual realities that give rise to these seasonal qualities. What are the cosmic metaphysical dynamics that cause or manifest as 'spring' in the month of Nisan? A certain permutation of the Divine Name, a certain letter of the Aleph Beis, a sign, a tribe, and so forth, are symbolic interfaces that reveal a multidimensional complex of energies and ideas that undergird and inspire the "season of our freedom." Now let us explore these details in depth, and discover the Divine potential of this month and season.

PERMUTATION OF HASHEM'S NAME

Yud-Hei-Vav-Hei, the four letter essential name of G-d referred to simply as *Hashem* / the Name, is the Divine Source of all Reality. The last three letters of the Name, Hei-Vav-Hei, create the word *Hoveh* / 'is', the present. The root of this verb means, 'to bring into being'. The first letter of the Name, Yud, serves as a prefix to the last three letters: *Yud-HoVeH*. In this way, the Yud modifies the verb to represent a perpetual activity. In other words, the Divine Name can be understood to mean, 'That Which is Continuously Bringing Being into Being'.

For numerous reasons, this Essential Name cannot be spoken. Therefore a common practice is to rearrange its four letters into an alternate construction that may be pronounced. This produces the word *HaVaYaH*, which literally means 'Being-ness'. This aspect of the Name refers to the Ultimate Being, who is the Source and Substance of all that is. The Ultimate Being does not depend on anything else to exist. It gives rise to all past, present and future manifestations, thereby bringing all things into existence ex nihilo, i.e. *Yesh meAyin* / being from non-being. Accordingly, the individual words *Hayah* / 'was', *Hoveh* / 'is' and *Yihyeh* / 'will be', are all encoded within the Essential Name.

As *HaVaYaH* is the Source of all Being and Time, it is thus *connected with* actual time. Because of this, each unique period in time is imbued with a special connection to the Essential Name. In terms of the months, this quality is expressed through a unique permutation of the four letters that comprise the Name — each month has an inner light that shines through the prism of a permutation of the four letters of the Name. Each permutation communicates a different spiritual dynamic which is part of the Divine signature encoded within that particular month.

The sequence of the four letters in Hashem's name which corresponds to the month of Nisan is the original sequence of the Four Letters of the Name: Yud-Hei-Vav-Hei.* This is the 'perfect' sequence of the letters and it represents a downward flow of Chesed (*Zohar* 2, 186a. Whereas "Backwards is the secret of Gevurah": *Zohar* 2, 52a).

---

* The vowels in the sequence of Hashem's name for the month of Nisan are Chirik-Yud, Patach-Hei, Sh'va-Vav, Kamatz-Hei.

Yud is a letter shaped as a point or a dot (י), whereas the letter Vav is a line (ו). Both of these are considered 'masculine' letters, called *Mashpi'im* / givers. The letter Hei (ה), shaped as a receptacle or open box, is a 'feminine' letter, called a *M'kabel* / receiver. This month's sequence represents the proper flow of Divine influx, from 'givers' to 'receivers'. For example, if these four letters are written vertically, the Yud is on top giving to the Hei below it, which gestates that which has been received before 'birthing' it in a new form back out into the world, and the Vav is then giving to the Hei at the bottom, which fulfills the same developmental function as the first Hei. This sequence embodies a flow from the Giver Above to the receiver below, from Heaven to earth, from inside to outside, and from hidden to revealed. This flow has two stages; first there is a downward motion from the Yud to the Upper Hei, then another downward motion from the Vav to the Lower Hei. In Nisan, the dynamic of Giver and receiver is thus clearly laid out; the Creator is defined as the ultimate Giver, and we creations are the ultimate receivers of the Creator's giving.

Nisan is referred to as the Month of Miracles. On Pesach we celebrate that Hashem took us out of Egypt, a miraculous event in which the Transcendent One descended to the depths of Egypt, so to speak, to take us out of our lowliness and physical-mental-spiritual slavery. This type of movement is called *Isarusa d'le'Eila* / 'awakening from Above', for it is an unearned gift of kindness flowing down to us from Heaven, arousing and awakening us from our slumber. Despite our not being prepared for it, we were lifted out of our bondage and redeemed from our enslavement. This same uplifting quality manifests for us every year.

At the peak of the month of Nisan, on the 15th day of the month, we celebrate Pesach. During the Seder night, the latent freedom that has been hidden deep within us, whether by suppression or oppression, is released and revealed. We are given this freedom, this *Gadlus* / greatness, as a gift, as will be explored further on.

Night is generally not a time to recite *Hallel* / the songs of praise (it is recited only during the 'day', and only when the redemption is complete: *Megilah*, 14b). But on Seder night, because of the overwhelming Gadlus — the expansion into redemption, freedom, and clarity — we recite a blessing and sing Hallel, despite it being nighttime. We amplify our joy and gratitude openly, thanking Hashem for giving us the gift of freedom, the gift of Gadlus that is given to us on Seder night.

TORAH VERSE

Each sequence of the four letter Divine Name that shines during each month is rooted within a particular verse in the Torah (*Tikunei Zohar*, Hakdamah, 9b. *Eitz Chayim*, *Sha'ar* 44:7). In other words, there is a 'verse of the month' consisting of a four-word sequence, in which each word either begins or ends with the letters of the *Tziruf* / name-formation for that month, and the order of the Tziruf follows the corresponding verses (*Mishnas Chasidim*, Maseches Adar, 1:3). The meaning and context of the verse connected with each particular month is, of course, also part of the revelation of that month's guiding light.

In Nisan, the permutation of the Divine Name of the month, Yud-Hei-Vav-Hei, is found in the beginnings of four words in *Tehilim* / Psalms (96:11): ישמחו השמים ותגל הארץ / ***Yismechu HaShamayim V'sageil HaAretz*** / "the Heavens will be happy and the earth will rejoice." During this time, there is joy and happiness all around, in Heaven and on earth, above and below. The nouns in this verse also allude to a flow from the Giver Above to a receiver below; it begins with *Shamayim* / Heavens, and concludes with *Aretz* / earth, showing that the Higher Reality is "happy" and therefore desires to bestow kindness upon the lower reality, and cause it to "rejoice."

The verbs in this verse also describe this same type of energetic flow. First comes *Yismechu*, from the word *Simchah* / happiness, and then comes *V'sageil*, from the word *Gilah* / rejoicing. *Yismechu* refers to an inner joy, hidden within the mind, a subtle 'intellectual' joy, a type of *Yishuv haDa'as* / settledness of consciousness (*Sheim Meshmuel*, Moadim 139). For this reason, the word בשמחה / *b'Simchah* / 'with happiness' has the same letters as the Hebrew word מחשבה / *Machshavah* / thought (*Tiferes Shelomo*, Sha'ar haTefillah, p. 10), suggesting an interior, mindful joy of consciousness itself. *Gilah* is related to the word *Gilu* / to reveal, suggesting that *v'Sageil* refers to a form of joy that is expressed outwardly, in the world (*Imrei Tzadikim*, p. 65). First comes *Yismechu haShamayim* — the 'hidden' joy of the Heavens, and then *v'Sageil haAretz*, the revealed joy of the body and the earth.

There are ten general types of joy expressed in the Torah (*Avos d'Rebbe Nasan*, 43:9), each one slightly different from the others. Simchah is the subtle mental joy of knowing you are doing the right thing and are in the right place in your life. This form of joy is felt in the mind and does not show up in the body. The outward expression of Gilah is present for example when a person is laughing at a joke or rejoicing at good news. His body shows signs of joy, yet, it is possible that inwardly or 'intellectually' the person is actually feeling depressed. The novelty of the Simcha-to-Gilah flow described in the previous paragraph is that one's inner joy filters down and is expressed outwardly, making one's outer joy into a faithful reflection of one's inner joy. This represents a smooth movement from one's internal state to one's external appearance, a flow from one's highest reality to one's lowest or most material sphere of expression, from invisible subjectivity to revealed objectivity.

In this month, there is a perfectly effortless flow from the Divine Above to Klal Yisrael below. The inner light of our soul becomes tangible in our body and we are given priceless gifts from Above.

LETTER

As the Torah, the 'blueprint of creation', is written in *Lashon haKodesh* / the Holy Tongue of Hebrew, the Sages teach that each of the 22 letters of the Aleph Beis contains a host of metaphysical energies and creative potentials. According to the *Sefer Yetzirah*, a profound book of early Kabbalah that pays particular attention to the inner dimensions of the Hebrew letters, the 22 letters are divided into three categories: three "Mother Letters," seven "Double Letters" and 12 "Simple Letters." Each month is connected with one of the 12 Simple Letters.*

---

* For a more in-depth analysis of all three categories of Hebrew letters and their relationship to the calendar, please see the introductory volume in this series, *The Spiral of Time: Unraveling the Yearly Cycle*.

The letter associated with Nisan, the first month of the monthly cycle, is the first Simple Letter, the letter Hei. Hei is the sound similar to an *'H'*. It can sometimes create a subtle consonant sound, and it can also be a silent letter, usually at the end of words. Sometimes a 'silent Hei' is present to indicate a vowel and sometimes it is just for emphasis, but in any case, it is not pronounced, rather it is expressed as a silent rest, as it were.

Even when the consonant sound of Hei is pronounced, it mimics a sigh of tiredness or relaxation (Rav Baruch of Kosov, *Amud haAvodah*, Kuntreisim leChochmas Emes, p. 328). Simply, Hei represents a state of rest.

Within the name of Hashem (the Yud-Hei-Vav-Hei) there are the two 'active' or 'masculine' letters, the Yud, a point or dot, and the Vav, a line, and there are two 'passive' or 'feminine' letters, the two Heis.

HaVaYaH (the Yud-Hei-Vav-Hei) refers to the Ultimate Being, which is the Source and Substance of all that is, all of space and time. Within the experience and flow of time, there are active elements, such as the six days of productive work and engagement in bettering the world, and there are the passive elements of time, such as the seventh day of Shabbos and *Yamim Tovim* / holidays.

This dynamic between 'six' (active) and 'seven' (resting) is reflected in the rhythm of every week, and within the cycle of every seven years. For six years we are instructed and empowered to work the land, but in the seventh year we need to leave the land to rest and reset. This seventh year of rest is known as the *Shemitah* / Sabbatical year in the Land of Israel. "Six years you shall sow your field, and six years you shall prune your vineyard, and gather in its fruit, but the seventh year shall be a Shabbos of rest to the land" (*Vayikra*, 25:3-4). The six days, and more broadly the six years of work and toil, are connected with the active letters in the Name of Hashem (especially the letter Vav, which has a value of 6), and the Seventh Day and seventh year are connected with the Lower Hei of Hashem's name.

The Lower Hei symbolizes the type of rest that manifests with each *Shemitah* / Sabbatical year. During a Shemitah year, the earth is given rest from planting and sowing. The resting of the earth corresponds to the Sefirah of Malchus and the lower Hei. In our personal lives, this means resting from action — non-doing.

This is a lower freedom; the land is free from being planted and worked (so that the earth can replenish itself: Rambam, *Moreh Nevuchim*, 3:27). Ceasing from work in this way allows us to recognize that the earth belongs to Hashem (*Sanhedrin*, 39a. *Sefer haChinuch*, Mitzvah, 84), and also to focus more on spiritual work.

Yet, there is a larger cycle, which is seven times seven. After seven cycles of seven years (49), the fiftieth year is the year of *Yovel* / Jubilee, which is a manifestation of the Higher Hei in Hashem's Name (the *Zohar*, 3:108a, says that the complete freedom of Yovel corresponds to the upper Hei in the Name of Hashem). In the fiftieth year, not only does the land rest, but during ancient times when most of the Jewish People lived in the Land of Israel, each in their designated tribal territories, slaves were set free. In this case, not only does Malchus, the World of Action, the Lower Hei rest, but *Binah* / understanding, the World of Thought or higher consciousness, the upper Hei, rests as well. This is a higher form of rest. In our personal lives, it means resting one's mind from restless or self-enslaving thoughts; a mindful, contemplative Shabbos of consciousness.

Thus, the Higher Hei represents a kind of 'existential' rest and freedom; a release from the bonds of mental 'slavery', including dependency, addiction and constricted consciousness.

When, in the Shemitah year, the land is allowed to rest, the lower Hei of the Divine Name thus experiences a degree of redemption. In our own lives, this lower, relative type of freedom manifests as freedom from reactive behavior. If someone insults you, and you choose not to react but remain silent, you are refraining from planting new seeds of conflict. However, although you did not act in retribution, your mind and heart might still be upset. This is a mere 'one-dimensional' freedom. You have merely silenced your reaction, but you have not yet transformed your reactivity at its root. Your will and desire was to react, and this may indeed remain your will deep down. You just controlled yourself in the world of action. This is no small feat, but it is not the ultimate level of freedom.

Shemitah brings freedom for the land — freedom in terms of outer action and reaction, symbolizing the body. Yovel, however, brings freedom for enslaved human beings, symbolizing human consciousness. We can become free in the world of 'thought' or consciousness, as well as in action. This is the complete freedom that comes from Binah, the higher Hei.

Binah contains seven permutations of each emotional attribute within itself. This internalized 'multi-dimensionality' has a balancing effect, freeing one from mindless reactivity. In a state of clear understanding, our emotions are contained and balanced by a higher perspective sometimes called 'intellect'. For example, even when you are experiencing the expansive emotion of *Chesed* / giving, from a higher perspective you can simultaneously be in touch with the contractive emotion of *Gevurah* / withholding. You are 'thinking out of the box' of whatever you might be feeling, free to respond with awareness, rather than merely reacting or repressing your reaction.

This freedom of Yovel is gifted to us, unearned and undeserved, like the miraculous gift of spring which follows the long, barren winter. In Nisan, and specifically on Pesach, we are gifted the fiftieth level, albeit temporarily. This gift is more gradually integrated on Shavuos, 50 days later (as explored in The Month of Sivan, at length). As an allusion to this idea, the Going Out of Egypt is mentioned in the Torah exactly 50 times (*Zohar* 2, 85b. 3, 262a. *Tikkunei Zohar*, Tikkun 32), representing the higher freedom of Yovel.

HEI & THE POWER OF BIRTH

The letter Hei is connected with rest and freedom from enslaved actions and constricted ways of thinking. It is also appropriately associated with the concept of birth, as is the month of Nisan in general (*Tanchuma*, Ha'azinu 1. בתחלה כשנולד, נדמה כטלה שהוא רך). Primarily, Nisan is the month of the 'birth' of Klal Yisrael.*

---

* In our generation, which is, G-d willing, the last generation of exile and the first generation to be birthed into Geulah, the Rebbe of blessed and righteous memory, was born on the 11th of Nisan.

Klal Yisrael was 'born' in *Yetzias Mitzrayim* / the Going Out of Egypt, much like a baby being pulled out of the womb (*Medrash Tehilim*, 114:6). In fact, the entire unfolding of the Ten *Makos* / Plagues, with the water turning into blood and the sounds of the frogs and so forth, are similar to the contractions and difficulties of childbirth (Arizal, *Likkutei Torah*, Shemos, p. 121). While still enslaved in Egypt, Klal Yisrael was asked to perform the *Korban Pesach* / the Paschal Lamb, and it was sacrificed immediately preceding the Exodus. In order to eat of it, the offering needed to be roasted over a spit, "with its head upon its legs" (*Shemos*, 12:9), meaning in the fetal position like a baby in the womb (*Nidah*, 30b. *Derech Mitzvosecha*, Korban Pesach. Arizal, *Ta'amei haMitzvos*, Bo). This tells us that while we were still in Egypt we were in a condition of *Ibbur* / like a fetus in a mother's womb (*Sha'ar haKavanos*, Derushei Pesach 1), and *Yetzias Mitzrayim* was the difficult labor leading to our birth.

And not only are we born as a people during the month of Nisan, but, according to the sages, the entire 'external' world is birthed in the month of Nisan. There is a well-known debate among the sages of the Mishnah, Rebbe Eliezer and Rebbe Yehoshua, as to when the physical world of time and space was created: was it in Nisan, the first of the months, or was it in Tishrei, the head of the year? (*Rosh Hashanah*, 11a). Parenthetically, this is more than a literal question; it is rather a deep philosophical and existential question: in what energetic reality is Creation birthed? What is the basic quality at the foundation of the world, the quality of Tishrei (nature and responsibility) or Nisan (miracles and faith)? Either way, Rebbe Eliezer's opinion is that the Creation was on the first day of the month of Tishrei, whereas Rebbe Yehoshua asserts that it was the first day of the month of Nisan.* In addition, they also argue over when the *Avos* / the Patriarchs, Avraham, Yitzchak, and Yaakov, were born. Rebbe Eliezer says they were born in Tishrei, and Rebbe Yehoshua says they were born in Nisan. This extends into a further argument about when the ultimate Redemption will take place. Rebbe Eliezer says it will be in Tishrei, and Rebbe Yehoshua says it will be in Nisan.

Reconciling these two opinions, and diffusing their argument, Tosefos (the classic commentary on the Gemara from the Ashkenaz scholars from the 12th to 15th centuries) writes that both opinions are correct and there is no contradiction (Tosefos, *Rosh Hashanah*, 27a). There is first the Creation that occurs within the Creator's mind, as it were — the thought to create — and then there is the actual articulation of this thought, which after a period of gestation is revealed. The thought of creating was 'born' in the Creator's mind, as it were, in the month of Tishrei, whereas the actual Creation took place six months later, in Nisan.

---

* All, however, agree that Tishrei is the "seventh month," and in this way, within the context of months, it is the middle month of the year. Thus, whereas Nisan is the "head," the 'top' of the lunar cycle, Tishrei is like the 'heart' or 'stomach' of that cycle, the place of the womb. The debate between Rebbe Eliezer and Rebbe Yehoshua is thus about whether the world is created from the head or the heart / stomach / navel / womb. This is an argument in the world of *Shanah* / time, and similar debates are found within the worlds of *Nefesh* / Soul and *Makom* / Space. Regarding the dimension of *Nefesh* / soul, human beings, Chazal / our sages, debate about where the fetus is created, from the 'head' or the middle, the 'navel': הולד נוצר מטיבורו או מראשו, *Sotah*, 45b. Regarding the dimension of *Olam* / space, Chazal also debate from where the world was created, from the sides (beginning) or from the middle, the center, עולם מאמצעיתו נברא או עולם מן הצדדין נברא: *Yuma*, 54b.

In terms of revealed reality, Nisan is the "birth of Creation."*

Some time later, the holy Arizal expanded and further revealed that in Tishrei the world is in a fetal state in the womb, and in Nisan the child is born (*Sha'ar haKavanos*, Rosh Hashanah, Derush 1. *Pri Eitz Chayim*, Sha'ar haShofar, 5. *Sefer haBris*, Ma'amar 2:8. In the context of many Halachic issues, Nisan precedes Tishrei; see, for example, *Rosh Hashanah*, 4b). In this way, Tishrei is when the seed of creation is implanted within the mind/womb of Hashem, and Nisan is the 'Exodus' from the womb: the actual birth of Creation, the birth of humanity as a whole, and the birth of Klal Yisrael.

All forms of birth are thus connected with Nisan and with the letter of the month, the letter Hei. Hei is a letter of birth and Creation (Pesach is also connected with the letter Hei: *Aderes Eliyahu*, Emor 23).

Indeed, it is with the letter, the sound-vibration, of Hei from which Creation emerged, as our sages say, "With the letter Hei this world was created" (*Menachos*, 29b). אלה תולדות השמים והארץ בהבראם: אל תקרי בהבראם אלא בה' בראם / "'These are the chronicles of the Heavens and the earth בהבראם / *b'Hibaram* / when they were created' (*Bereishis*, 2:4); do not read בהבראם / *when they were created*, rather read בה' בראם / *with a Hei* He created them" (*Menachos*, ibid. *Medrash Rabbah*, Bereishis, 12:1).

---

* Rav Yonasan Eybeschutz has a wonderfully novel approach to reconcile this argument. Both opinions maintain that the 'world' was created in Nisan, the first month of the year, and in the Mazal of *T'leh* / Aries. Yet, during the first Six Days of Creation, the sun was moving through the *Mazalos* / zodiac very quickly, and so on Friday it was already the zodiac sign of Scales, the 'month' of Tishrei. Thus, 'man' was created in Tishrei, whereas the world was created in Nisan, and there is no argument. Today, on the first day of Tishrei, Rosh Hashanah, we celebrate the creation of man.

"Things" in Hebrew are called *Devarim* / words. Everything in Creation is a manifestation of a particular spiritual sound vibration, another combination of 22 letters of the Aleph Beis, a Divine 'word'. Hashem 'speaks' the world into being: "Let there be light, and there was light." The physical phenomenon called *Ohr* / light is an outward expression of the spiritual vibration of the three letters that comprise the Hebrew word *Ohr*: Aleph-Vav-Reish. Darkness arises from another Divine vibration, one formed from the letters that make up the word *Choshech* / darkness.

On a deeper level, all of the letters of speech are articulations of the simple outward flow of breath, which is the '*hhh*' sound of the letter Hei. When we speak, forming vowels and consonants with our mouth, we are harnessing and directing the exhale through the five 'potentials' of the mouth: the lips, tongue, teeth, palate and throat. The same processes are mirrored in the Divine 'mouth', Above. The root of all the 'sounds' that make up Hashem's words is the Divine breath, the 'hhh' sound of Hei.

Just as the outbreath moves from the lungs to the mouth even before we articulate a word, so the Divine breath is the beginning of the movement of Divine speech and Creation, before it is articulated. As this silent Hei travels from the belly and lungs into the mouth, it is 'shaped' into other sounds. In this way, each of the 22 letters is a crafted articulation of the subtle 'hhh' sound of the breath. When this 'hhh' sound vibrates the vocal cords and passes through clenched teeth, for instance, it becomes the 'zzz' sound of the letter Zayin, and when it meets closed lips, it becomes the 'mmm' of the letter Mem, and so forth. The letter Hei is at the root of all Divine creative processes, vibrations and utterances.

Words are letters that are streamed together in specific ways. The undifferentiated sound of the outbreath, the Hei, is filtered through a series of contractions and pressures creating a complex of meaningful differentiations of sound. But Hei in itself is free of contractions and pressures. It is a restful, effortless sound, as the Medrash says, כל האותיות יש יגיעה בקריאתן, עקימת פה ונענוע לשון ושפתים, אבל ה"א אין בה נענוע כלל / "All the letters demand exertion when reading them: movement of the mouth, the tongue and lips. But with the sounding of the Hei there is no movement (just breath)" (*Pesikta Zutrasa*, Bereishis, 2:4. Or, "All letters are created through contracting the mouth, not so the letter Hei, which is released from the mouth without contracting the mouth." *Tanchuma*, (Buber) Bereishis, 16). This is another reason that our sages speak of Creation via the letter Hei. The Rif, Rabbeinu Yitzchak Alfasi (1013–1103), one of the early Rishonim, writes (on *Sanhedrin*, 16b) that Hashem created the world with the letter Hei, "because for all other letters a person needs to strain his mouth when he utters them. However, this is not so with the letter Hei (it is merely an outbreath); similarly, HaKadosh Baruch Hu, the Holy One, created the world without strain and without exertion." The root of Creation is rest.

Hei is the letter of creation; its power can even allow a person to bear children (*Igeres haTiyul* [brother of the Maharal], Sod, Hei). We find with Avraham and Sarah, the grandparents of Klal Yisrael (לא בסבי טעמא *Shabbos*, 89b), that they were well-advanced in years and Sarah was not able to have a child with Avraham. When the Creator added a letter Hei to their names, Avram became AvraHam, and Sarai became SaraH, they miraculously gave birth to a child, Yitzchak. Although Avraham was able to father Yishmael even before the addition of a Hei to his name, this was only possible because of the letter Hei in the name of Hagar, Yishmael's mother.

In fact, all the matriarchs of Klal Yisrael, Sarah, Rivkah and Leah contain a letter Hei in their names. The only matriarch not to have a Hei in her name was Rochel, and that is why she also had extended difficulty in becoming pregnant. (Regarding Rivkah's difficulty, *Bereishis* 25:21 says, כי עקרה הוא. The *Kri* / the way this phrase is read, is "*she was barren*", but the *K'siv* / the way it is written, is הוא / "*he was barren.*") When Rochel gave her maidservant בלהה / Bilhah as a wife to Yaakov, Rochel as well was able to give birth, as the name Bilah contains two letter Heis; one Hei giving her the ability to give birth and one for Rochel, to help her give birth.

All objects and subjects are created through particular letter combinations, yet everything is rooted in the *Hevel haElyon* / The Supernal Divine Outbreath. In breath itself there is the potential for all articulations and sounds. Since everything is rooted in the Hei, the Hei represents the pure potential of all things. In the dimension of Hei, everything is possible. It is the dimension of *Ayin* / no-thing-ness, in which nothing is defined or differentiated, and therefore the letter Hei is the womb from which all things emerge. It is the miraculous, the unpredictable, the Exodus.

Nisan is therefore considered the month of *Nisim* / miracles (In fact, Nisan and Nisim have the same numeric value, 170). A miracle is often an exchanging of one particular manifestation for another, for example, when *Mayim* / water is turned into *Dam* / blood. The energy and matter of blood comes to being through the spiritual vibration of the letters Daled and Mem, together spelling the word *Dam*. Water, on the other hand, is called *Mayim* because the energy and matter of water comes to be through the spiritual vibration of the letter sequence of Mem, Yud, Final Mem. Yet from a place of Divine breath, before there is any articulation or diversification into different letters and sounds, water can be blood and blood can water. In breath, all is undifferentiated oneness; in speech, the specificity and multiplicity of creation is manifest.

As will be explored further on, this power of Hei, the power to manifest miracles, is accessed through the experience of the Divine *Ayin* / no-thing-ness. This is an experience of deep humility and a lack of any real separation between us and HaKadosh Baruch Hu, the Source of both the unmanifest and all concrete manifestation. In this space of no-space, all returns to its root, and can therefore reemerge as something completely different, transformed.

INTERNALIZING THE LETTER HEI

Like the restful letter Hei, we too rest during the week of Pesach from eating חמץ / *Chametz* / leavened breads and foods which represent inflated egocentrism. Instead we eat מצה / Matzah. The words *Chametz* and *Matzah* each contain three letters. They share two of these letters, the Mem (מ) and Tzadik (צ\ץ), and they differ in one letter. The different letters are the Ches (ח) in *Chametz* and the Hei (ה) in *Matzah*. There is only a tiny difference between a Hei and a Ches in their graphic design: the left leg of Hei is suspended in mid-air (ה), whereas the left leg of Ches rises up to the top (ח).[*]

---

[*] כל אות צריכה להיות גולם אחד / "Every letter needs to be of one substance… besides the letters Hei and Kuf. …And if the left leg of the Hei or Kuf touches the roof, the Sefer Torah is *Pasul* / void": *Tur* and Mechaber, *Shulchan Aruch*, Orach Chayim, 36, from the Rosh, *Sefer Torah*, 12. The *Beis Yoseph* (on the

The empty gap in the Hei represents humility, and an openness to receive from and connect to the Infinite Source of the Unmanifest. The closed gap in the Ches represents arrogance or ego, being shut down and shut in. On Pesach, we need to puncture and deflate the Ches of *Chametz*. (Significantly, בדיקת חמץ / checking for Chametz, is related to the word בוקע / pierce, thus, בדיקת חמץ means to 'pierce the Chametz', i.e., piercing the Ches and making it into a Hei.) We need to create an opening in our arrogance and sense of entitlement, and transform our Ches into a Hei, our Chametz into Matzah. And when we deflate and humble our ego, we become open to receive from the deepest level of creation, the Supernal Hei, the root of infinite potential and

---

Tur) writes that this is the ruling of the Rosh, based on the Gemara in *Shabbos* 104a, and this is also the opinion of the Rashba (*Teshuvas haRashba*) and the Ramban and the Ran writing on the Gemara in Shabbos. Yet, the Rivash rules that בדיעבד if the Kuf touches the roof, the Sefer Torah is Kosher, as suggested from *Menachos*, 29b. אמר רב אשי חזינא לספרי דוקני דתלי לכרעא דה״א ומדקאמר ספרי דוקני נראה שאינו לעיכובא אלא למצוה מן המובחר: *Teshuvas haRivash*, Teshuvah 120. The Tashbetz also rules that בדיעבד it is Kosher: *Teshuvas haTashbetz*, Part 1:50-51. In fact, he brings an interesting story from the Ran: עוד שמעתי כי הרב ר' נסים גרונדי ז״ל שהי' בברצלו״נא והיה רבם של רבותי ז״ל שכתב ס״ת לעצמו והיו רגלי הקו״ף דבוקות לגגם. ואנוידל סופר שהי' ש״ץ במיורק״ה שאל אותו על זה כמדומה לו שהוא פסול ושתק הרב ז״ל ולא ענהו / "I heard that the Ran when he was in Barcelona (and was the teacher of our teachers) that he himself wrote a Sefer Torah and the left leg of the Kuf was actually touching the roof. And the Sofer who was the Shaliach Tzibur in Mallorca once asked the Ran about this, and the Ran just remained silent and did not answer" (Regarding this Sefer Torah, see also, the Rebbe, *Igros Kodesh* 15, p. 189). This is a very interesting story, as the Ran himself rules in *Shabbos*, 104a in his commentary on the Rif, that the left leg must not touch the roof, and yet, he himself wrote such a Torah with the left leg of the Kuf touching the roof. Perhaps, there is a difference regarding other people — outside of Spain writing such a Torah (where the Mesorah is not to attach the left), and in Spain, where the Mesorah was to write with the Kuf touching the roof.

miracles. On Pesach we draw the Hei down into our own name and identity and internalize it, enabling us to 'give birth', to renew life, and to manifest miraculous events.

NAME OF THE MONTH

*A*CCORDING TO THE TORAH, NAMES ARE VERY powerful (*Yuma*, 83b. *Tanchuma*, Ha'azinu. *Berachos*, 7b). Composed as they are of Hebrew letters, they represent and define the energy or attributes of that which is named (*Tanya*, Sha'ar haYichud ve-haEmunah, 1). Our names, for instance, unlock and reveal hidden potentials present within our own spiritual makeup. Similarly, names of other people, places and periods of time provide subtle hints as to their deeper purpose or poetic significance. Additionally, changing one's name is akin to a kind of rebirth; some might even say that a change of name initiates a change of *Mazal* (Rashi, *Bereishis*, 15:5. *Rosh Hashanah*, 16b. Yerushalmi, *Shabbos*, 6:39. Rama, *Yoreh Deah*, 335:10).

Each of the 12 months of the year has a distinct name, and every name has a meaning. According to our Sages, the current names we have for the months were imported to our tradition upon our return to Israel from the Babylonian Exile (They can in fact be traced to ancient Babylonian or Akkadian names. See Yerushalmi, *Rosh Hashanah*, 1:2. *Medrash Rabbah*, Bereishis, 48:9. Tosefos, *Rosh Hashanah* 7a. *Even Ezra, Chezkuni*, Shemos, 12:2). In the times before the Babylonian Exile, the names of the months were mostly known by their number in the sequence of the year. For example, the month of Av was called 'the Fifth Month', and Cheshvan was known as 'the Eighth Month'.

Nisan is one of the names of the months of the year that is mentioned in Tanach, in post Babylonian Exile writings, first called as such in the *Megilah* / scroll of Esther (*Megilas Esther*, 8:9), along with Adar (*ibid*, 3:7) and Teves (*ibid*, 2:16. Elul and Kislev are mentioned in *Nechemyah*, 6:5 and 1:1). Nisan is also mentioned in the Book of *Nechemyah* (2:1). Prior to the Babylonian exile, Nisan was simply called *Chodesh haAviv* / the Month of Spring.

THE NAME *Aviv*

Before exploring the name of Nisan, a few words about the name אביב / *Aviv*. Aviv simply means 'spring', as Nisan begins the spring months. *Aviv* begins with the letters Aleph and Beis — the first and second letters of the Aleph Beis. As mentioned, sounds, letters and vibrations are the conduits and transmitters of Divine flow. When the letters of a word appear in the sequence of the Aleph-Beis, this represents Divine Compassion, which is an uninterrupted flow from Above to below. When letters appear in a sequence opposite to the Aleph-Beis, it reveals an element of *Din* /

restriction and judgment (*Zohar* 2, p. 51b). The sequence of the beginning letters of *Aviv* suggests a flow from Above to below. Indeed, the entire month of Nisan is a revealing of Hashem's Light and Compassion from the Heavens Above, to us, below.

Everything that we receive from Above flows from Nisan. Rabbeinu Bachya (*Shemos*, 13:4), breaks down the word אביב / *Aviv* and interprets it to mean: אב / *Av* / the father of, יב / the letters Yud-Beis. Yud-Beis is the number 12, signifying the 12 months of the year. In other words, Nisan is the Av, the source, of the 12 months of the year. All of the months of the year flow from Nisan.

Additionally, the word *Aviv* itself means 'father' (Aviv from the word Av / father, first. *Rashi*, Shemos, 23:15). In Hebrew, when a word is doubled it can indicate a smaller version of the thing. For example, עץ is tree, and עציץ / is a small plant. The same is with אב /*Av* and אביב /*Aviv*; Aviv is a small *Av*. The 'smallness' of Aviv indicates its quality of humility and no-thing-ness, which is the silent breath of the Hei, the letter of the month, as discussed.

Nisan, the month of Aviv, is the first, the father of the *months* of the year. The first *day* of the year, which follows the solar count of the seasons, is Rosh Hashanah, the first day of Tishrei. In contrast to the forward flow of the word אביב, the word תשרי / *Tishrei* is spelled Tav-Shin-Reish-Yud, which is the last three letters of the Aleph Beis in reverse order, and then an earlier letter, Yud. This demonstrates that Tishrei is characterized by a movement from below to Above and is a time of Judgment and Teshuvah / returning, as in Rosh Hashanah and Yom Kippur. It is the opposite of Aviv, which is the correct order and a time of miracles and revelations.

Nisan is the first חדש / *Chodesh* / month and is thus the headquarters of all חידוש / *Chidush* / newness. Months follow lunar cycles, and the moon is renewed every month with Rosh Chodesh, the first day of the new month. The newness of the moon is a breaking out of the monotony of linear time, of 'day-in day-out' sameness. It catapults us into a sense of the miraculous *Hischadshus* / renewal of life. Things are going in a certain direction, the moon is waning, and then all of a sudden there is a glimmer of hope, a miraculous reappearance of the moon in the sky. This is also the gift of the spring, of Aviv, and the gift of יציאת מצרים / the Going Out of Egypt.

THE NAME '*Nisan*'

Since the end of the Babylonian Exile, and even before the completion of the building of the Second Beis haMikdash, the Month of Aviv has been called Nisan. A question remains, though, whether *Nisan* is a Torah derived word, or non-Torah derived. There is a general argument over the source of the current names of the months. Are they originally Hebrew names, rooted in the Torah, that were lost over history and then rediscovered (*Divrei Torah* [Munkatch], Mahadurah, 2:7), or are they names that we borrowed from our hosts in Babylon, as noted in some sources (*Yerushalmi*, Rosh Hashanah, 1:2, and so forth). If the name *Nisan* has a Hebrew root, it would be the word *Nes*, meaning 'miracle'.

Even if the word *Nisan* is not a Torah word originally and comes from a non-Hebrew word, the custom of *Chazal* / our sages is to tease out Hebrew meaning from the words of other languages (Rav

Yaakov Emdin, *Lechem Nikudim*, Avos, 2:14). Even though the names of the months are Babylonian or Akkadian in origin, our sages interpreted and explained these names according to their Hebrew cognates. *Nisan* is the perfect example, as Chazal say the name reflects the *Nisim* / miracles which were revealed during that month (*Pesikta Zutresa*, Bo, 12:2. *Medrash Lekach Tov*, Shemos 12:2). In the words of Rashi (*Berachos*, 56a), שע"י נסים נקרא ניסן / "*Nisan* is called *Nisan* because of the miracles." (The Rebbe coined a saying [based on the Gemara, *Berachos*, 57a and Rashi, regarding seeing חנינא / *Chanina* in a dream, see also *Maharsha* ad loc.], that "One who sees the word ניסן / *Nisan* [another word with two Nuns] in a dream, many *Nisim* / miracles will be performed for him": *Sefer haSichos*, Tav / Shin / Nun / Aleph, 1. p. 383. *Haggadah, Likutei Ta'amim u'Minhagim*, 2. p. 689. Many quote this saying without knowing its source.)

Nisan is by definition the month of miracles, and the month of *Geulah* / redemption. If the word *Nisan* is not indigenous to Hebrew, then it comes from the Akkadian word *Nissanu* / 'to move' or 'to start'. In Nisan, HaKadosh Baruch Hu inspires us with revealed miracles, and moves us, from Above, out of exile into Geulah.

There is actually a notable distinction between ניסן / *Nisan* and נס / *Nes*. In Hebrew, when the final Nun ן is placed at the end of a noun, it implies a person or doer. For example, when a final Nun is placed at the end of שקר / lie, it becomes שקרן / liar, and at the end of the word פחד / fear, it becomes פחדן / fearful person. ניסן / Nisan is thus the 'agent of' ניסים / miracles; it has the character and constitution of the miraculous. Whereas the month of Tishrei is the month of Creation and Sivan is the month of Revelation, Nisan is the month of Miracles.

Every letter in the Torah represents a number: Aleph is 1, Beis is 2, and so forth. The first nine letters in the Aleph-Beis are the single digits, the next nine letters in the Aleph-Beis are double digit numbers, and the last four letters are triple digit numbers. The letters in the word ניסן / Nisan are Nun (50), Yud (10), Samach (60), and Nun (50). In regular *Gematriya* / numerical value, these add up to 170, but in the system of *Mispar Katan* / small numerical value (in which 50 is 5, and 60 is 6), the total is 26. This is the same value as the Name 'Hashem': Yud (10), Hei (5), Vav (6), Hei (5) = 26.* As described in the section on the letter permutation of the month, the correspondences between Nisan and the Name of Hashem express an unimpeded Divine flow from Above to below that is present during this month. This dynamic lays the foundation for a month of miracles and new beginnings, as explained above.

---

* Another way to correspond the Four Letter Name of Hashem, the Yud-Hei-Vav-Hei, to the four letter word *Nisan*, is as follows: The Yud in Hashem's Name corresponds to the Yud in the word *Nisan*. Yud is 10 and in every letter in the name of Hashem there are ten dimensions, alluding to the 10 Sefiros. Within Hashem's Name there are two letters Hei. Hei is 5, which, multiplied by 10, is 50. Two Heis is twice 50. In Nisan there are two Nuns, Nun being the number 50. Within the name of Hashem there is a Vav (6), and multiplied by 10, it is 60 — corresponding to the Samach (60) within the word Nisan.

SENSE

THE CONVENTIONAL WORLD IDENTIFIES FIVE SENSES, YET *Sefer Yetzirah* speaks of 12 *Chushin* / senses. In addition to the more commonly understood definition of what comprises our 'senses', the word *Chush* can also mean, 'a sensitive level of perception, understanding, appreciation and skill' in relation to a particular psycho-spiritual process or function. For example, a 'sense of sleep' is a deep understanding and appreciation of sleep which includes both: what sleep represents spiritually, as well as the practical skills and abilities that make one's experience of sleep both peaceful and beneficial. (Indeed, the definition of 'sleep' can also include preparations for sleep, in the words of Rashi, דאית ליה בשכבך כל זמן שבני אדם עוסקין לילך ולשכב / "(according to Rebbe Eliezer) who maintains that 'when you sleep' refers to the entire time that people are busy going to sleep: Rashi, *Berachos*, 4a).

Overall, these 12 *Chushim* are also the 12 activities that the Torah describes the Creator performing in the perpetual process of maintaining the world (*Pirush haRa'avad, Sefer Yetzirah*). As we are created in the Divine image, we also possess all 12 Chushim, at least in potential. Even if a person is born blind, for example, he always has the potential for sight and thus can give birth to a child who can see; it is just that he is currently missing the physical vessels (capacity) for sight (*Pirush haGra*, Hakdamah, Sefer Yetzirah). However, the sense of sight is included in the person's Divine image, as it were.

There are 12 Chushim and every month gives us the ability and strength to expand our vessels or potentials for a particular Chush, along with its corresponding Divine Attributes. When we align and refine our consciousness via these Chushim, we can harness the qualities of each month in a most profound and meaningful way.

According to Sefer Yetzirah, the *Chush* / sense or faculty corresponding to Nisan is speech. Interestingly, the Mazal / astrological sign of the month, which we will discuss more in depth, actually alludes to an inability to speak: Aries, like all other signs besides Gemini, is depicted without a mouth (*Zohar* 2, p. 78b. See Chida, *Midbar Kedeimos*, 41). To more deeply understand the relationship between speech and Nisan, we need to look to the time when the month of Nisan was established as the first month of the lunar year. The command to establish Nisan as the first of the months was introduced by the Torah as the first Mitzvah, given on the very cusp of liberation. Leading up to this moment, the Jewish people were enslaved, physically, emotionally, mentally and spiritually, in Egypt.

Indeed, the Zohar teaches that in Egypt the notion of "speech" was in exile (*Zohar* 2, 25b).

A slave has no voice. The Torah's account of the People of Israel's time in Egypt suggests that they were silent until late in the period of their exile. Perhaps they were too overwhelmed to feel anything, or perhaps they had become so accustomed to their harsh subservience, that they no longer noticed it enough to describe or protest it. In any case, they were completely stuck, and not even a cry or groan could escape their lips.

This exile of speech, this inability to give voice, even to oneself, to one's wants, needs and feelings, is the deepest exile possible. To be human is to be a *Medaber* / a speaking being. When we cannot express ourselves, never mind articulate to others what we are thinking or experiencing, we are, in a sense, less human. Taking away the ability to speak robs people of their humanity. Speech implies choice, for through language we define our reality. A slave cannot really listen to another, nor hear the possibility that his life could change for the better.

Even Moshe, who was essentially above slavery — as he was born into the un-enslaved tribe of Levi and raised as an Egyptian prince — even he could not speak easily. At the Burning Bush, Moshe says of himself, לא איש דברים אנכי /I am not a man of words" ..., כי כבד־פה וכבד לשון אנכי / for I have a כבד / hard (or heavy) mouth and a hard tongue" (*Shemos*, 4:10).

Significantly, the word פרעה / *Pharaoh* can be permuted and broken into two words which spell פה רע / *Peh Ra*, meaning 'negative mouth' (Arizal, *Sefer haLikutim*, Shemos 2). This symbolizes the force of negativity and reactivity that sought to keep us stuck in Mitzrayim, with no voice. Our reality and narrative were imposed upon us.

In Egypt, the slaves were forced to do *Avodas Perech* / harsh labor. The word *Perech* can be broken down into the two words, *Peh Rach*, meaning 'weak mouth' (*Sotah* 11b). Having a weak mouth means that even when the yearning for freedom was awakened, Klal Yisrael was not able to articulate their thoughts, dreams, and yearnings. Their mouth was in a weak condition. The *Ra* / Negative, harsh, enslaving mouth of Pharaoh weakened the mouths of Israel, causing an exile of speech.

The book of the Torah that speaks about our release from Egypt is called *Shemos* / Names. This book begins when the children of Israel are still free people, and it lists the names of each family. ואלה שמות בני ישראל הבאים מצרימה... ראובן שמעון לוי ... and goes on to name all the 12 Tribes. They enter Egypt a proud people, with distinct names and expressions of identity. Then they descend physically, mentally and spiritually into a condition of slavery, a state of *Tumah* / stuckness, to the point that they no longer have names.

During the period of Klal Yisrael's slavery, when the Torah seems to give names to the two midwives, Shifrah and Puah (1:15), our sages understand that these are not really names, but descriptions of their work: they were שמשפרת את הולד / beautifying the children, and שהיתה פועה / they were 'cooing' to them (*Sotah*, 11b), and these women were either Yocheved and Miriam or Yocheved and Elisheva (the wife of Aaron).

When the Torah mentions the parents of Moshe (2:1), it only says, "A man from the house of Levi married a daughter from Levi." No names are given. When they have a child, the Torah does not say that his parents gave him a name (Chazal, in *Sotah*, 12a, tell us that his name was Tov or Tuvia, but he is not named clearly in the Torah, at this point). He is only named later by his adoptive Egyptian (albeit, converted) mother — a person who is not enslaved, and is thus able to speak and bestow a name.

Up until this point in the Torah, upon the birth of a child, it immediately narrates the mother or father giving a name. Here, in stark contrast, the greatest prophet and leader of Klal Yisrael is born, but is not overtly named. Not only are they a nameless people, they cannot give names either.

Being able to name things is a most essential human trait. One of the first acts of Adam is to name and define the animals: ויבא אל־האדם לראות מה־יקרא־לו וכל אשר יקרא־לו האדם נפש חיה הוא שמו / "And (Hashem) brought them (the animals) to the man to see what he would call them, and whatever the man called each living creature, that would be its name" (*Bereishis*, 2:19). By naming the world around us, we, like Adam, are able to navigate our reality more easily, and define our space.

A human being names, defines, and contextualizes his reality. Losing the ability to name and be named represents a state of existential exile from one's humanity. Free people have names and give names. A slave is a speechless, nameless statistic, with no independent personal identity or sovereignty.

Klal Yisrael starts off proud, with unique names and expressions and strong identities, and then descends into a condition of mental and spiritual slavery, a state of stuckness and *Tumah* / impurity, paralysis and silence.

As slaves, Klal Yisrael was forced to build פתם ואת־רעמסס / Pisom and Ramses (*Shemos*, 1:11). These are two cities, but their names are also indicative of this enslavement. פיתום can be split into two words, as in פי תום / Pi Tom, shut mouth, a closed mouth (פי תהום / the mouth of the abyss: *Sotah*, 11a), and Ramses can be split into is רע ממס *Ra Moses* (Moshe is 'Moses' in Egyptian). This refers to a 'negative Moshe', a constriction of the capacities of Moshe to become the great 'speaker' on behalf of Hashem and Klal Yisrael.

Essentially, there are three levels: פה רע / *Peh Ra* / negative month, פה רך / *Peh Rach* / weak mouth, and פה סח / *Peh Sach*, 'a mouth that speaks' (*Zohar Chai*, Tazria). These form a narrative; the force of Peh Ra causes the weakness of Peh Rach, but then the *Geulah* / redemption breaks through by means of Peh Sach, thus פסח; the liberation and empowerment of speech.

Sometimes, the best form of 'speech' is taking up self-mastery and remaining silent. The middle letters of the word מצרים / Egypt are יצר / inclination, referring to our negative inclination. The first letter is an open Mem (מ) which represents an open mouth, and the final letter is a closed Mem (ם) which represents a closed mouth, a mouth that is silent. A spiritually, emotionally, mentally healthy *Peh* / mouth (פ is numerically 80) is one that knows when to be open and when to stay closed (two Mems also equal 80). The exile in Egypt represents a separation, disunity and confusion between these two potentials of the mouth, symbolized by the two Mems. In a state of Mitzrayim, our yetzer leads us to express *Peh Ra* / negative speech, words which would be best unspoken, and this leads to a weak, powerless mouth. At the same time, when we need to speak up or articulate our experience, we are unable to do so. The redemptive experience of Pesach brings about a healthy Peh Sach, a balanced, wise power of expression.

As Klal Yisrael leave Egypt, they come upon a place called פי החירת / Pi HaChiros (*Shemos*, 14:2). Why is it called such? Says Rashi, in the name of the Mechilta: הוא פיתום, ועכשיו נקרא פי החירות על שם שנעשו בני חורין / "This place is actually פתם but now it is called פי החירת / the mouth of Cheiros / freedom, as they have become a free people."

A transformation occurs in the very place of constriction. What was once פי תום / *Pi Tom*, sealed mouth, or "the mouth of the תהום / abyss" (*Sotah*, 11a, the buildings they constructed sunk, one by one, into the mouth of the earth), is now Pi HaCheirus, the mouth of freedom. The people's mouth was opened, they were redeemed from the abyss of exile, and they could now speak the truth and praise HaKadosh Baruch Hu for their freedom.

SPEAKING & FREEDOM

Any act of speaking is an act of free choice, for it is through language that we come to define our reality. A slave, or anyone in a physical, emotional or mental state of exile, does not have this luxury. A slave cannot express or reveal who he really is, or what he is really thinking and dreaming about, for his 'narrative' is externally imposed upon him.

While the ability to speak freely is an expression of freedom, on a deeper level, speaking itself facilitates freedom. We create the reality of freedom when we speak of it. In this way, we can liberate ourselves through speech. The ability to speak and articulate our feelings is a vital key to redemptive, healing catharsis and mindfulness.

Just as the Creator created the world through the medium of Divine speech, we too create our world, or at least our experience of it, through our words. We can only experience freedom when we are able to proclaim ourselves or refer to ourselves as free. On Seder night, which is the full moon and the essence of the entire month of Nisan, we recite the Haggadah with a full voice. Ever since the opening of redemption from Egypt during this month and especially on the night of Pesach, we too are gifted with the ability to proclaim our freedom on all levels of our being, and to actually begin to live from a place of freedom.

The main Mitzvah of the Seder is *l'Sapeir* / to tell the story, and *veHigadeta leVincha* / to tell it to your children, and pass on this experiential knowledge of freedom to each and every person at our Seder table and in our lives. As the Haggadah itself says, "Anyone who elaborates in speaking about the Exodus from Egypt, he is certainly praiseworthy." When we have 'a mouth that speaks', we can liberate ourselves from our own 'weak mouth' and 'negative mouth', and allow others to do the same.

A CHUSH IN REFINED SPEECH

Redeemed speech is actually more than being able to express yourself when you need and want to. It is more than the ability to express your deepest desires and yearnings, and more than the mental, emotional headspace to express who you are. Redeemed speech is also a quality of 'how' you speak.

How we use our voice, the manner in which we speak, indicates whether we are inwardly free or not. The way a person speaks tells us a lot about the person, revealing inner freedom or inner slavery, whether they are enslaved to their whims and instincts or in control of them. The wise Shlomo haMelech / King Solomon says, דברי חכמים בנחת נשמעים מזעקת מושל בכסילים / "Words spoken softly by wise men are heeded sooner than those shouted by a ruler in folly" (*Koheles*, 9:17). Not only are wise words spoken softly more effective, as the simple reading of this verse tells us, but, in general, a wise person speaks softly, without screaming (Rambam, *Hilchos De'os*, 2:5), and this is a quality of freedom. In fact, you can tell a wise person by the gentleness of their speech (*Otzar Medrashim*). Beyond the tonality of the voice, is also the refinement of their voice. An inwardly empowered individual also speaks בלשון נקיה / clean language, whereas an unredeemed, unrefined individual uses coarse or foul language. This is the deeper reason that Chazal's teaching about speaking בלשון נקיה is recorded in the beginning of *Maseches Pesachim* / the tractate dedicated to the laws of Pesach. Clean, noble speech is a mark of a redeemed and empowered person — one free from Peh Ra and the sense of conflict and reactionism that flow from it.

THE HIGHEST FORM OF SPEECH IS SINGING HASHEM'S PRAISE

In the Seder, at the end of the Maggid section, which is the bulk of the 'speaking' part of the Haggadah, we lift up a cup of wine and declare, "Therefore, it is our duty to thank, laud, praise, glorify, exalt, adore, bless, elevate, and honor the One who did all these miracles for our ancestors and for us!" At this point our power of speech has been redeemed; we speak openly and clearly, with a refined but confident voice, and we use our voice to sing Hashem's praises. Singing Divine praise is related to the tribe of the month, the *Sheivet* / tribe of Yehudah. The name Yehudah is from the word *Hoda'ah* / giving thanks, as will be explored. Praise and thanksgiving is the highest form of speech and expression. In fact, it is the very reason our mouths were created, in the words of the Arizal and later Poskim: הפה נברא להודות לה / "The mouth was created to offer thanks and praise to Hashem" (*Kaf haChayim*, Shulchan Aruch, Orach Chayim, 60:4, in the name of the Arizal. Chida, *Midbar Kedeimos*, Zayin).

This is the Chush of speech of Nisan and the Chush of speech of the Seder night: gratefully recounting our going out of Egypt, speaking deeply about all the miracles* that occurred then, and

---

* The Rambam (*Hilchos Chametz uMatzah*, 7:1) begins explaining the laws of the night of Pesach as follows: מצות עשה של תורה לספר בנסים ונפלאות שנעשו לאבותינו במצרים בליל חמשה עשר בניסן שנאמר זכור את היום הזה אשר יצאתם ממצרים כמו שנאמר זכור את יום השבת / "It is a Torah command to speak, on the night the 15 day of Nisan, about the miracles and wonders that were performed for our forefathers in Egypt. As it is stated, 'Remember this day that you went out of Egypt'; just as it is stated, 'Remember the day of the Shabbos.'"

Many scholars have wondered, why does the Rambam add that we should remember Yetziyas Mitzrayim, as it is stated, "Remember the Shabbos?" What does that add? Let the Rambam just write that on the night of Pesach there is a Mitzvah to speak about the miracles of the Exodus, as the verse says, "Remember this day that you went out of Egypt."

The source for connecting the remembrance of Yetziyas Mitzrayim with the remembrance of Shabbos is from the Medrash (*Shemos Rabbah*, end of *Bo*) which says that HaKadosh Baruch Hu told Moshe, "Go and inform Klal Yisrael that just as I have created the world and told them to remember the day of Shabbos as a remembrance of (My) creation, in the same way, they should remember the miracles that I performed for them in Egypt."

This is the source, but it still does not answer the question. It just seems now there is a question to be asked on the Medrash, as well.

When the Rambam writes that we need to remember *Yetzias Mitzrayim* / the

Going Out of Egypt as we remember Shabbos, it behooves us to see what the Rambam writes earlier, in the laws of Shabbos, regarding remembering Shabbos. In the laws of Shabbos (*Hilchos Shabbos*, 29:1), the Rambam writes, מצות עשה מן התורה לקדש את יום השבת בדברים שנאמר זכור את יום השבת לקדשו. כלומר זכרהו זכירת שבח וקידוש / "It is a Torah command, to sanctify the day of Shabbos with words, as it states, 'Remember the day of Shabbos to sanctify it.' This means, 'Remember it with praise and sanctity.'"

When the Torah tells us to remember the days of *Yetzias Mitzrayim*, and that there is a Mitzvah to do so on the night of Pesach, maybe the Torah just wants us, as simply stated, to "remember" that we left Egypt — and just *think* about the Exodus. How do we know that the Torah wants us to a) do so with words, to speak about it? And b) how do we know that on the night of Pesach we need specifically to לספר בנסים ונפלאות שנעשו לאבותינו במצרים / "speak about the *miracles and wonders* that occurred to our ancestors in Egypt?" In other words, if there is a Mitzvah to not only think about it, but also speak about it, maybe the Mitzvah could be just to articulate the fact that we left Egypt on this night many years ago. How do we know that there is a Mitzvah to speak about the miracles and wonders?

Perhaps this is what the Rambam is suggesting. Regarding Shabbos we learned, זכור את יום השבת לקדשו. כלומר זכרהו זכירת שבח וקידוש / "'Remember the day of Shabbos to sanctify it,' meaning, 'Remember it with praise and sanctity.'" There is a specific type of remembrance of Shabbos, and the purpose of this remembrance is to sanctify Shabbos: זכור...לקדשו / "Remember...to sanctify." The Mitzvah is thus not simply to "remember" Shabbos, but to remember in order to bring us to a point of sanctifying Shabbos, and to do so with words. A similar purpose is behind the remembrance that we perform on Pesach; we need to remember the Going Out of Egypt to bring us to a point of לספר בנסים ונפלאות שנעשו לאבותינו במצרים / "telling, verbally, of the miracles and wonders that were performed for our ancestors in Egypt".

Just as Shabbos is about *Kedushah* / sanctity — as in *Shabbos Kodesh* / "holy, sanctified Shabbos" — Pesach is about miracles. Just as the *Etzem* / essence of Shabbos is Kedushah, the Etzem of Pesach is *Nisim* / miracles.

Pesach Night is a time to open our mouths and speak at length of all the miracles, physical and spiritual, that occurred to our ancestors. We also need to speak of the miracles that continue to occur to us, as we need to envision ourselves as having left Egypt, and are leaving Egypt in every generation, and every day. This night is the redemption of speech.

continue to occur for us every day. On the night of the Seder, we should speak "about all the kindness and miracles Hashem has done for us, both collectively and individually, and one who does so fulfills a Mitzvah" (*Peleh Yoetz*, Erech Dibbur).

We need to express gratitude every day and night, but Seder Night is a vital moment to give thanks to HaKadosh Baruch Hu for all the miracles in our lives, and all the kindness that Hashem has shown us and continues to show us. In this way, as will be further explained, we open ourselves to even greater wonders and miracles. The *Kli* / vessel to receive more and more of Hashem's infinite kindness and blessings, even to a level beyond imagination, is to give continuous, humble offerings of thankfulness and gratitude. Pesach night is the redemption of speech.

SIGN

*E*ach month contains a zodiac influence of a particular constellation, called a *Mazal*. A constellation is a perceivably patterned grouping of visible stars. Today, we count 88 constellations in the night sky. Out of all of these, one constellation is predominantly visible on the horizon at the beginning of each month.

Indeed, each constellation refracts the light of the cosmos differently, alternately reflecting times that are more conducive to war and times that are conducive to the flourishing of peace, for example (*Yalkut Reuveini, Bereishis,* Oys 56). The *Zohar* teaches that each sign can manifest positively or negatively (*Zohar* 3, 282a). In other words, the constellations can have either a productive or a destructive influence in one's life. It is important to keep in mind, however, that even if our proclivities are innate or celestially influenced, we still possess the free choice of response to the situations that arise in our life. In other words, we have the ability to steer the outcome of the conditions that have been projected onto us. For example, a person born under the influence of Mars may have a tendency to be involved with blood, but he or she also has the ability to employ this inherent tendency for good or ill; such a person could therefore choose to be a violent criminal or a life-saving surgeon.

Due to the prevailing popular belief that the stars exert a kind of fatalistic influence upon world history and human development, we need to repeatedly emphasize that anyone can rise above these influences altogether and be unaffected by them. Despite all the forces and influences in our life — physical and psychological conditions, upbringing, education, environment, financial status, and so forth, we always have the freedom to choose. We have the choice to live as either the *effect* of our conditions (as passive receivers of what life serves us), or as the *cause* of what comes next, thereby becoming proactive co-creators of our lives. When we begin to live more proactively, the influences of our birth constellation and the Mazal of each month function less as positive or negative *influences*, and more as *tools* that can help us climb ever higher into our freedom of being.

The astrological influence of Nisan is the *T'leh* / the Lamb or Aries (see also Rashi, *Bava Metziya*, 106b). A lamb is a weak animal, depicted as being silent or 'not having a mouth' (although in the language of the Gemara a lamb is called אימרא, in Hebrew suggesting 'word'). To have the 'weakness' of a lamb means to be an 'undeserving', passive recipient. In the month of Nisan, Hashem, in His Infinite kindness, lifted us out of Egypt, from the place of our oppression and enslavement, despite the fact that we were so sunken into our condition, that we barely had the tools to even imagine ourselves as free.

At the time of our redemption, we were all likened to sheep (*Yirmeyahu*, 50:6. Rabbeinu Bachya, *Kad haKemach*, Rosh Hashanah 2); we were physically and mentally, emotionally and spiritually meek and feeble, trudging along lifelessly without a desire or dream for freedom. Hashem, so to speak, *Pasach* / passed over all these issues, skipped over our pathetic physical and spiritual state, and catapulted us to redemption.

We were commanded to forever after commemorate our redemption from Egypt with a *Korban Pesach* / Pascal lamb offering. Even if we were, or are, meek or ambivalent about our physical, emotional, mental, spiritual need for freedom, on Erev Pesach we are to present a lamb offering. Today, when we do not have the ability to make an actual animal offering, we are to offer ourselves up to the experience of Hashem's Redemption.

Aries is also a Mazal of growth and movement (Ramban, *Shemos* 12:3: כי מזל טלה בחדש ניסן בכחו הגדול, כי הוא מזל הצומה). This is reflected in Klal Yisrael's wandering through the desert for forty years following their liberation, before entering the Promised Land. Those who are born under the sign of Aries are generally energetic and enthusiastic. They are often leaders or pioneers, people who like to start new projects, perhaps even a bit impulsively. All these traits are consistent with the primary spiritual quality of Nisan, which is

Chidush / "newness", being that it is the first *Chodesh* / month of the year. Nisan signals the beginning of spring, the return of enthusiasm, of new life, possibility, energy and vitality.

ניא
TRIBE

EVERY MONTH OF THE YEAR IS CONNECTED WITH ONE OF the 12 Tribes of Klal Yisrael, the 12 sons of Yaakov (*Sefer Yetzirah*. Medrash, *Osyos d'Rebbe Akiva*, Dalet). Nisan is associated with the *Sheivet* / tribe of Yehudah. The meaning of the name Yehudah is 'to give thanks' and specifically giving thanks to Hashem (*Bereishis*, 29:35). When Yehudah was born, his mother, Leah, said (*Bereishis*, 30:35), הפעם אודה את ה' / "This time I will give thanks to Hashem," and thus she called him יהודה / Yehudah, י-הודה / continual praise and thanks-giving. When the letter Yud is placed before a word as a prefix it modifies the verb to represent a perpetual activity. For example, the word עשה / *Aseh* means 'do', whereas with a Yud, as in יעשה / *Ya'aseh*, it means to 'continually do' (Rashi, *Iyov*, 1:5. Rashi, *Bereishis*, 24:45, *Shemos*, 15:1. *Tanya*, Sha'ar haYichud ve-haEmunah, 4). The name *Yehudah* means to continuously offer praise and thanks to Hashem, to be perpetually expressing gratitude.

Leah's voicing of her gratitude is also consistent with the sense of the month, the sense of speech (*Pirush haRavad*, Sefer Yetzirah). An elevated and redeemed sense of speech is characterized by thanksgiving and praise.

Dovid HaMelech / King David, the archetype of kingship, is a descendant of Yehudah. Kingship also alludes to speech, for a king rules over his people through his words, which are received as commands: "For the word of the king is his rule" (*Koheles*, 8:47). Nisan initiates "the New Year of Kings" (*Rosh Hashanah*, 2a). It is thus a new beginning for power and leadership, for creative, empowered speech, and also for expressing thanks.

Originally, the term *Yehudim* / Jews applied only to the descendants of Yehudah, the son of Yaakov and Leah. However, since the destruction of the First Beis HaMikdash, all of Klal Yisrael have been called Yehudim, including those that we know to be descended from another Sheivet, such as Levi. We are named with the word *Hoda'ah* because the essence of Klal Yisrael is our sense of gratefulness and our continuous offering of Hoda'ah and thanks to HaKadosh Baruch Hu, who calls us, עם־זו יצרתי לי תהלתי יספרו / "This people I formed for Myself; My praise they will declare" (*Yeshayahu*, 43:21). According to Rashi, this means, עם זו יצרתי לי למען תהלתי יספרו / "This people I formed for Myself *so that they will* declare My praise." In other words, 'This is the reason I have formed Klal Yisrael, this is the reason I made them a nation: to sing My praise amid the world, and thereby bring My praise into the mouths of all nations.'

We became a nation in Nisan, at the Going Out of Egypt; we were birthed as a people in a month connected with Hoda'ah, as this is our collective mission and purpose. Yehudah is thus the Sheivet that includes all the other Shevatim, providing us all with a collective identity and orientation, in addition to all our individual particularities.

BODY PART

Each month is connected with the general energy and particular vibration of a specific body part. This inter-inclusion of the body within the structure of time empowers us to focus on and refine the spiritual properties and functionings of our physical body, as the spiral of the yearly cycle continues to turn on its Divine axis. The body part associated with Nisan is the right foot, representing *Chesed* / 'loving-kindness' and expansive giving. Pesach is deeply connected with Divine *Chesed*. In fact, one meaning of the word Pesach is 'loving' or compassion (Rashi, *Shemos*, 12:23).

Another meaning of the word Pesach is to 'skip over' (Rashi, *ibid*), since HaKadosh Baruch Hu skipped, as it were, over the doors and homes of Klal Yisrael during the Plague of the Firstborn. A person skips by using one foot at a time to leap, unlike when walking, in which travel is more of a two-footed procedure. In this way, *Dilug* / skipping alludes to a miraculous *Kefitzas haDerech* / collapse of distance, a sudden arrival at the goal, while normal walking represents natural and deliberate progression from level to level. To skip is to jump over or hurry through a process of change, and to attain what is beyond what can be normally reached. Nisan is a time of miracles and skipping over all processes; we spontaneously experience *Gadlus* / greatness, on both a physical and a spiritual level, without our own agency or even participation. All of this is represented by our right foot, the body part of the month.

ELEMENT

There are four primary elements, four fundamental building blocks of Creation: fire, air, water and earth. Each month is associated with one of these four elements. However, it is important to note that while manifesting physically, these elements are also meant to be understood in a much more metaphysical sense as well, as they represent numerous properties, allusions, and correspondences.

Fire is the element of Nisan. 'Fire' means hot and dry and Nisan begins the spring and summer months, when the days become hotter, dryer, and less rainy.

Fire also represents passion and desire. Nisan is the month we were drawn out of Egypt, taken from our physical, emotional and mental state of constriction and brought deeper into freedom and closeness to Hashem. This drama ignited our desire and passion toward HaKadosh Baruch Hu, calling us out of our enslavement to what is familiar, out into the wilderness of our souls.

Fire, the Arizal teaches, is also connected with creativity and innovation. Fire and the manipulation of fire is the engine of human invention. Nisan, being the first of the spring months, following the long cold months, represents new beginnings, the blossoming of the new.

TORAH PORTIONS

Over the course of a month, 4-5 weekly Torah portions or *Parshiyos* are read by the community. These individual portions can be combined and viewed as a single unit based on the particular month in which they are most commonly read. Indeed, one finds, when viewing the Parshiyos through this calendrical lens, that an astounding array of thematic elements consistent with the spiritual energy of the month is revealed.

During the month of Nisan (besides on the actual days of Pesach) the Torah portions that are normally read are the first portions of the Book of *Vayikra* / Leviticus. This book of the Torah primarily speaks of the various offerings that were offered in the Temple and relevant laws of ritual purity and impurity. The offerings hint to the Exodus from Egypt, which began with an offering, the Paschal Lamb, and the ideas of *Taharah* / purity and *Tumah* / impurity are related to the entire narrative of *Yetziyas Mitzrayim* / the Exodus from Egypt. In Egypt, Klal Yisrael was stuck in the deepest abyss of Tumah, the 49th level of impurity (*Zohar Chadash*, Yisro. *Chesed l'Avraham*, 2:56. *Shaloh*, the *Alshich, Siddur Rebbe Shabtai*, and *Chayei Adam*, in their respective Haggadahs, on "Matzah Zu." Ramdu, *Eis laChenina. Ohr haChayim*, Shemos, 3:8. *Beis haLevi*, Derush 2 and many places in Chassidus. Note, *Sefer haDeiah*, 2, Derush 5:2, 5. See *The Month of Adar* for further exploration). As a result of Yetzias Mitzrayim, they were lifted to the peak of the fiftieth level of Taharah, where all the Tumah of the "snake" left them (*Shabbos*, 156a. Tosefos, *Avodah Zarah*, 22b). Then they went on to transcend even death, the meta-source of Tumah itself (*Medrash Rabbah*, Shemos, 41), when, 50 days later they arrived at Sinai.

In general, many of the offerings were brought to atone for past intentional and unintentional *Chata'im* / sins or 'veerings'. In the Torah context, 'sin' leads to ritual impurity, and through the offerings one attains atonement, purity, and an opportunity to begin again, to reset and realign one's life and consciousness.

When young children begin studying Torah, they start with reading the beginning of the Book of Vayikra, as the Medrash (*Vayikra Rabba*, 7:3) says, "Let the pure (the children) come and study the pure — the laws of the offerings, which bring purity" (*Tanchuma*, Tzav

14. *Col Bo*, 74. Shach, *Yoreh Deah*, 245:8). In fact, because of this association between purity and children, Rebbe Yehudah haChasid writes that there is a custom of putting the Book of Vayikra in the crib, near the baby's head, at his Bris (*Sefer Chassidim*, 1140).

Vayikra, and the offerings that are described in it, represent new beginnings, rebooting and recalibrating the system, and starting afresh.

ויקרא אל־משה / "And Hashem called to Moshe..." this is the way the Book of Vayikra opens. In the Torah scroll, the final letter of the word ויקרא / *Vayikra*, the letter Aleph, is written smaller than the other four letters. Why? What does this mean?

There are two similar terms in the Torah which indicate that someone is receiving prophecy: ויקרא / *Vayikra* / called out, and ויקר / *Vayikar* / happened upon. The difference between the words is that *Vayikra* has an Aleph at the end, and *Vayikar* does not. *Vayikra* is of course a higher level of prophecy, as expressed in the verse, ויקרא אל־משה / *Vayikra Hashem el Moshe*, "Hashem called out to Moshe...." Rashi says that the word Vayikra is לשון חיבה / *Lashon Chibah* / "a term of affection." It is an intentional calling out, a reaching out from Hashem to man. ויקר / *Vayikar* is a lower level of prophecy, as expressed in the verse, ויקר אלקים אל בלעם / *Vayikar Elokim el Bilam* / "Elokim happened upon Balaam" (*Bamidbar*, 23:4). The term ויקר comes from the root קרה, connected with the word מקרה, which denotes a 'chance occurrence'. It is also connected with the word קרי / *Keri*, meaning 'occurrence'— an involuntary act which happens unexpectedly or suddenly, without the subject's *Da'as* or full awareness.

Moshe's prophetic experiences were of the highest order. He was the greatest prophet in history, and yet the Aleph at the end of *Vayikra* is written with a small Aleph, showing his humility. The Baal HaTurim (*Vayikra*, 1:1) suggests that Moshe considers it as if he is only on the level of Vayikar, an unmerited prophet to whom prophecy is just 'happening', and Hashem's expressed affection is an unearned gift from Above. For this reason, Moshe wanted to write ויקר the way it is written regarding Bilam's 'chance' prophecies. Hashem, however, told him to write the א, so Moshe wrote it, but small. This sense of humility, thinking that perhaps you are not worthy of *Gadlus* / greatness and *Geulah* / redemption, and yet you are receiving it from Above, is consistent with the entire theme of Nisan. Springtime is when we are 'redeemed' from the physical constrictions of winter, and also from the constrictions of *Mitzrayim* / Egypt — even when we are not yet deserving or possessing the desire and vessels to be redeemed. Nisan is an awakening from Above, a movement from Above that arouses us below.

SEASONS OF THE YEAR

INTRICATELY RELATED TO THE SEASONAL QUALITIES OF A given month are the month's spiritual qualities. When daylight lasts for longer or shorter periods, different kinds of spiritual light are being revealed on a subtle level. The physical experiences of spring are external expressions of an internal reality emanating during that time, such as the vital pulse of new life and growth. All dark and dank months reflect a quality of corresponding spiritual 'coldness', stimulating us to seek warmth. People tend to keep to themselves when winter begins and are more outgoing when summer starts. All of these psycho-physical weather patterns reflect deeper spiritual truths, as the mind-body complex is a reflection of the metaphysical qualities of the soul and the spiritual realms.

"For everything there is an appointed time" (*Koheles*, 3:1). In other words, everything happens according to Divine timing (Rebbe Rayatz, *Sefer haMa'amarim*, Tav-Shin-Aleph, p. 59). When we left Egypt, it was the appointed time for such liberation. Indeed, Nisan is the perfect month for the Exodus and redemption. Dovid HaMelech, in the Book of Tehilim, says, "Hashem מוציא אסירים בכושרות / sets free the imprisoned" (*Tehilim*, 68:7). The word כושרות is related to the word כשר / *Kosher*, meaning, Hashem took us out of prison, from Egypt, in a *Kosher* / appropriate month. Hashem took us out, says Rebbe Akiva (*Medrash Rabbah*, Bamidbar, 3:6), in a month that is perfect to be taken out to travel in the Desert, a month that is not too hot nor too cold (see also *Rashi*, ad loc.).

Beyond the pleasantness of the month, Nisan is the first month of spring. And when spring arrives, something about the increasing light, the warmer air, and the sprouting vegetation enhances our feeling that life is a gift and a blessing and we should be grateful.

Shelomo haMelech / King Solomon, in the book of *Shir haShirim* / Song of Songs, sings, "My beloved resembles a gazelle or a fawn of the hinds; behold, he is standing behind our wall, looking from the windows, peering from the lattices" (2:9). Regarding these words Rashi writes, "I had expected to remain detained for many more days, and behold, he informed me that he was standing and peering from the windows of Heaven at what was being done to me, as it is written (*Shemos*, 3:7) 'I have indeed seen the affliction of My people,' etc."

Shelomo haMelech continues: "For behold, the winter has passed; the rain is over and gone. The blossoms have appeared in the land, the time of singing has arrived" (*Shir haShirim*, 2:11-12). Here are the words of Rashi on these verses: "The days of summer are near, when the trees blossom and the travelers enjoy seeing them… when the birds give forth their song, and the sound is pleasant for travelers…It is customary for the birds to sing and chirp in the days of Nisan."

We left Egypt in the month of Nisan, when the birds start chirping and creation is coming alive again following the long cold winter months. With this visceral sensation of reawakening comes a recognition that life is given to us whether we 'deserve' it or not. Hashem alone gives us life, and all is Divine grace and compassion. With this humility comes a deep sense of gratitude. During the eight days of Pesach, as we eat the unleavened bread of Matzah, the bread of humility, we strive to internalize the trait of humility, and to sing praises and thanks to Hashem for all the blessings and miracles in our life.

THE HOLIDAY OF THE MONTH

WHILE THE YOM TOV OF PESACH BEGINS ON THE 15th of Nisan, the entire month is permeated with Pesach. Our sages even debate whether we should begin to celebrate, or at least begin to remember, the Going Out of Egypt on the first day of the month, from Rosh Chodesh, rather than waiting for Pesach in the middle of the month.

The Shaloh haKadosh teaches that every day of Nisan is like Rosh Chodesh, containing the *Kedushah* / holiness and sacredness of Rosh Chodesh (*Shaloh*, Maseches Pesachim, 21).

One unique feature of the month of Nisan is that during the entire month, *Tachanun* / the daily prayers of penitence are omitted. We are also not allowed to fast during this month, except in certain specific situations. Many have the custom to refrain from eating Matzah from the first day of the month until Pesach, while others do not eat Matzah a full 30 days prior to Pesach.

FIRST 12 DAYS OF NISAN

Being that Nisan is the first month of the lunar year, the first 12 days of the month correspond to the 12 upcoming months of the year (*Igra d'Kala*, Pikudei). This is similar to the concept that the final 12 days of the month of Elul, the end of the solar year, correspond to the 12 months of the year that has almost passed (the Rebbe Rayatz). For example, the first day of Nisan corresponds to the entire month of Nisan, the second day of Nisan corresponds to the subsequent month, Iyyar, the third day to the month of Sivan, and so on. We can use this inner correspondence to projectively sow each month of the new year with positive action, speech and consciousness. Moreover, the Avnei Neizer teaches that every hour of those first 12 days of Nisan have the power and potential of a full day. We need to use them wisely.

In 12 days there are 288 hours. This number alludes to the רפ"ח / *RaPaCh Nitzutzos* / 288 sparks of Divine Light that humanity needs to 'raise up' to their source in order for the Final Redemption to occur. This meta-historical process is recapitulated within the life of each individual — we all have personal traits to elevate, relationships to heal, blessings to make, Mitzvos to perform, and mistakes to correct, in order to activate our *Ge'ulah Pratis* / individual redemption.

Everything that will transpire during the upcoming 12 months is manifest on a seed level during these 12 days. According to our *Avodah* / work of raising the sparks of our own lives, we receive kernels of blessings for living a 'redeemed' life in the upcoming year. This is the meaning of our declaration at the end of the Seder: *L'Shanah haBa'ah b'Yerushalayim* / 'In the coming year may we live — individually and collectively — in the redeemed Jerusalem.'

The least we can do is be conscious and mindful of the power of these days and hours, and take some small steps in creating positive potentials for the experiences that we will have in the months ahead. Some who are more refined and spiritually attuned can meditate during these 12 days and intuit what will occur during each month of the year. It is said that the great Tzadik, the *Chozeh* / Seer of Lublin, would write in a journal on each of the first 12 days of Nisan what would occur during the corresponding month of the year. He did so not only as intuitions regarding what would occur, but also as hopes and prayers, to help bring those realities into being. In the year that he passed away, he only wrote entries for the first four days; up until the fifth corresponding month of Av. In that year, he passed away in the month of Av.

Truly, the entire month of Nisan is a powerful portal into the depths of our potential for redemption. The entire month is celebratory, beginning with the anticipation of the redemptive power of Pesach, continuing with the actual days of Pesach, and concluding with a period of unpacking and integrating what we have experienced.

PESACH AS SHABBOS

The Torah calls the holy day of Pesach "Shabbos" when it speaks of the counting of the Omer. The verse says וספרתם לכם ממחרת השבת / "Count (seven weeks of the Omer) from the day after *Shabbos* (meaning the day after the first day of Pesach)" (*Vayikra*, 23:15). Because of this ambiguous reference to Shabbos in the text, the *Boeshusians*, otherwise known as the *Tzedukim* / Sadducees, read the verse literally, suggesting we count the seven weeks always from the Sunday after the first day of Pesach. If the first day of Pesach was on a Monday, they would wait until after the following Shabbos, and then begin to count seven weeks (*Menachos*, 65a). Through the *Torah she-b'al-Peh* / the Oral Torah transmitted in an unbroken chain from teacher to student beginning with Moshe Rabbeinu, we know that *Shabbos* in this verse refers to Pesach. Logically speaking, Pesach can be called *Shabbos*, as *Shabbos* simply means 'a day of rest'.

There are many reasons offered in the Gemara, as well as in the Rambam and later sources, that prove the accuracy of our oral tradition, that the command to "Count the Omer from the day after Shabbos" can only refer to Pesach, but why is there an ambiguity in the text of the Torah? Why does it not state clearly, "Count the Omer from the day after (the first day of) Pesach," and leave no room for error?

Throughout the ages many reasons were offered; perhaps we can add one more reason, and through exploring this reason, understand more deeply the nature of Nisan and Pesach. The Torah says, "And… / וקצרתם את־קצירה והבאתם את־עמר ראשית קצירכם אל־הכהן

(when) you reap its harvest, you shall bring the עמר / *Omer*, the first sheaf of your harvest, to the priest" (*Vayikra*, 23:10). In simple language, the Torah is telling us that in the time of the year when you reap your harvest, in the month of Nisan, the beginning of the spring, you shall bring an Omer-measurement of barley to the Kohen. A few *Pesukim* / verses later, the Torah says: וספרתם לכם ממחרת השבת מיום הביאכם את־עמר / and you shall count to yourself (each individual) from the day after Shabbos, from the day the Omer is offered" (Ibid, 15).

The Torah wants us to bring the Omer when we reap the harvest, but the winter harvest changes from year to year. The harvesting of winter wheat occurs in Nisan, in the beginning of spring, but sometimes it occurs in the beginning of Nisan and sometimes at the end of Nisan. A principle of Torah is that it generally establishes things in the middle (see, *Chazon Ish*, Orach Chayim, Moed, 138:4) and so, the Torah establishes that the reaping of the winter harvest is in the middle of the month, the 15th of the month. On the other hand, there is a technical issue, as the 15th of Nisan is Pesach, and it is a day of "rest from work" and we are not allowed to reap the harvest, and thus, the Torah pushes off the reaping until the 16th day: "You shall count…from the day *after*.…"

If the Torah would say, 'Cut the harvest on the 16th day,' it would not be accurate, because the Torah wants us to do such Mitzvos in the middle of the month. Thus, the 15th is the 'real' date, not the 16th. A technical issue of Yom Tov prevents us from cutting the harvest on the 15th, and more importantly because Yom Tov is a day of Shabbos (וימים טובים נמי שבתות איקרו / "and the Yamim Tovim are called Shabbos": Rashi, *Shavuos*, 15b. Or in the words of the Rambam, 'שכולם שבתות ה' הן / "for they are all Shabboses to Hashem": *Hilchos Shabbos*, 29:18), therefore, on this day, we need to 'rest from cutting'. Thus the Torah says, ממחרת השבת / "from the day after Shabbos," to stress the 'Shabbos element' within Yom Tov.

Let us now take this idea a little deeper. Not only is Pesach called "Shabbos" with regards to the cutting of the Omer, stressing the element of Shabbos within Yom Tov, but on a deeper level, Pesach is intimately linked to the quality of Shabbos.

Pesach is a *Bechinah* / element of Shabbos. Shabbos on the seventh day of the week has a *Kedushah* / holiness that comes into the world on its own. It is מקדשא וקיימא / *Mikadshah v'Kaymah* / "sanctified and established" from Above (*Beitzah*, 17a). This is in contrast to Yamim Tovim, which are to a certain extent established by human observation of astronomical events. The holiness of Shabbos comes on its own; Hashem creates it and makes it sacred without human participation. Shabbos is from Above. Yom Tov, on the other hand, is described in the blessing, *Mekadesh Yisrael v'haZemanim* / "...Sanctifies Israel and the (holy) days." This is a hint to the fact that 'Israel sanctifies the holy days'; we participate and create the holiness of the Yamim Tovim by 'helping' to determine when they begin.

Weeks are not up to us. In fact, the structure of weeks has no astronomical or agricultural pattern or correlation, and thus they are a purely objective Divine creation. Months, although they are related to an astronomical cycle, the phases of the moon, are up to our confirmation and declaration regarding when they are to begin. It is the testimony of an eye witness who has seen the new moon that determines the first day of a new month. The weekly Shabbos, on the other hand, is a gift that comes on its own, entirely apart from our involvement and even desire. The seventh day of the week comes every week, whether or not we counted the days leading up to it.

The holy days, which occur on specified days of the month, are thus created with some measure of human collaboration: we are given the responsibility to establish when exactly the new moon has occurred, and the new moon determines when the *Yom Tov / Holiday* of that month will occur. In other words, if the Yom Tov begins on the 15th day of the month, only once Rosh Chodesh has been established as the first day of the new month, can it be determined when the 15th day of that month will be. The actual lunar cycle is 28 days, yet, because of the solar cycle, it takes approximately 29.5 days for the new moon to be revealed to someone situated on the earth's surface. In times past, when two witnesses would see the new moon following the 29th and half day, they would come to the High Court, offer testimony that they observed the new moon, and that day would be established as the first day of the new month. If no witnesses came forth, the 30th day would be considered part of the previous month, and the 31st day would become the first day of the new month.

This is the meaning of *Mekadesh Yisrael v'haZemanim* / "...Who sanctifies Israel and the (holy) days": Hashem sanctifies us with the Mitzvah and ability to establish new months and determine which days are Yomim Tovim and which days are not. While this is certainly the case with Pesach, a Yom Tov, the 15th day of the month of Nisan, Pesach also contains a unique spiritual quality of Shabbos. *Ge'ulas Mitzrayim* / the Redemption from Egypt was given to us, like the day of Shabbos is given to us, and Pesach thus represents an awakening from Above similar to Shabbos. This is the deeper reason the Torah calls Pesach "Shabbos" — it is indicating the *Nekudah* / point of Shabbos within the Yom Tov of Pesach.

On a deeper level, not only does the Yom Tov of Pesach contain a Nekudah of Shabbos within it, but even the establishment of Rosh Chodesh Nisan has a quality of Shabbos, and this quality is reflected forward onto the Yom Tov of Pesach. To explain: Normally a Yom Tov depends on the sighting of the new moon, in the beginning of the month. We who observe the new moon, together with the high court who accepts and confirms the testimony of the people, together establish the new moon, the first of the month, and thereby determine when Yom Tov will occur. Yet, with regards to the Pesach narrative, the first time Klal Yisrael heard the command to "sanctify the new moon" was on Rosh Chodesh Nissan, a mere 15 days before the Exodus from Egypt. It was therefore not the testimony of the people that established Rosh Chodesh Nisan, rather, HaKadosh Baruch Hu was the one to establish it. Why? Moshe was troubled, not knowing what exactly the people would have to see in order to sanctify the new moon, and so Hashem showed Moshe the new moon in the evening (Rashi, *Shemos*, 12:2) or in a prophetic image (Rambam, *Hilchos Kidush haChodesh*, 1:1), and said, "Like this ('when you see this') you shall declare it holy" (*Mechilta*, Bo). And so, it was HaKadosh Baruch Hu's testimony, as it were, that established the first Rosh Chodesh Nisan, which is the foundation of all the months of Nisan that follow. This is consistent with the theme of Pesach being like Shabbos, an intrinsic holiness, a miraculous *Gadlus* / expansiveness, an infinite gift, which is given to us from Above.

In Nisan, Hashem "skips over" all gradual and natural processes and reveals to us *Gadlus* / greatness, expansiveness, beyond our merit or expectation. HaKadosh Baruch Hu takes us out of our own Mitzrayim, our own confinement, narrowness and smallness, and lifts us into Gadlus. Like Shabbos, this elevation is 'beyond us', not caused in any way by our Avodah or actions. In reality, *Avadim Hayinu l'Paro b'Mitzrayim* / "We were slaves to Pharaoh in Egypt" — we did not have the choice or capacity, or even the time, to act in a way which could have initiated our release from confinement. It was all from Above. Shabbos, too, redeems us without our effort. In fact, we relinquish 'work' on Shabbos, and this is reflected in the 'non-doing' of Ge'ulas Mitzrayim. Indeed, we were 'taken out'.

Mochin d'Gadlus / big mind, expansive consciousness, inner freedom, is the gift of Pesach. And this is offered to us as a gift of pure *Chesed* / freely-given generosity, a giving without the participation of the *M'kabel* / receiver.

Nonetheless, right away, on the night after the first day of Pesach, we begin to count the Omer; to work on ourselves in order to fully receive the coming revelation at Mount Sinai, on Shavuos. Similarly, right after Shabbos, we begin to do *Melachah* / weekday work; we light a flame for Havdalah and we gradually begin again to refine the world and ourselves through spiritual and physical work, to open ourselves to fully receive the coming revelation of Shabbos.

Understanding the Shabbos nature of Pesach, and how the entire spring season of Nisan is connected with the meek lamb, the silent Hei, humility, the idea of simply receiving and being grateful

(*Hoda'ah* / Yehudah) for what we receive, the gift of life and freedom, will help us understand a great thematic truth encoded in the structure of the *Seder* / order of the night (a full exploration of these ideas will be published in a two-volume Haggadah, G-d willing soon). Namely, why we begin the Seder on a very 'high' note (Kadeish), without first experiencing any of the 'lows' that we will later recount over the course of the night.

THE *Seder* / ORDER OF PESACH NIGHT

On the night of Pesach we enact a Seder, where we move through fifteen steps, which were defined by the school of Rashi. 1) The first step is *Kadeish*: we recite Kiddush. Then 2) we perform *Urchatz* / wash our hands. Then 3) *Karpas*, we eat an onion, or the like, dipped in salt water. 4) *Yachatz*: we break the middle Matzah. 5) *Magid*: we recite the bulk of the Haggadah. 6) *Rachtzah:* we wash our hands for bread. 7) We recite the blessing of *Motzi*, and 8) the blessing over the *Matzah* and eat the Matzah. 9) We eat the *Maror*. 10) We eat the *Korech* 'sandwich'. 11) *Shulchan Orech*, we eat the festive meal. 12) *Tzafun*: we eat the previously hidden broken Matzah. 13) *Beirach*: we say grace after the meal. 14) *Hallel*: we recite the special Psalms of praise. 15) *Nirtzah*: we recognize that everything has been accepted. This is the *Seder* / order of the night.

Rav Meir Leibush ben Yechiel Michel, better known as 'the Malbim', writes (*Haggadah*, Ma'amar Yesod Mussar): "The beginning of all knowledge and the source of all wisdom is to have an understanding of the Seder," the order and structure of the text and process of Pesach. He notes that some commentaries on the Haggadah focus on explaining each passage and delving deep into the passages of the Haggadah, but to really understand the Haggadah we have to find the *Seder* / the order, the inner structure within it.

In the stage of Magid, a core principle is expressed: מתחיל בגנות ומסיים בשבח / "We begin by recounting our disgrace and concluding with our glory" (Mishnah, *Pesachim*, 116a); there is a thesis and antithesis, an arc, a narrative, a process. This general structure is consistent with the entire movement of Pesach, which is a movement from negativity to positivity, slavery to freedom, spiritual and physical hardship followed by redemption.

The great sages of the Gemara, Rav and Shmuel, argue regarding the definition of "our disgrace." Rav says we should begin by saying, 'At first our forefathers were idol worshippers.' And Shmuel says it means we should begin by saying, 'We were slaves….' Rav is looking at our spiritual disgrace, our ancestry of idolatry, and Shmuel focuses on our physical dishonor, our enslavement.* The *Halacha* / law follows Rav, as in all sacred matters, yet, the Haggadah also includes the opinion of Shmuel, and we also begin the Seder with our story from *slavery* to redemption.

Clearly, the opposite of idol worship is to serve Hashem, and it would seem that the opposite of slavery is simply freedom, yet

---

* This is consistent with Rav and Shmuel's opinions throughout the Gemara; Rav focuses on the spiritual aspect of the issue, between man and G-d, and Shmuel on the more mundane, between man and man: *Likutei Sichos*, vol. 16, Shemos 1, p. 9. In general, Rav was more involved and scrupulous with ritual law, and Shmuel with civil issues: ששמואל היה רגיל תמיד לפסוק דינין ולכך היה מדקדק בהן ויורד לעומקן ומשכיל על כל דבר אמת. וכן רב היה רגיל לדקדק בהוראת איסור והיתר לכך סמכו על הוראותיו לעניני איסור והיתר: Rosh, Bava Kama, 4:4. Thus, the Halacha follows Rav in 'ritual' debates and Shmuel in 'money' issues, הלכתא כרב באיסורי וכשמואל בדיני: *Bechoros*, 49b.

the Rambam adds an important subtle addition. The Rambam writes that we begin the Seder by relating, "Originally, our ancestors were *idol worshipers*," and then conclude this statement with שקרבנו המקום לו והבדילנו מהאומות וקרבנו ליחודו / "Hashem has drawn us close to Himself, separated us from the nations of the world, and has drawn us close to His Unity." And immediately after, we state that we were slaves to Pharaoh in Egypt and remember all the evil done to us, ומסיים בנסים ובנפלאות שנעשו לנו ובחירותנו / "and conclude with the miracles and wonders that were wrought upon us, and that we were chosen" (Hilchos *Chametz U'Matzah*, 7:4). In other words, for the Rambam, the opposite of being a slave in Egypt is more than 'freedom'; it is closeness. Hashem performs miracles for us and shows us miracles as Hashem takes us out of Egypt and chooses us as His 'intimate People'. Hashem's love is the essence of true freedom.

So far, this all makes sense; a movement from negative to positive, from slavery to freedom, from being alienated idol worshipers to "intimate" servants of Hashem. Yet, in the structure of the Haggadah it is all out of sequence. In fact, there is something peculiar about the entire *Seder* / order of the Seder night. On this night we are celebrating our going out of Egypt, both the historical event and the inner 'event' of our being empowered to go out of our own personal *Mitzrayim* / Egypt. Pesach night is about our *freedom*. We drink four cups of wine, corresponding to the four levels of freedom that we experienced going out of Egypt, we eat the Matzah and drink the wine reclining, as kings and free men of old would do. We adorn our tables with the finest silverware and wear our finest garments. Yet, we also contrast this sensation of freedom and royalty with a taste of the bitterness and lowliness of our slavery:

we eat *Maror* / bitter herbs, and *Karpas* / a traditional vegetable dipped in salt water, symbolizing our tears. This is because we can only recognize a new experience through contrast with its opposite: we can only feel as free as we have felt enslaved in the past.

It would thus make perfect sense to first eat the Maror / bitter herb, to grind our teeth and feel the physical pain and general bitterness of our enslavement, and then to eat Matzah, the bread of freedom, and drink wine, which induces sensations of the joy and pleasure of redemption. This way we would begin by feeling the pain of having been beaten down, and speaking about our exile and hardship in Egypt — only after that would we lift a beautiful cup filled with fine wine and recite *Kiddush* / the sanctification of the joyful Yom Tov, recline luxuriously and drink like a king or queen. One could then freely continue with the story of the Exodus from Egypt, sing the praises of Hashem, our Redeemer, envision our complete freedom, and experience a miraculous closeness to HaKadosh Baruch Hu. In the actual Seder, however, this is not how it is done. We begin with Kiddush and wine, and only then mention being slaves and idol worshippers.

Toward the end of Magid, we explain the Mitzvos of the night, Pesach (the *Korban Pesach* / Pesach Offering, brought in the time of the Beis HaMikdash), Matzah, and Maror. The Nodah beYehudah asks; why are these three Mitzvos listed in this order? One would think that the correct order would be first Maror, symbolic of the bitterness in Egypt, then the Matzah and the Pesach offering, which are each expressions of freedom (*Tz'lach*, Pesachim, 116b).

Indeed, when the Rambam speaks about this Halacha, Maror

does appear before Matzah (although Pesach comes first): ומגביה המרור בידו ואומר מרור זה שאנו אוכלין על שם שמררו המצריים את חיי אבותינו במצרים שנאמר (שמות א יד) וימררו את חייהם. ומגביה המצה בידו ואומר מצה זו שאנו אוכלין על שם שלא הספיק בצקם של אבותינו להחמיץ עד שנגלה עליהם הקדוש ברוך הוא וגאלם / "He lifts up the Maror in his hands and says, "This Maror that we eat [is] because the Egyptians made the lives of our forefathers bitter in Egypt, as it (*Shemos*, 1:14) states: 'and they embittered their lives.' And he lifts up the Matzah in his hand and says, 'This Matzah which we eat [is] because the dough of our ancestors was not able to leaven before the Holy One, blessed be He, was revealed to them'" (Rambam, *Hilchos Chametz uMatzah*, 8:4). As the *Kesef Mishnah* (ad loc.: שתחלה מררו חייהם ואח"כ נגאלו) comments, this order follows the story of the Exodus; first comes the bitterness, the Maror, and then redemption, the Matzah.

Furthermore, as we currently do not bring a Korban Pesach, today we first eat the Matzah, and then eat the Maror. Once again, it would make more sense if we ate the Maror before the Matzah, tasting bitterness and *Katnus* / smallness, before tasting redemption and *Gadlus* / greatness.

A simple reason that we eat Matzah before Maror is that today eating Matzah is the night's main Mitzvah from the Torah, whereas Maror, without the *Korban Pesach* is, according to most opinions (perhaps not the opinion of the Yerushalmi), a Mitzvah from our sages, and the most essential Mitzvah is performed first. But the question can also be contemplated philosophically: what does it mean that Matzah precedes Maror? And why do we start the whole Seder with a royal Kiddush? Halachically, we cannot eat before Kiddush, so, practically, it needs to precede the ritual foods, but why not have the children ask questions, and then start to tell the story of our exile, slavery and idol worship, before making Kiddush?

Even more puzzling regarding our Seder, according to the Arizal, is that the four cups are in descending order (The First Cup is Chochmah (of *Ima* / mother, the Chochmah within Binah), the second is Binah. The Third cup is Chesed, and the Fourth cup is Gevurah (both within Da'as). *Pri Etz Chaim*. Sha'ar haMitzvos, 2. See also *Shaloh*, Maseches Pesachim, p. 188. A similar 'descending' order of the four cups is found in the teaching of Rabbeinu Bachya, who writes that the four cups correspond to the Name of Hashem, from Yud to Hei, first cup Yud last cup Hei. *Rabbeinu Bachya*, Shemos, 12:23). Meaning, the first cup represents higher cosmic levels and the fourth cup represents lower levels. Why — and how — can we start the Seder on a higher level and then descend? How is it possible to experience *Gadlus* / greatness and spiritual expansiveness, drinking a cup of wine evoking liberation and maturity, before experiencing *Katnus* / smallness, spiritual contraction and immaturity? We stand proudly in our best attire, with the finest silver cup we can afford; our table is set for kings and queens, some even don a beautiful white garment symbolizing the *Kohen Gadol* / the High Priest, who served in the holy of holies with white garments. We declare "For You have sanctified us...desired us... *chosen* us." We begin the Seder as a noble prince and priest, not as an oppressed and silenced slave.

This, however, is the very meaning of *Pesach* / passing over; skipping over all levels and stages to directly encounter our Gadlus, our physical and spiritual greatness. Kiddush is an expression of freedom and restfulness that skips over any sense of exile or strain. It is the confident answer that comes before we even consider our nagging questions. Similarly, Matzah before Maror reflects the

"Shabbos" nature of Pesach.

On Pesach we are given a level of freedom called *Gadlus Rishon* / first level expansiveness, which is the sense of being a *Melech* / sovereign, a master, a person who has everything they need and want. A Melech or *Malkah* / queen has self-mastery, freely flowing *Mochin* / higher awareness, and a sense of being chosen and treasured. We receive the state of the noble Kohen Gadol. All of this occurs in the Seder even before we experience *Katnus Rishon* / first level smallness.

In a state of Katnus, we feel *Katua* / broken, disjointed and immature, whereas in Gadlus there is a sense of unity. The etymological root of Gadlus, Gimel-Dalet, represents a unit, a continuation. In a Gadlus state, one has a global sense of clarity. In Katnus, things are mixed up and broken apart, like the paradigm of the Tree of Knowledge, of Good and Evil, the world of duality. In this experience of life, everything seems partly good and partly or potentially bad, and thus there is never complete moral clarity. The perspective of Gadlus is the complete clarity of unity-consciousness, the wholeness of the Tree of Life. On Pesach night we receive a great *Tikkun* / healing, a rectification of the *Chet* / sin of eating from the Tree of Knowledge. This inner Tikkun comes to us by means of the Gadlus that we are given to experience, so long as we open ourselves up to it.

In the normal course of events, first comes night, then day, as the order of Creation, "It was evening, it was morning, day one." First comes darkness and then light; first Katnus then Gadlus; first question then answer. Similarly, in the course of human development, first comes childhood and then adulthood. First we are immature, guided by our emotions, and only when we become a *Gadol* / adult are we potentially guided by our rational faculties. A child is not just physically *Katan* / small, but is also without *Mochin* / higher capacities of awareness. A child's life is intensively guided by their parents (for good reason); the child does not decide where to live or when to go to sleep. Within this parental container, they are guided by their emotional reactions. If, G-d forbid, a child is traumatized, they can be trapped in their trauma, without an ability to see life from a more intellectual perspective, to make some sense of their experience and thus free themselves enough in order to choose their responses. They are stuck in 'smallness' without Da'as. Once they become mature, they can try to make sense of their past, learn new responses to life, and free themselves, G-d willing, from their trauma. Without this practical Mochin, this Gadlus, we are stuck in a state of Din, constriction, limitation and exile.

This is true of all of life; first comes Katnus and only later, Gadlus. But on the night that we left Egypt, and from that point forward, every year on this night, the order is reversed. First we are miraculously elevated into utter Gadlus, the 'answer', and only then do we come down and revisit Katnus, the 'question', the bitterness, the brokenness. In this way, we taste the bitterness of Maror within a context of sweetness, wholeness and expansiveness. We experience the sting of lack within a state of luxuriant fullness.

LEAVING IN HASTE & KATNUS AFTER GADLUS

Now we can understand the reason we left Egypt in great haste. As Hashem had "skipped" over the houses of Klal Israel, we experienced a leap, "passing over" all spiritual and emotional levels, directly attaining Gadlus. Since we were steeped in the Egyptian culture of *Kelipah* / impurity, we needed a radical shift to lift us out instantaneously. We needed to be 'blasted' out — especially because our Da'as itself was in exile, in Kelipah. The normal, gradual, progressive path from Katnus to Gadlus would not have allowed us to leave.

A person who is 'enslaved' to a negative pattern of behavior cannot escape his Katnus if he begins by slowly working out his issues or gradually reducing his indulgences. Rather, he needs to begin by going to an extreme in removing himself from the behavior and its context and triggers. Only after sustaining his distance and transcendence for a little while, does he have the inner resources to descend and begin unlearning his Katnus behavior. For example, if a person finds himself becoming angry, he should try for a certain period of time to stay away from anger all together, being almost stoic or indifferent to life. Then, from this place of relative expansiveness, he can go back and explore the beliefs, fears and sufferings underlying his reactivity.

Spiritually, Klal Yisrael was sunk into the lowest depths of *Tumah* / impurity and *Avdus* / slavery, and to become free they needed a radical, dramatic shift to break the ingrained pattern and perspective of slavery. They needed to leave in haste, and to be suddenly catapulted into a taste of Gadlus, an awareness of their latent potential for freedom, clarity, faith and empowerment. This is Gadlus Rishon.

Klal Yisrael experiences this same dynamic every year on the night of Pesach. We start the night with Gadlus, in a state of *Shabbos* / restful release of *Meitzarim* / constrictions. Our first act is Kiddush, a term which comes from the word *Kodesh* / holy, separated. We stand up in the presence of this holy night, hold a beautiful cup of wine in our hands and declare that tonight is the night of Gadlus, expansive freedom; tonight we are completely separated from exile, from *Mitzrayim* / Egypt, from any internal or external slavery.

Only then do we go wash our hands to rid them of any remaining ritual impurity and plunge right back into Katnus and constricted consciousness. We eat Karpas, a small (as in Katnus) piece of bitter onion or parsley dipped in salt water. This is a 'lowly' vegetable, plucked from the ground where people tread, too insignificant to nourish or energize us. Then, we proceed to break the middle Matzah, acknowledging the *Katu'a* / brokenness in our lives. Finally, the *Katan* / child, or our inner child, asks questions, raises uncertainties and calls out seeming contradictions. We begin to answer by confessing our own painful Katnus: "In the beginning, we were idol worshipers…."

On this night, we do not travel the normal route, beginning from lower states and progressively elevating ourselves upward. Rather, we leap to the very high level of Gadlus Rishon and then abruptly descend and start dealing with extremely low levels — idolatry representing the most degraded state that a human being can reach.

Starting with Gadlus and then 'dipping' into Katnus is actually the way to ensure that our transformation over the course of this night is complete. From the state of Katnus Rishon, we gradually step higher and higher until we are established, at the end of the Seder, in *Gadlus Sheini* / second level expansion, a place of deep clarity and answers, joy and connection, gratitude and ecstatic praise of HaKadosh Baruch Hu, our All-Powerful Redeemer.

Once we have already tasted the maturity of Gadlus, we can go back into the immaturity of Katnus and not be scared that we will stay stuck there. In order to meet the needs of our confused inner *Katan* / child self, we need to have a foothold in the relaxed maturity of our inner *Gadol* / adult, our benevolent parental self.

The Arizal teaches a deep meta-physical and psycho-spiritual truth, that if you start a process of growth with Katnus, there will always be a worry of *Yenikah* / leakage into the *Chitzonim* / external, unwanted forces. Inwardly, this means that if you attempt to deal with Katnus while you are still in a place of Katnus, you may end up dealing with Katnus the rest of your life. People who think of themselves in a Katnus paradigm, as a failure, as inadequate, as powerless, and they speak and think all day about their Katnus, even though their intention of speaking about it is to get out of this stage, they can end up just reinforcing and remaining in Katnus. For example, forms of therapy that propose to heal people by having them repeatedly detail their experiences of trauma or conflict, what is wrong, what hurts, and what others did to them — can end up simply perpetuating that same kind of experience in their lives. Higher consciousness is not accessed, so there is nowhere to go but round and round.

On Pesach night we are gifted freedom from Above, as we are on Shabbos. We are gifted immediate access to Gadlus without first working to climb out of Katnus. When, after a sustained glimpse of pure, higher consciousness, we descend into our problems, pettiness and impurity, there is no fear of going lost there.

KATNUS WITHIN A CONTEXT OF GADLUS

Knowing how it is to stand upon the roof of our being, and as a result, no longer being afraid to visit the basement, we can courageously begin to reclaim and include our Katnus within the context of our Gadlus. Eventually, we will be able to experience lack within a context of *Sheleimus* / wholeness and fullness, a sense of drive within a context of having already arrived, yearning within settledness, questioning within a greater sense of knowing.

WE ARE GADLUS

After passing through an initial Gadlus, then an initial Katnus and then a deeper Gadlus, we conclude the Seder with *Beirach* / Grace after Meals, *Hallel* / singing Hashem's praises, and finally *Nirtzah* / acceptance, the realization that the whole process is complete and Divinely accepted. We no longer mention or even hint at past exiles, enslavement, hardship, bitterness, questions, or lack of clarity. The essential element in all of this, though, is that we started with Gadlus, declaring who we truly are at the outset: a chosen, free and proud people, and an individual who is a king and a Kohen Gadol, experiencing the greatness of the Source of existence. Gadlus is who we are, and how we can fully manifest ourselves throughout the entire year, if we so choose. Seder night is our chance to imprint that Gadlus into the fabric of the rest of the year.

As individuals and as a nation, we also have experiences of brokenness, sadness, bitterness, and nagging uncertainty. But when we know deep down who we truly are, and what we can become, our collective and individual Gadlus will eventually shine forth. Because we *are* Gadlus, we can start from Gadlus, and we can and will always reclaim Gadlus. Collectively, we know that Hashem will redeem us, and the Geulah will come, because Geulah is what we are in essence, and it is our destiny that this essence will be revealed.

People sometimes choose a path of spiritual constriction, lowliness, poverty, slavery, or even "idol worship," but Pesach night reveals to our hearts that anyone, at anytime, can reclaim their birthright, their inner Gadlus.

THE NIGHT OF THE SEDER:
AS THE KOHEN GADOL SITTING IN GAN EDEN

In the times of the Beis HaMikdash, on the night of Pesach we would eat the *Korban Pesach* / Pesach offering. Today, the Seder takes the place of the feast of the Korban Pesach, and thus in a way, in both cases we are eating משולחן גבוה / "from the supernal Divine Table" (as the opinion of Rashi, *Bava Kama*, 12b, and Rambam, regarding Kodshim Kalim such as the Korban Pesach). When we eat from the Divine table, we need to do so with special garments (Netziv,

Imrei Shefer, Pesicha). On this night, as we are especially linked to the Kohen Gadol, some people dress in a white *Kittel* / light overcoat, or in other white clothing. This is because the Kohen Gadol who entered into the Holy of Holies wore white garments (Maharal, *Gevuras Hashem*, 51. Not (only) to remember the day of death, as the *Taz*, Orach Chayim, 472: 3, writes).

In our finest garments, we sit down to celebrate the Seder. The table sparkles with fine dishes and cutlery reserved for this holy festival. We are like kings and queens, and on a spiritual level, we are like the Kohen Gadol, rejoicing at the Divine Table. We are also like Adam and Chavah, dressed in the brilliant garments of light bestowed upon them from Above, basking in the bliss of Gan Eden, tasting from the Tree of Life the fruits of clarity, connection, openness, expansiveness and *Deveikus* / unity with HaKadosh Baruch Hu. Whether we fully sense any of this, or whether it is beyond sensing, it is the true inner reality of our Seder.

Our sages tell us (*Megilah*, 29a), עתידין בתי כנסיות ובתי מדרשות שבבבל שיקבעו בא״י / "In the future (in the times of Moshiach), all the houses of prayer and houses of study in Babylonia, those in exile, will be transported and reestablished in Eretz Yisrael." The great Tzadik and scholar, the Chasam Sofer, writes (*Derashos* 2, p. 236) that every home in which a Seder was performed will also be transplanted to Eretz Yisrael when Moshiach comes — included in the category of "all the houses of prayer and houses of study."

This points out the fact that the Seder transforms our homes into sacred spaces. Upon the above Gemara, the Maharsha writes, לפי שבירושלים הבנויה לעתיד יהיה חוברה לה למקדש יחדיו כל מקומות של

בתי הכנסיות שהיו בעוה"ז ונמצא עתה בגלות שאני עומד בבית הכנסת הרי הוא מקום המקדש גופי׳ דלעתיד / "In the future, in the (spiritually and physically) rebuilt Jerusalem, the Beis haMikdash will be a collection of all the houses of prayer and learning from our current reality. As such, even now, in exile, when we are standing in a Shul, we are actually standing within the Beis haMikdash of the future."

Tying these two teachings together, a home that houses a Seder will be transported together with all the Shuls and sacred study halls to Yerushalayim, and will become a part of the greater Beis haMikdash. As such, when we are sitting in the comfort of our own home, celebrating the Seder, we are actually sitting in a part of the future Beis haMikdash. We are the elegant, royal priests serving the Master of the Worlds. We are the primordial human beings celebrating in Gan Eden at the beginning of time prior to any *Cheit* / misalignment, and in the ultimate future, in the Beis haMikdash.

This is the gift (the *Shabbos*) of Pesach, the gift of our first Geulah, when we left Egypt with great physical and spiritual riches, with Gadlus expressed on a material level. This is our birth as a nation, in which each individual is a Kohen Gadol.

ואתם תהיו־לי ממלכת כהנים / "And you shall be to Me a nation of priests" (*Shemos*, 19:6). Says the Baal haTurim, אילו זכו ישראל היו כולם כהנים גדולים ולע"ל תחזור להם / "If we would have merited (and not created the Golden Calf), then we would have all been *Kohanim Gedolim* / High Priests. And in the Future, this will be so." The Kohen Gadol is the most spiritually wealthy person possible, and a king or queen is the most physically wealthy person possible. We are all born with infinite, free-flowing resources, rooted in a place of Gadlus, clarity, connection, Deveikus, and certainty, with open minds and hearts. This is our birthright, it is who we truly are, it is who we will become. We can manifest this today if we choose our greatness, and we will in any case manifest this at the end of time, in the World to Come. On the first Night of Pesach in Egypt, we are gifted this Gadlus as our birthright, and on the holy night of Pesach ever since, this force descends upon us with greater power; we only need to make ourselves a vessel to receive this infinite blessing.

SUMMARY OF NISAN

*I*N THE MONTH OF NISAN, THE BEGINNING OF SPRING, THE **season** when the world is brimming with new life and hope, we naturally adopt the attribute associated with the **tribe** of the month, Yehudah: *Hoda'ah* / humble gratitude. This quality of consciousness is expressed through the **letter** of the month, Hei, a quiet, humble letter, yet the letter through which the world is created and new life flows.

In this month we also become like the *T'leh* / lamb, the **sign** of the month, representing an open posture of simply receiving life from Above. Indeed, the **letter sequence of Hashem's name** for this month, Yud-Hei-Vav-Hei, reveals a direct flow of Divine light, from Above to below, received in this world in simple humility and gratitude. The **verse** of the month describes this downflow in terms of joy: "The Heavens (Above) will be happy, and (then) the earth (below) will rejoice."

The **body part** associated with Nisan is the right foot, representing *Chesed* / 'loving-kindness' and expansive giving. Pesach, the **holy day** of the month, is also connected with Divine *Chesed*. *Pesach* means skipping over, as when HaKadosh Baruch Hu, with great Chesed, skipped over the laws of nature to take us out of *Mitzrayim* / Egypt, displaying many profound miracles. The **name** Nisan itself means *Nisim* / miracles. The **Torah portions** read in this month discuss issues of Tumah and Taharah, hinting at our abrupt, miraculous liberation from the Tumah of Egypt, when we did not 'deserve' such Chesed. Something of this Taharah is given to us as a free gift from Above every year on Pesach Night.

Receiving the gift of freedom ignites in us a passionate love for Hashem, like fire, the **element** of the month. Our liberated faculty or **'sense'** of speech, which was at first used to express an awareness of our story of suffering and contraction, now becomes expansively joyful, erupting into exuberant songs of praise — praise to our Creator for the unimaginable miracle of life, of freedom.

Summary

12 DIMENSIONS OF NISAN	
Sequence of Hashem's Name	*Yud-Hei-Vav-Hei, symbolizing unimpeded flow from Above.*
Torah Verse	*Yismechu HaShamayim V'sageil HaAretz / "the Heavens will be happy and the earth will rejoice."*
Letter	*Hei, signifying creation and humility.*
Month Name	*Miracles*
Sense	*Speech*
Zodiac	*T'leh / Aries / Lamb*
Tribe	*Yehudah*
Body Part	*Right leg*
Element	*Fire*
Parshios / Torah Portions	*The first portions of the Book of Vayikra / Leviticus, detailing offerings and issues of ritual purity and impurity.*
Season	*Aviv / Spring*
Holy Day	*Pesach*

PRACTICE
Becoming a Vessel for Miracles

NISAN, AS EXPLORED AT LENGTH, IS CONNECTED WITH *Nisim* / miracles. It is the headwaters of the flow of miracles into this world. As the month of Geulah, Nisan initiates the season of spring, with its redemptive sense of renewal, fresh possibilities, and blessings from Above.

Generally speaking, there are three steps to create the proper vessels to receive the miracles that the Source of all of Life wants to bestow on us. We can learn these three steps from the story of our collective redemption from the exile in Egypt. They are also intricately related to the *Ko'ach* / power and potential of the month of Nisan, and so this is an opportune time to study and practice them.

Before exploring these steps, another important point is worth mentioning: we reawaken the power of the miracles described in the Torah simply by reading the verses in the Torah connected with those miracles. When we recite the story of Yetziyas Mitzrayim and the miracles and wonders that occurred, it stimulates the same *Hashpa'ah* / downflow of Divine influence that was originally revealed. In the words of the Chozeh of Lublin (*Beshalach*), "Through reciting the letters in the Torah which speak about the miracles, we awaken the source of those miracles."

The metaphysical source of everything that occurs, of all of life and history, and all time, space and consciousness, is the Torah, the Divine blueprint. When the Torah narrates the splitting of the sea, for example, the Torah is not merely 'describing' an event, rather it is speaking of the spiritual source of this miracle. Because a spiritual source of this miracle exists, the miracle itself can also come to exist in the natural world. Furthermore, HaKadosh Baruch Hu creates through 'speech', and Torah is a condensation of this creative speech. For this reason, when we pronounce the words of the Torah about the Splitting of the Sea, it gives rise to the creative power that can split a sea, as well as whatever the Splitting of the Sea represents in our lives and world. When we read the portion of the *Mon* / Manna, it opens the channel for *Parnasah* / livelihood. Similarly, when we pronounce words of Torah that speak about the Going Out of Mitzrayim, we are tapping into the power source that gives us strength to go out of our own personal *Meitzarim* / constrictions and limitations. The Torah narrative is the root cause, the initial vibration and Divine flow, through which all blessings and miracles flow down into this world and to us.

What follows is the three-step process for receiving miraculous blessings: 1) Speaking, 2) Dreaming, and 3) Surrendering.

FIRST STEP: SPEAKING

1) Speech is the sense of the month, and Pesach represents the liberation and realignment of speech. In Egypt, Klal Yisrael was so mired in exile that their ability to speak about their current situation, not to mention any possibility of freedom, or even to speak with a degree of basic authenticity, was suppressed.

They thus remained there stuck and paralyzed, until the overwhelming burden of it all built up within them to such an extent that they could only cry out in agony. Only when they let out a groan did Hashem 'notice': ויאנחו בני־ישראל מן־העבדה ויזעקו / "And Bnei Yisrael groaned from the labor, and they cried out..." וישמע אלקים את־נאקתם / "and Hashem heard their groan..." (*Shemos*, 2:23-24). There is a profound connection between this groan, a preverbal and preemptive form of 'speech' or prayer, and their salvation. Only once a sound could break forth from their lips, a cry recognizing the weight of their predicament, could they even conceive of a potential reality with no slavery. Their cries thus opened the possibility of even dreaming of an alternate reality. Like a mirror image, along with their cry below there was a corresponding hearing or 'understanding' Above, and thus began the process of their redemption.

Bnei Yisrael were slaves for over 200 years, but because there was no movement or opening within them, there was also no opening from Above, *Kaviyachol* / as it were. During the first period of exile, Klal Yisrael actually just accepted their situation; although begrudgingly, they silently bore the load of their oppression assumed it was their lot. They uttered no prayers, nor meaningful words nor gave voice to any aspirations. As they did not speak of their suffering, nor express any personal or collective yearnings for change, they blocked out their own understanding of themselves and their real circumstances. The moment they were able to groan, however, even though it was not in the form of a Tefillah (*Ohr haChayim*, ad loc.), Hashem heard their groan as a prayer for help.

The Above mirrors the below. The very moment there was an opening below there was an openness Above. As they cried, they could hear themselves, and Hashem in turn heard them as well. In the same way, we need to open up to Hashem regarding the issues that are bothering us. We need to learn to speak to Hashem as we might speak to our most beloved, most non-judgmental friend, to share anything and everything that is hurting or constricting us. We must find a way to speak openly about whatever we are wanting and needing, whatever is alienating us or holding us back. When we speak about our life in this way to Hashem, we will both gain self-understanding and we will be simultaneously 'heard' Above.

Beyond being the time of *Peh Sach* / a mouth that speaks — a time when we need to speak to Hashem — the entire month of Nisan is a month of perfecting and fully redeeming our speech. In numerical value, the word Nisan is 170 (Nun/50, Yud/10, Samach / 60, Nun/50 = 170), twice the word *Peh* / mouth (Peh is Pei/80, Hei/5 = 85). Nisan is thus the 'fullness' of the mouth that speaks words of self-awareness and authenticity. This is the first stage; verbally opening ourselves up to need as well as the possibility of miracles in our life. We need to state verbally that 'the situation is not good'; we need to enter a state of prayer and say, 'Hashem, I need help, this is not working, I need something to shift.' We also need to know that HaKadosh Baruch Hu hears all of our prayers and understands us completely.

SECOND STEP: DREAMING

2) The next stage is to create in your mind a visual image of the reality you need. Imagine it in detail, and couple this visualization with verbal declarations and prayers. Know that you are creating a vessel to receive the miraculous blessings of HaKadosh Baruch Hu.

"Sanctify the new months" — this was the very first instruction Klal Yisrael received as a nation. It is the Mitzvah to sanctify and thus establish the first day of the month of Nisan, the first month of the year, the month of *Geulah* / redemption and *Nisim* / miracles. Months are created and defined by the cycling of the moon. "There is nothing new under the sun" (*Koheles*, 1:9), and yet, as the Zohar adds, "...But the moon *is* new" (*Zohar* 1, p. 123b). The sun represents rigidity, linear structure and inevitability, as it rises and sets in the same way each day. The moon, on the other hand, waxes and wanes, sometimes it is observable and sometimes not. The moon represents a paradigm of renewal and the potential for novelty that breaks the monotony of linear 'sun' time. The moon represents *Chodesh*, meaning both 'month' and *Chidush* / newness. The moon represents the world of dreams, of imagination and the miraculous.

'Sun', in Hebrew, is *Shemesh*, which is related to the word *Shamash*

/ servant or minister, as the sun serves and ministers to the earth, consistently providing necessary light, nourishment and warmth. *Shemesh* is also rooted in the word *Mash* / touch, tangible. The word *Levanah*, one of the terms for moon, comes from the word *Lavan* / white or transparent, suggesting an elusiveness and unpredictability, the very opposite of tangible consistency.

שמש ידע מבואו / "The sun knows its setting" (*Tehilim*, 104:19). This, too, is in contrast to the moon: שמש הוא דידע מבואו ירח לא ידע מבואו / "The sun knows its setting and its movement, whereas the moon does not know" (*Rosh Hashanah*, 25a. Rambam, *Hilchos Kiddush HaChodesh*, 17:23). The moon represents a reality beyond knowing, beyond predictability, beyond what can be seen. "All the work (movement) of the sun is done slowly, whereas all the work (movement) of the moon is done suddenly" (*Pirkei d'Rebbe Eliezer*, 7). The sun moves in predictable and gradual ways, while the moon comes and goes in haste, from 'beyond' the world, beyond the regular course of time, outside the confines of solar time. This points to the moon's association with surprise and the miraculous, and this is why living with lunar time gives us an awareness of the possibility to imagine, to dream, to hope and to pray for fulfillment.

Before we can stand outside of the assumed predictability of life and imagine a new reality, we first need to believe our dream is possible. In the free spontaneity of the moon paradigm, everything is indeed possible.

During the story of the Exodus from Egypt, to become a free people, we first needed to imagine the possibility of freedom. We were slaves for such a long time that we started believing it was the only life possible for us, that our slavery was inevitable. Slavery was no longer just our physical condition, rather we began to think of *ourselves* as slaves. We identified with the narrative that was forced upon us. An external voice became our own internal reality.

To become redeemed, we needed to first redeem our imagination and open our minds up to the possibility that Hashem, the Infinite One, could *Schlep* / pull us out of our *Galus* / exile, despite our habitual investment in being enslaved.

As the moon of Nisan swelled to fullness, we stepped out into the night and dreamt of no longer being enslaved to anyone or anything. We prayed to let go of our strictly predictable and hierarchical ways of being. 'If the moon can change', we declared, 'so can we'.

By commanding us to observe the new moon of Nisan in Egypt, HaKadosh Baruch Hu wanted us to start believing in the potential for miracles, supernatural and unpredictable events. Hashem wanted our *Da'as* / awareness and imagination to be inwardly liberated; to intuit that it was possible for us to be physically and spiritually free. Hashem wanted us to understand that, in truth, nothing is routine, old, predictable, or even 'natural' in essence. At every moment there is a completely renewed Creation, a miraculously novel world before us. Nature is nothing but a continuously renewed miracle, giving it the illusion of static immutability.

Nisan is the new year of the months, the first of the new moons; a time for dreams that soar beyond all expectation and prediction. This is why Nisan is the month of Geulah and the month of *Nisim* / miracles. Geulah and Nisim are possible for us when we can open ourselves, even if just a sliver, like the first glimmer of the new moon. The enveloping night sky is the canvas upon which our dreams may be imagined and envisioned by the constantly shifting light of the moon.

LETTING GO OF OUR CURRENT LIMITED PERCEPTION

Nisan is the first of the new moons, 'the renewal of newness'. בניסן נגאלו בניסן עתידין ליגאל / In Nisan we were redeemed (from Egypt) and in Nisan we will be redeemed (from this current exile)" (*Rosh Hashanah*, 11a, the opinion of Rebbe Yehoshua). Nisan, the novelty of newness, is the context for Geulah in the past, present and future.

For our past Geulah to occur, merely connecting with the Chodesh, the new moon, was sufficient to create a context in which the seemingly impossible redemption could occur. The question is, what do we need in order to leave the extreme state of Galus that we are in right now. This Galus is 'extreme' in relation to time, as it has been more than 2,000 years, and it is 'extreme' in relation to space, as Klal Yisrael is dispersed all over the globe. Most significantly, however, it is 'extreme' in relation to consciousness. The Da'as of Klal Yisrael is so alienated and concealed from its proper orientation that many people don't even know they are in exile. The concealment itself is concealed. Because of this, we require a radically powerful way of opening to the 'impossible'. We actually need a miracle in order to open our eyes to the miracle of the Future Geulah. This is the Yom Tov of Purim.

Purim occurs in Adar, the last month of the previous year — 30 days before Pesach. Our sages debate (*Megilah*, 6b) about when Purim is to be celebrated during a leap year, a year that contains two months of Adar. Do we celebrate Purim during the first Adar or the second? Based on the principle that one should not forgo an opportunity to perform a Mitzvah, when presented with such an opportunity, one should do it immediately — one would think that in this case, we should celebrate Purim on the first Adar. However, there is another principle of מסמך גאולה לגאולה / juxtaposing the celebration of one redemption to the celebration of another redemption.

The Halacha follows the second opinion, as we need to connect the redemption of Purim with the redemption of Pesach. When our sages teach משנכנס אדר מרבין בשמחה / "When the month of Adar enters we increase in joy" (*Ta'anis*, 29a), Rashi writes, ימי נסים היו לישראל פורים ופסח / "Miraculous days for the Jewish People were Purim and Pesach." In this way, Pesach and Nisan are subtly enfolded within Purim and Adar (perhaps, since Moshe was born in the month of Adar: *Megilah* 13b. Whether he was born in the first or second Adar is debated: *Sotah*, 13b). Pesach in a sense then emerges from Purim, although the miracle of Purim occurred many centuries after the Exodus from Egypt.

Purim opens us up to receive the Geulah of Pesach, and by extension the Geulah of the future, which will also be revealed in the month of Nisan, as בניסן נגאלו בניסן עתידין ליגאל. We can therefore only truly experience miracles and *Gadlus* / expansiveness on a physical and spiritual level on Pesach, based on how we experience Purim.

As explored in great detail in the book *The Month of Adar*, the month of Adar is connected with *S'chok* / holy, productive, life-affirming laughter and merriment. Purim, and in fact the entire month of Adar, wages battle with Amalek, doubt, cynicism, apathy, indifference. The story of Purim took place in a time of 'concealment within concealment' — it therefore directly addresses the dynamic that we still experience today, of many people being unconscious of the fact that our consciousness is in exile. To remedy this 'extreme' Galus, the Purim experience grabs our attention with complete surprise, miraculously reversing a decree to destroy Klal Yisrael in one day.

With such an unexpected, sudden miracle, in the place of our negative doubt, uncertainty, sarcasm and pessimism, we laughed. The experience of holy *S'chok* / laughter is an unhinging of all limiting perception and conceptions, in response to the shock of the revelation of the Infinite Light of Hashem. This is why *S'chok* is numerically 414, the same as the words *Ohr Ein Sof* / Infinite Light.

Yitzchak is connected with holy laughter. Sarah says, upon his birth, ...לי-יצחק השמע-כל לי עשה צחק / "(Hashem) has brought me laughter; everyone who hears will laugh with me" (*Bereishis*, 21:6,) and she thus names him יצחק / Laughter. Due to her age and apparent inability to have children, neither she nor anyone else could have believed it was possible for her to conceive, much less to give birth. This radical surprise enlightened the eyes of many other childless women, and they too laughed, and they in fact began having children as well. The word the Torah uses to describe Hashem allowing Sarah to become pregnant is *Pakad* / remembered, which can also mean 'redeemed'. In order for us to be redeemed, sometimes the element of surprise, which inspires holy laughter, is necessary.

Avraham and Sarah were both advanced in age, and they certainly overheard "the mocking and cynical laughter of the ליצני הדור / scoffers of the generation, who laughed and said, it is impossible for Avraham, such an old man, to have a child" (*Tanchuma*, Toldos, 1. Rashi, *Bereishis*, 25:19). When they were separately told that they were going to have a child, they each laughed: "And Avraham fell on his face and he laughed, and he said in his heart, can a hundred year old give birth" (*Bereishis*, 17:17)? When Sarah heard, "Sarah laughed in her heart, and she said, after I am worn out and my lord is old, will I now have this pleasure" (*Ibid*, 18:12)? Whether their laughter was warranted or not, and whether it was a laughter of joy or of disbelief, their laughter served to break a certain tension, a finite, defined inner mold or identification with limitation, which in turn allowed for the birth of Yitzchak to occur, for the miracle to be revealed.

All opinions agree that Yitzchak was born during the month of Nisan, on the day that would become Pesach (*Rosh Hashanah*, 10b-11a). The birth of Yitzchak in Nisan thus follows the month of S'chok, Adar, the month that would become the context for Purim. After positive and holy S'chok connected with a revelation of the Ohr Ein Sof, the possibility is created for infinite, 'impossible' miracles to occur.

Purim is the holy laughter in which everything is possible; this leads to Pesach, when the 'impossible' actually became a reality.*

---

* Laughter and drinking (in a proper context, such as on Purim) can also be a way to reach לא ידע / 'unknowing', letting go of what you 'know', what you think is possible, so that you can be open to so much more. There is a Halachah that the Matzah of Pesach has to be eaten with desire and appetite, meaning without a full stomach: *Pesachim*, 99b. There is also a Halacha that since a little bit of wine satisfies hunger (*Berachos*, 35b), one is not allowed to drink a

Positive laughter shakes you out of what you 'think' is possible and gives you the ability to have Emunah in the 'impossible'. Rational thinking is obviously indispensable, however, if rationality leads us to getting stuck in what we think is real or possible, we can become our own worst enemy, arresting our growth in all levels of life — material, interpersonal, emotional, mental and spiritual. We rationally delineate limitations on our potentials, and then think, 'This dream is not possible, it will never happen'. This thought can become a self-fulfilling prophecy, and indeed it will not happen. For miracles to happen, we need to let go of rational limitations on what we think is possible. This is why Nisan follows Adar. Our past Geulah, as well as our future Geulah, follows Purim. We might have a little Amalek voice, an inner skeptic whispering, 'Oh, do you really think the world can change, and that Moshiach and Redemption will come? How naive and foolish!' To shake ourselves out of this, we need to stop and laugh at our own limited perception, and say, 'Ah, it seems I really must know everything!

---

little wine before the Seder. However, a 'lot of wine' does not satisfy, rather it stimulates more hunger (*Ibid*), and for this reason one can drink a 'lot' before the Seder (the Alter Rebbe, in *Shulchan Aruch*, adds, "although not too much"). In fact, as the Gemara tells us, רבא הוה שתי חמרא כל מעלי יומא דפסחא כי היכי דנגרריה ללביה וניכול מצה / "Rava drank a lot of wine on Erev Pesach in order to stimulate his heart (create a bigger appetite for the Matzah)." This can also be understood on a more allegorical level: drinking "before the Seder" refers to Purim. Rava drank a lot on Purim (maybe he drank a lot on Erev Pesach, as well) to let go of his *Da'as* / rational awareness, so that he could be open to truly have a mental, emotional, spiritual and physical appetite (as the physical and spiritual are linked) for the Geulah on Pesach Night. Indeed, it is Rava himself who rules that מיחייב איניש לבסומי בפוריא עד דלא ידע בין ארור המן לברוך מרדכי / "A person is obligated to become intoxicated with wine on Purim until he is so intoxicated that he does not know how to distinguish between 'cursed is Haman' and 'blessed is Mordechai'": *Megilah*, 7b.

What a joke!' Holy laughter opens us up to unimaginable possibilities, preparing the way for redemptive miracles.

The Baal Shem Tov once said that if we had true Emunah all the seas in the world would split for us. The reason such miracles do not occur for us, is because we don't really believe that they can actually happen. We become so invested in the conventional, empirical world that we lose our ability to appreciate the mysteries of life.

We need Emunah like that of the women of Klal Yisrael. Women, who are more connected with the rhythm of the moon, and thus, with Rosh Chodesh and hope for renewal, have an inherent capacity to believe in and dream of redemption. בשכר נשים צדקניות שהיו באותו הדור נגאלו ישראל ממצרים / "It was in the merit of the righteous women in that generation that the Jewish people were redeemed from Egypt" (*Sotah*, 11b). Their merit, courage and vision of the future was powered by Emunah. This unmovable faith and inspiring hope became the foundation of that redemption, and it will be the foundation of the coming ultimate redemption, with the arrival of Moshiach. Emunah is the power that overcomes all *Safek* / doubt and skepticism, only faith can overcome the inner voice that whispers, 'Geulah is not possible, it is clearly a lost cause after these 2000 years; there is no hope for this world'. Emunah is the power that guided Queen Esther to approach the king, uninvited, to request the salvation of her People. Emunah is the light ignited by women around the world, which ushers in Shabbos well before sunset, and which confidently welcomes in the complete redemption, the swiftly arriving day of eternal perfection and unity.

GEULAH COMES FROM THE EIN SOF (AND BEYOND), THE AYIN BEYOND THE YESH OF REALITY

Yesh / existence is the reality of things as they appear. The situation and details of your life, and all of life, with its physicality and seemingly individual, separate existences. Yet, Yesh is not merely 'illusory' appearance; it is actually a particular manifestation of the Infinite *Ayin* / no-thing-ness. Creation as a whole comes into existence as *Yesh meAyin* / somethingness from no-thing-ness. Being continuously unfolds out of the Transcendent, Unmanifest, Unformed, Divine Ayin or *Ein Sof* / Infinity into a dazzling array of defined forms within a space-time-consciousness continuum. In other words, Yesh is real, but it is not as opaque and impenetrable as we may think. It is like the open, ever-fluctuating moon. It is a matrix of the miraculous.

In a person's Yesh reality, they may seem enslaved or trapped, with no possibility of salvation, stuck in a bad job without growth opportunities, or, G-d forbid, stuck in an illness with little hope of improving. Such a person needs to lift up their eyes to the One Above (as it were) to the Ein Sof, the Ayin, and recognize that "Even / אפילו חרב חדה מונחת על צוארו של אדם אל ימנע עצמו מן הרחמים if a sharp sword rests upon a person's neck, he should not prevent himself from praying for mercy" (*Berachos*, 10a). There is always hope, because the Source of this world of Yesh is *Ein Sof* / unlimited and there are thus *Ein Sof* / infinite possibilities available. What we need to do is strengthen our Emunah by cultivating a stronger connection to the Truth beyond the observable world of Yesh — to the ever-present freedom of Ayin. We need to know and trust that our lives themselves are like the moon, ever-evolving and flowing with the power of *Chidush* / renewal.

Dovid HaMelech / King David sings, "I lift up my eyes to the mountains and ask, מאין / *meAyin* / from where will my help come? My salvation comes from Hashem, the Creator of the heavens and earth" (*Tehilim*, 121:1-2). Most often this passage is read as a question and answer, Dovid asks, where will my salvation come from, and then he answers that it will come from the Creator. On a deeper level, Dovid is not posing a question, he is making a statement: מאין / *meAyin* / 'from Ayin' will come my help, from the Ein Sof, the 'Infinity' of Hashem, which is the unmanifest potential of all potentials.

When Rebbe Yochanan and many of the sages declare that אין מזל לישראל / "there is no *Mazal* / constellation for Israel" (*Shabbos*, 156a), it also means that אין / Ayin *is* the Mazal of Klal Yisrael. The reality of Ayin itself is our source of guiding influence (*Likutei Torah*, (Alter Rebbe) Haazinu, 71d. Rebbe Rayatz, *Kuntres Chanoch laNa'ar*, p. 48). We are, in fact, one with the Ayin of HaKadosh Baruch Hu, as in the words of the Maharsha (*Bechoros*, 8b) regarding Klal Yisrael, שאין להם מזל בשמים... אבל הם בת מזלו של הקב"ה / "They do not *have* a Mazal in the celestial spheres... they *are* the Mazal of HaKadosh Baruch Hu."

We need to train ourselves to "lift" our eyes up to the mountains, and beyond; to lift our vision above seeming impossibility, above the challenges and hardship that overshadow our lives like foreboding, unclimbable mountains. We need to look beyond ourselves and connect to the Infinite Ein Sof with resolute Emunah.

When the Torah contrasts the land of Egypt with the Land of Israel, the Torah says, "The land which you are about to conquer is not like the land of Egypt from which you have come, where, when you planted your field, you watered it with your foot... The Land which you are about to conquer, a land of hills and valleys, receives its water from the rains of the Heavens" (*Devarim*, 11:10-11). The Torah is pointing out that the Egyptians were dependent on an irrigation system, drawing water from the Nile ("from under your feet"), whereas in Israel you will become dependent on rainfall from the heavens. Israel lacks a mighty river such as the Nile to provide the land with a continuous, predictable supply of water. The agriculture in the Land of ancient Israel was utterly dependent on natural rainfall. In Egypt your water came from your 'legs', meaning from your 'feet', a natural, more predictable source. So long as you maintained a good irrigation system, your fields would flourish. By contrast, Israel was, and is, a land of 'dreaming' and yearning, where one must lift their eyes upward in prayer. In general, rain is not predictable or controllable (to date, even manipulations such as 'cloud seeding' are not proven to be reliable methods of increasing precipitation). This makes you continually 'lift up your eyes to Heaven', to the true Source of earth's bounty. The Land of Israel forces one to live in direct and continuous relationship to the Ayin, to the miraculous, to the Ein Sof.

FOR MIRACLES TO OCCUR WE NEED TO BELIEVE THAT THEY CAN OCCUR

To put it simply, the second step in revealing miracles is Emunah. For miracles to occur, we need to believe that they can occur, as belief is part of the *Kli* / vessel that draws down the Light of miracles.

To be an instrument of miraculous or unforeseeable blessings, we need to have faith in such a possibility. Rebbe Pinchas of Koritz (*Imrei Pinchas*, 57) teaches that when a person has faith in Hashem, the Source of all possibilities, this itself is a miracle. Through the miracle of having faith the person draws down further miracles.

Before proceeding to the third step, let us briefly recap. The first element that we need to activate is 'speaking', giving voice to our frustration over current circumstances in prayer. As we pray to the Source of our reality, we open ourselves up to the miraculous, the 'impossible', that which is beyond our normal modes of knowing. We make a conscious connection with the Ein Sof, the Ayin beyond the Yesh of the world. This connection allows us to dream of and visualize what could be. The third stage is to surrender to Hashem's will, which is an actual experience of Ayin.

THIRD STEP: SURRENDERING

3) The third and most detailed stage in the process of becoming a vessel for miracles is to be humble, as suggested by the Mazal of the month, Aries / the Lamb. Part of being humble is being grateful and giving thanks, which is the theme of the tribe of the month, Yehudah. Indeed, gratefulness comes from humility, as a deeply humble person takes nothing for granted and receives everything as a gift.

After speaking our hearts in prayer and dreaming with faith that the 'impossible' is possible, the next step is *Bitul* / ego-nullification and entering *Ayin* / no-thing consciousness. This is a surrender to and acceptance of Hashem's will, which opens us up to HaKadosh Baruch Hu's Infinite potential for blessings.

MOSHE IS AYIN

Nullifying personal desires in Ayin allows for miraculous and unforeseen salvations to occur. The greatest and most profound instrument and facilitator of miracles in the Torah is Moshe Rabbeinu / Moshe, Our Teacher. The *Miluyim* / 'filling letters' of the name Moshe confirm this fact, as follows. The three letters in the name Moshe are Mem, Shin and Hei. *Mem* is spelled Mem-Mem (thus, the 'filling letter' is Mem). *Shin* is spelled Shin-Yud-Nun (the filling letters being Yud and Nun). *Hei* is spelled Hei-Aleph (the filling letter being Aleph). The letters Mem, Yud, Nun and Aleph, rearranged, spell *meAyin* / from Ayin (Rav Menachem Tziyoni, *V'Zos haBerachah*. Also cited by the *Shaloh*, Shemos, 2). The power to bring salvation to Klal Israel, to draw unexpected and miraculous blessings down into the world, is rooted in Moshe's deeply humble Bitul and constant connection to Ayin.

Ayin is the formless potential that precedes the creation of any particular form of some-thing-ness. Creation is existence and form, flowing from Ayin. When a person humbles himself with extreme self-sacrifice, his self becomes a selfless self. He becomes the embodiment of Ayin, entering the silence that comes before the sound of the Divine Utterances that create the world. He becomes the stillness before movement, the emptiness before the fullness. In this way he is able to be a conduit channeling a new flow of revealed blessings, new Divine Utterances, so-to-speak; new Yesh from the infinite Ayin.

The root of the word Nisan is *Nes* / miracle. The numerical value of the word *Nes* (Nun/50, Samach/60), with the *Kollel* / addition of 1 representing the word itself, is 111. This is the numerical value of the name of the letter Aleph (Aleph/1, Lamed/30, Pei/80 = 111). The miraculous manifestation of new forms is rooted in the Aleph, the silent first letter, the 'beginning', or the 'thought' that precedes the *Beis* of Creation (*Degel Machaneh Ephraim*, Chukas). Aleph represents the Ayin, the unmanifest no-thing-ness that precedes manifestation.

THE PARADOX

This may seem quite paradoxical; first you say what is bothering you, then you faithfully imagine a better reality, and now it is being suggested that you let go of control and nullify your will in Ayin, which implies a humble acceptance and thankfulness for what is. However, we cannot allow miracles beyond expectation to occur if we are still engaging in *Yesh* / egoic will and personal expectation. If we are still focussing on whether our prayers are answered or not and constantly seeking their results, we are still attempting to assert our own will, which closes our connection to Ayin, our conduit of blessings. (One should not think: "I prayed with such intention, certainly my prayers will be answered," and in this way wait for the answer: *Rosh Hashanah*, 16b. This is called 'negative *Iyyun Tefillah*' according to Rashi and Tosefos.)

We need to surrender control if we want to allow change to occur. We need to give up our expectations, our images and ideas of what we really want, and even think we need. The word 'wanting', in English, also means 'lacking' — if we 'want' something, we paradoxically block ourselves from 'having' it. Our hand remains clenched instead of open to receive. Our own expectations limit the manifestation of Hashem's unexpected possibilities. Hashem is Infinite and therefore knows of infinite ways to give us gifts. If we persistently hold a distinct image of what we think we need before our mind's eye, we are limiting what we can see.

It was of course vital that we began by defining and knowing what was bothering us. And we do need to have a clear awareness of what our Egypt, our constrictions, are, be they physical, mental, emotional or spiritual. We do need to voice our desire and prayer for change. We do need to draw within our mind an image of what we would like to see and dream with Emunah in the Infinite Source of All Life that everything is possible — that even a sea can split. But then we need to let it all go, even if just momentarily, and say, 'Hashem in Your Infinite Wisdom do what is best for me and I hereby completely accept Your will.' We need to be able to say, 'Hashem You are Infinite, and even beyond Infinite; let me not limit the manifestation of Your blessings by defining them in my limited comprehension. I am willing to let go of the image I have created and put it in Your hands.'

Up until now, the process has been described in terms of a sequence of steps, but the truth is, letting go in Ayin can be paradoxically practiced even while engaged in steps one and two. Even when we are yearning, praying and visualizing images of what we think we want and desire, we can simultaneously surrender our perceptions, statements and images, as if to say, 'Hashem in Your Infinite reality, bring us the blessings we need in any of Your infinite ways, and if my specifications are not what are best for me, please let me be open to whatever is truly best.'

Even while persistently praying for and imagining a specific miracle or salvation, we need to acknowledge our powerlessness, our sense of being *Ayin* / no-thing, in order to be open for the Ultimate and Infinite power of Hashem to run through us. Our vessel needs to be cleared if it is to be filled.

AYIN AS LETTING GO OF ALL ATTACHMENTS & RESULTS

One aspect of Ayin, as has been suggested, is surrendering our limited perception of what we think is good for us, or *how* something is good for us; surrendering our preconception of what blessings should manifest. For example, 'I need to make this or that business deal, I should get into this or that school, get this or that job, enter a relationship with this or that person.' The blessings of the Infinite One are themselves infinite and transcend any context or vessel that we can create.

Any difficult situation in life represents Yesh; that is the way circumstances are manifest in a particular moment. Let's say someone is struggling with making ends meet or struggling with their health. For a miracle to occur, there needs to be a new and different manifestation, a new Yesh, namely a different form of prosperity or health. Yet, for one Yesh to disappear and another Yesh to manifest, there needs to first be an emergence of or immersion in *Ayin* / no-thing-ness. A seed disintegrates in the soil before it can sprout new life, and if a person wishes to use the wood of a table and make it a chair, he first he needs to deconstruct the table (*Likutei Amarim, Ohr Torah*, p. 21). In order for one form to change to another form, it needs to go through a process of shedding its first form; the old Yesh has to become Ayin before a new Yesh can appear. And here is the secret: an object can only become Ayin through our relationship to it. If we are Ayin in our relationship to a certain Yesh, then that object too becomes Ayin as it were.

Spirituality and physicality mirror each other. Just as changing a silver plate to a cup requires flattening out the old form, to alter a spiritual reality you need to 'elevate' the existing Yesh to a state of open potential in Ayin. This elevation is accomplished primarily by the observer of the spiritual object themselves becoming Ayin, including being personally unattached in relation to that object. The observer affects the observed, at least in its relationship to the observer, and thus the observed also becomes Ayin. Then from this state of Ayin a new Yesh can become manifest.

Say, for example, you want to change your habit of being distracted in prayer, and begin to experience Deveikus in the Amidah. The way your attention is functioning now is the current Yesh, and this needs to be elevated and dissolved in Ayin in order to allow a new level of attention to emerge. For you to be Ayin in relation to your stream of thoughts, one approach is to simply declare yourself above them, unattached and unconcerned. Be nothing, and give stray thoughts no landing place. In other words, do not fight the mental distractions, nor show any interest in them; just let them be while calmly ignoring them like an absentminded host. You are not actively avoiding or suppressing your thoughts. You are above them and they cannot touch you. Keep your eyes on the words of the Siddur, and if necessary keep your finger on the place you are reciting, as thoughts rise and vanish into Ayin.

If this strategy of ignoring thoughts does not seem to help, you may need to submit your thinking to Hashem altogether, both the 'words' of distracting thoughts, and the words of the Siddur. Neither the distracting thoughts nor the words of prayer are yours; you are placing them both in Hashem's hands. This way you become the Ayin 'prior to' the Yesh of all thoughts, before all words you are no more than a silent listener. Before beginning the Amidah, you can contemplate the opening sentence, *Ado-noi Sifasai Tiftach uv'Fi Yagid Tehilasecha* / "Hashem, may *You* open my lips and my mouth speak *Your* praise." The words and praises of Tefillah are Hashem's own words and praises; you are just a bystander, allowing Hashem to speak through you, as it were. You are a self-empty conduit for Hashem's praise of Hashem. You might not even *Shukel* / sway or move in the Tefillah, because it is not 'your' Tefillah; there is no more you, Only One, Only Hashem.

Either way, once you are nullified, along with all of your so-called 'distractions,' now you can fill your mind with the new Yesh: the awareness that the words of Tefillah have profound meanings and intentions, whether you know the details or not. The words of the Siddur are invitations to Deveikus. Listen for and accept one or more of these invitations. Come back, again and again, to the Ayin above thought, whenever needed. Every word is a doorway to the deepest depths. All is contained within every one.

To draw down miracles, we need to *be* Ayin in relationship to our presently projected Yesh. This means, on one level, to simply observe our life from a place of *Ayin* / no-thing-ness; a detached, objective witness state, without investment in the Yesh and drama of life.

Naturally, from the place of ego and self-centeredness, we are all very much attached to the things of our lives, our homes, cars, money, gadgets and so forth. And we are also very much invested in and attached to the narratives of our lives, our careers, relationships, thoughts, emotions, sensations and desires. This can be called a 'lower Yesh consciousness'. On this level of operating, there is tremendous reluctance to surrender to, or even just relax our grip on, all the 'things' in our lives. There can also be a tenacious resistance to let go of certain aspects of our inner life: what we think we 'know', our deeper thought patterns and perspectives, our history and identity — it can be difficult to release these even for a few moments.

It is usually from the context of this 'lower level Yesh consciousness' that we go through the first two stages, the speaking, praying, imagining and dreaming of our lives changing for the better. Yet, again, for change to occur we need the Ayin stage, the place where we let go of the results, and all the attachments to the 'things' in our lives, including our thoughts, feelings, possessions, and personal identity.

In this place, we learn to become mere observers of our lives. Life continues to happen, we still eat, sleep, work, have thoughts and feelings and perform mundane activities; we still perform Mitzvos, study, pray and refine ourselves and our relationships. Still, it feels more like watching our life than being enclosed within it. In this, there is an existential relinquishing of the anxiety-ridden, obsessive attachment to the 'things' in our life. It is like seeing a film; things come and go on the screen, thoughts and feelings arise and fall away, yet your attention is always focused on the film. Life then feels more free and light, empty of tension, and with less self-centered ambition and desire. This is Ayin consciousness.

STAGE 3 COUPLED WITH STAGE 1 & 2

It is important to keep in mind that although the Ayin stage is ultimately required to tap into the Infinite Source of Blessings, steps one and two are equally important. The process of voicing, demanding, dreaming and envisioning a new Yesh, is equally as important as releasing it all in Ayin. Furthermore, although it seems that steps one and two are polar opposites of stage three, and thus they can only function in sequence, the truth is all three can be practiced simultaneously.

One might think that the Yesh of demanding and picturing, and the Ayin of surrendering, are mutually exclusive. Yet, from the perspective of *Etzem* / essence, this is not so. Etzem, otherwise known as the *Yesh haAmiti* / Ultimate Yesh, is beyond all expressions, yet includes all expressions. From the perspective of Etzem the formless Ayin and the form of Yesh are equally existent. From an *Etzem* consciousness, form and formless, finite and infinite, fullness and emptiness — all polarities — are embraced and included within a greater unity.

Both stages 1 and 2, without a good sense of stage 3, are lacking. When we approach life merely from our ego, from our Yesh, there is inevitably some level of unhealthy dependency and attachment to objects. Merely having ambitions, dreams, desires, without any sense of surrender or humility, leaves a person in an anxiety-filled, and even paranoid, existence. Yet, if we live only in stage 3, in Ayin-consciousness, with complete surrender of all attachments, unmoved by anything, unconcerned and unambitious, we cannot and will not accomplish anything in life. We will not help build institutions or give charity, nor refine our character, nor strive to make this world a place where Hashem's presence can be felt by all, as everything is already experienced as perfect and whole. True *Gadlus haMochin* / expansive consciousness includes these two paradigms simultaneously.

We need to learn to unite all three stages as one. From a place of non-attachment, we must also experience holy re-attachment. We must grow in our capacity to dream, and ask Hashem for the fulfilment of all the physical, material, mental and spiritual needs of those around us, and of all human beings, while at the same time we need to ensure that we ourselves achieve our purpose in being created.

AYIN AS A LETTING GO OF THE BODY & ITS NEEDS

It cannot be stressed enough that it is not sufficient to simply think about the idea of Ayin, to 'connect' to the Ayin, or even to experience some measure of Ayin and detachment. In order to effect miracles, one must actually 'be' Ayin in order for the new Yesh to appear. One therefore needs to experience some level of *Hispashtus haGashmiyus* / divestment of materiality. In this spiritual state, one is internally detached and isolated from bodily sensations, thus transcending the constrictions of the physical world. This is also called 'living in *Tzurah* / abstract form', as opposed to indulging or being preoccupied with the world of *Chomer* / substance and materialism.

You cannot lose yourself in consuming a steak or any other 'compulsion', nor blow up in anger when someone insults you, and then expect to right away 'be' Ayin or become immersed in the *Yuli* / ethereal layer of existence sometimes associated with Ayin. To be a facilitator of miracles, you need to exercise discipline in cultivating a 'hovering' kind of existence, being within the world but always one step 'above' it. This is the reason the prophets were the vehicles through which miracles occurred, because they lived in a constant state of Hispashtus, and identified more as pure, unbounded consciousness than as a body with insatiable urges and yearnings.

AYIN AS MESIRAS NEFESH

Beyond a general detachment from 'things' or a surrendering of one's thoughts, expectations and specific outcomes, although these are required, on a deeper level, Ayin is a total surrender of selfhood, a state of *Mesiras Nefesh* / giving one's life to Hashem's will. This means to be free of the drive to gain things for yourself, or to focus only on what you can get out of any given experience. Rather it means that all your drives and focus are directed to the thought, speech, action and states of consciousness that bring more *Kevod Shamayim* / honor of HaKadosh Baruch Hu into this world.

Some people are always asking, 'How can I get what I want?

How will this experience fulfill my needs? How will that encounter benefit me?' But for a person living with Mesiras Nefesh, the question is, 'What am I needed for? What does Hashem want of me right now? How can I 'benefit' Hashem, so-to-speak?' Mesiras Nefesh means giving up your personal will, and being an empty vessel for the *Kevod Hashem* / glory of the Divine Will.

Sometimes Mesiras Nefesh demands literally giving one's life, however, we are discussing 'the Mesiras Nefesh of the living', giving your entire self to HaKadosh Baruch Hu while remaining in this world. This is arguably harder than the Mesiras Nefesh of 'being martyred'. In any case, miracles occur to those who perform self-sacrifice for Kevod Shamayim. The sages ask, מאי שנא ראשונים דאתרחיש להו ניסא ומאי שנא אנן דלא מתרחיש לן ניסא / "What is different about the earlier generations, for whom miracles occurred, and what is unique about us, for whom miracles do not occur?" קמאי הוו קא מסרי נפשייהו אקדושת השם אנן לא מסרינן נפשין אקדושת השם / "Previous generations, had Mesiras Nefesh for the sanctification of Hashem's Name, while we do not have Mesiras Nefesh for the sanctification of Hashem's Name" (*Berachos*, 20a. In this context, *Mesiras Nefesh* means literally giving up one's life to sanctify Hashem's Name for reasons *other than* the refusal to transgress one of the three cardinal sins. Being *Moser Nefesh* instead of transgressing any of the three cardinal sins is an obligation and commandment even for us, the אחרונים / latter generations).

AYIN AS PUSHING BEYOND THE EGO'S COMFORT ZONE

Another way of living in a state of Ayin and Mesiras Nefesh is to push beyond what you think are your limits, or what you feel is your comfort zone, specifically in your *Avodah* / spiritual work. In the words of the Ramak (*Ohr Yakar*, Pekudei), if one breaks his *Teva* / nature and in his service of Hashem reaches beyond his natural comfort zone, then *Teva* / nature itself will break for him, and he can be an instrument to reveal miracles beyond nature.

In numerical value, *me'Ayin* / 'from Ayin' is 101. Our sages tell us that there is a great difference between one who learns and reviews their studies 100 times, versus one who learns and reviews them 101 times. The parable given is of a donkey whose job it is to take loads from one city to the next, a distance of 10 miles. For this, the charge is one coin. If the person renting the donkey wants to go just a little further than that, say 11 miles, he is charged two coins. If 10 miles is one's "comfort zone" or habitual pattern, going the extra mile is thus equal in effort to going 10 miles. Our sages say that to be a true servant of Hashem, to truly do the inner work, you need to extend yourself that extra mile, reviewing your studies just one extra time (*Chagigah*, 9b) even when you assume that you have already mastered them and can now take it easy. The number 100 represents completion. Going beyond 'completion', or reviewing a *Sugya* / subject for the 101st time, is the act that 'breaks your nature' and catapults you to the level of Ayin, beyond any trace of self-definition or egoic complacency. (Note that the difference between the word זכר / remember (227) and שכח / forget (328) is 101. To fully inscribe a lesson into our consciousness, we need to push beyond the urge to settle for a limited sense of accomplishment.)

When we break out of our laziness and push ourselves just a little beyond our assumed *Koach* / strength, we dip into the Ayin, beyond our Yesh, our normative sense of agency, and thus, we open ourselves up to become an agent or conduit of HaKadosh Baruch Hu's flow of miracles.

It is not by coincidence that the great Tzadikim throughout history who were known to be 'miracle workers' are those who pushed themselves tremendously, both spiritually and physically. Whether in the world of Chesed, sacrificing themselves in being kind and giving to others, or, if they were 'introverts', giving of themselves to their Torah students with Mesiras Nefesh. The essential element and common denominator is transcending their own Teva, becoming themselves a *Nes* / miracle.

After Klal Yisrael had left Egypt and escaped slavery, they found themselves standing at the banks of the raging sea, with the Egyptians nearing them from behind, they seemed stuck. The urgent question was raised: Should they battle against the fiercest power on the planet, surely a losing battle? Or should they rather lay down their arms and meekly return to Egypt? As both of those choices were doomed, should they defiantly commit mass suicide by jumping into the waters? Or, more aligned with their ancestral path, should they not stand and pray, and scream to Hashem for help? Various groups argued urgently for each of these options. At that moment, a prince of Israel, Nachshon the son of Aminadav, walked resolutely into the sea. Letting go of and nullifying all his notions of the properties of water and its nature to drown those submerged in it, having complete trust and faith in Hashem's affection for Klal Yisrael, he opened the way for perhaps the greatest miracle in world history to occur, and the sea split, allowing the entire nation to make it to the other side.

Nachshon's Emunah, coupled with his Mesiras Nefesh in breaking and transcending his natural survival instincts, his Teva, instantaneously made him the instrument of the miraculous salvation of

Klal Yisrael. All the men, women, children and animals surged after him, and they all marched through the waters on dry land, with an upraised hand of victory. Such 'Mesiras Nefesh of the living' requires piercing the limits and strategies of the ego and walking forward with unshakable faith.

Anyone can, at times, rise to the occasion in their way; like Nachshon transcending beyond what is currently imaginable and seemingly possible. For instance, you could stay up at night a few minutes later or awaken in the morning a few minutes earlier to learn Torah. If you calculate that you can give 100 dollars to charity, give 101 dollars. Sometimes, life itself forces us to either take the high road and meet a challenge, or to turn away and fall. When a test arises, we are presented with a choice to live 'bigger' or to buckle. The words *Nisayon* / test and *Nes* / miracle share the same root letters. Indeed, tests and miracles are closely related. A miracle is when the natural, rational or predictable surface of our reality is broken and something beyond our imagination occurs. A 'test' is when the Creator invites us to do the same, to *be* the miracle. A predicament can force us to do something that we never thought possible. That is why people who overcome great tests and challenges in life, become miraculous beings, around whom miracles can occur.

THE SIX DIMENSIONS OF AYIN

According to the exploration above, 'being Ayin', the third stage of opening to miracles, has six Dimensions:

1) Surrendering our perception of reality to the will of Hashem, including what we think we need, and how and when we need it;

2) Letting go of any attachments to outcomes and results, despite our dreaming, aspiring, imagining and praying for those very outcomes;

3) Surrendering all our attachment to the objects and Yesh in our life; relating to things from the standpoint of Ayin;

4) Letting go of our personal, egoic needs, in service of a higher cause; asking not what we can gain from life, but what we can contribute;

5) Living with Mesiras Nefesh on all levels and areas of life;

6) Pushing ourselves beyond our comfort zone, breaking our Teva and living beyond it to the extent that we become a living miracle and nature miraculously breaks for us.

LIVE AS IF THE MIRACLE HAS ALREADY OCCURRED

To these six, we could add one more: Sometimes, for the miracles and blessings to actually occur, we need to stop, pause, and even let go (so-to-speak) of Davening itself. We can become so fixated on the process, on the experience of yearning and longing itself, that we become stuck in a labyrinth of our own devising. When this happens, we are unable to create the necessary space within ourselves for the miracles to enter into our lives. We need to be open to receive the miracles, yet, paradoxically, sometimes it is our very desire and Davening that does not allow that opening to emerge. All of our striving to achieve a state of Ayin can end up filling that empty space with more Yesh. To counter this, we need to Daven intensely, and then stop waiting for our prayers to be answered (which is called *Iyun Tefillah*, a negative mode of absorption in prayer). Instead, at such a moment we must simply start living as if our Tefilos have already been accepted. Start living the miracle you requested.

Rebbe Elimelch of Lizhensk once said that Moshiach would come in his own days or in the days of his Talmidim/students. Decades later, the second Belzer Rebbe was wondering what this meant. One night, the Belzer had a dream of Rebbe Elimelech, and he asked him, "Rebbe, none of your students are still alive... where is Moshiach?"

Rebbe Elimelech told him to ask a question, and that way he would be his 'Talmid'. The Belzer asked, "When the Jewish people stood at the shore of the Sea and the Egyptians were coming up behind them, they cried out but were told not to pray nor to ask for rescue: 'Speak to the People of Israel,' said Hashem to Moshe, 'and they shall journey forward.' But Rebbe," continued the Belzer, "we were just developing this relationship with HaKadosh Baruch Hu through speaking, and it seems that we *should* have been praying at that moment." In the dream, Rebbe Elimelech then explained the answer with a story:

There was a princess in a great land who was going through a terrifying labor and the baby still was not being born. The king called all the experts and doctors but nobody was able to help. Finally, an old man came and said, "I have the solution!" He sent everyone out of the room and told the king and the princess to send out a message to the whole kingdom proclaiming that the baby had been born healthy. They did so, and immediately the baby was born and the mother and child were both well.

Reb Elimelech explained that when we pray and ask for something, there is still room for doubt whether it will happen or not. There is still an *Ayin haRa* / Evil Eye upon the situation, and there is still uncertainty in the mother that she will be successful. This doubt and negative context creates more panic and more negativity, which physically holds back the child even more, and thus holds up the birth. But when we act as though the thing we needed is already a fact and it has been accomplished, all concealments and negativity fall away.

HaKadosh Baruch Hu was telling Klal Yisrael that it wasn't time to ask for anything. They had to believe with all their hearts that they were meant to escape Egypt and receive the Torah, and therefore there could be no doubt that they would be saved, rather, they needed to act as if the sea had already split. Rather than praying for a miracle, they needed to act as if it already occurred, as if the 'baby' had already been born (Perhaps Reb Elimelech is also hinting at the idea of Moshiach as well).

We too need to believe that the miracles we need have already occurred — to go out and buy the baby stroller or happily imagine living in the new home. We should act as if the blessings that we were praying for have already materialized, and even celebrate and give thanks for them.

In this month of miracles and *Geulah* / redemption on all external and internal, collective and personal levels, may we merit to be truly freed of all constrictions and limitations and experience the ultimate miracle: the coming of Moshiach, speedily in our days.

PRACTICE: PART II

KAVANAH / MINDFUL INTENTION,
I: SPEAKING OPENLY AND FREELY WITH HAKADOSH BARUCH HU

Humility, gratitude, openness to new beginnings, miracles, and the power of speech, these all comprise the spiritual tapestry of the month of Nisan.

Pesach is about the concept of *Peh Sach* / 'a mouth that speaks' of redemption, a mouth that is no longer in exile, no longer alienated, constricted, or incapable of expressing one's inner desires, wants, yearnings. An exiled power of *Dibur* / speech feels *Kaveid* / heavy, closed, unable to speak freely. Redeemed Dibur is effortless, expressive and free flowing.

As mentioned, the process of becoming free from Egypt only began when Klal Yisrael was open enough to 'cry out'. Only once there was a movement, a groan and a cry, on the part of Klal Yisrael, was the process of redemption set into motion.

Crying is liberating in its own right. The arousal of emotion demonstrates an aliveness within. A person can be so stuck in their predicament, so numb, depressed or traumatized, that they even lose their ability to cry. If someone cannot cry, certainly they do not have the *Koach* / strength to look up to Heaven, as it were, and pray to Hashem for change and to articulate their needs and desires. Their inner voice, and even their desire for change, may have been silenced to the point that they have given up. They may even have stopped believing in the possibility of change altogether.

The most devastating sensation that comes with this form of alienation is the sense of isolation, of being all alone in the universe. This feeling magnifies the inability to self-express, and creates even deeper frustration and loneliness.

Just before the first groan emerged from the hearts of Klal Yisrael, the old king of Egypt died, and the monotonous drudgery of slavery was momentarily broken. In the sublte disruption of this event, Klal Yisrael suddenly noticed that there is indeed change, there are alternative realities, and perhaps even that slavery was not their necessary fate. Such a sudden, stark contrast to their cognitive biases made them cry out, and they spontaneously reached out to HaKadosh Baruch Hu with a primal, wordless, 'prayer'.

Maybe a life situation or a deeply felt need stimulates a movement and desire in you to reach out to the One who Hears, or maybe it is a good friend or a book that inspires you to do so. Either way, what is most important is to use this opening to begin a process of inward and outward redemption, to allow the impulse to reach out to grow into a cry or a prayer, a vibration or song. All the while, maintain the sense that you are not alone; Hashem is always with you, feels your pain, and wants to help you.

For some, full-fledged, formal Tefillah is not yet (or always) possible, while simply speaking to Hashem as one friend speaks to another, is much more accessible. This is fine; just keep the channel open between you and HaKadosh Baruch Hu. Furthermore, if one is not yet comfortable presenting a full 'monologue' to Hashem, just saying, "O my G-d" or "Hashem please help me," or even just repeating the phrase *Ribono shel Olam* / "Master of the World" over and over can help a person feel and know that they are heard. Remember: you are never alone. Whenever you feel there is a caring Presence listening, you have created an opening and you are on the path towards a deeper level of inner freedom and redemption.

PRAYER AND REDEMPTION

A human being is defined as a *Medaber* / speaker. When we cannot express ourselves, we are in exile and a little less 'human'. As we learn from *Yetziyas Mitzrayim*, our redemption begins with some form of vocalized expression of our desires, yearnings, hopes and dreams.

Formal Tefillah or Davening, at set times and using a set liturgy, can and should be an arena in which we cultivate a vibrant, living connection with *Elokim Chayim* / the Living G-d. This can be done in such a way that *enhances* one's ability to live in a fluid, dynamic, free flowing way. Yet, sadly, many people feel that the discipline of set Tefillah is another burden they wish to avoid, and they merely puppet the words and go through the motions, and at the end of Davening they feel just as alone, alienated, exiled, lost and forgotten as they did before, maybe even more. In this case, the informal prayer of openly and freely speaking to HaKadosh Baruch Hu as a 'friend' may help create a dramatic breakthrough.

In formal Tefillah, we often play the role of a servant pleading in front of their Master, but for many, it is necessary to engage in a more informal mode of Tefillah, in which they speak to Hashem openly, like a child speaking to a loving parent. These two typologies of Tefillah, the servant and the child, are reflected in the qualities of Gevurah and Chesed.

The profound teacher and moralist, Rav Elazar Azikri (Tzefas, 1533-1600), brings a tradition that at least once a week, a person, even a Torah scholar, should spend time alone with HaKadosh Baruch Hu, as it were: וידבר לא-ל ית׳ כאשר ידבר...ובן אל אביו / "and he should speak to Hashem… as a child speaks to his father" (*Sefer Chareidim*, 65. See also *Michtavei Chafetz Chayim*, pp. 96-97. *Mishnah Berurah*, Siman 571, Biur Halacha, 2. *Sheivet haMusar*, 20:39).

In truth, millenia ago, all Tefillah was 'informal' and spontaneous. In fact, according to the Ramban, the Mitzvah of Tefillah is not that one should Daven each day, but that one should Daven to Hashem when they need to. Spontaneous prayer is the essence of Tefillah, which is intended to help us cultivate a living, vibrant relationship with *Elokim Chayim* / the Living Divinity. It is only because of the inadequacy of most people's expression when living in Galus, that Tefillah, namely the Shemoneh Esrei, was formalized and written down. As the Rambam codifies: "When the People of Israel went into exile…they mingled with the Persians, Greeks and other nations. In those foreign countries, children were born to them, whose language was confused. Everyone's speech was a mixture of many tongues. No one was able, when he spoke, to express his thoughts in any one language, in a way that was not (somewhat) incoherent…. Consequently, when any of these people prayed in

Hebrew, they were unable to adequately express their needs or recount the praises of Hashem, without mixing Hebrew with other languages. When Ezra and his Council realized this condition, they ordained the Shemoneh Esrei in their present order" (Rambam, *Hilchos Tefillah*, 1:4).

For this reason, now that we use the standardized, fixed text of the *Siddur*, room for complete spontaneity is generally left only for the informal settings of prayer we may encounter throughout the day; meaning, not as part of the prayer "service." However, it should be noted that there were many pious Chassidim who would, spontaneously, or perhaps even unconsciously, vocalize their emotions in their own vernacular, even in the middle of the Shemoneh Esrei (See *Teshuvas Imrei Yosher*, 2:109. *Nemukei Orach Chayim*, 101:2. *Shomer Emunim*, Vol. 2, p. 402b. *Teshuvos haElef Lecha Shelomo*, Teshuvah 58), although, this is not today considered such a desired practice (the Rebbe, *Igros Kodesh*, Vol. 6, p. 262).

For most people, the informal modalities of Davening are engaged outside the context of formal Tefillah.

HOW TO OPEN YOURSELF TO SPEAK WITH HASHEM

"Informal prayer" suggests a free spontaneity of expression, however, some people with little experience, find such things difficult, or are too rigid, and they need guidelines for how to open themselves up so they can freely and honestly speak their minds to Hashem. The following outline may be helpful to those seeking to relax and enter into a more natural, free and spontaneous flow of communication with HaKadosh Baruch Hu.

Da' Lifnei Atah Omeid / "Know before Whom you stand." The first ingredient in free-flowing informal prayer is to contemplate Who you are speaking to. Simply become aware that you are standing or sitting in the presence of the Master of the World Who is your loving parent. Settle for a moment and appreciate what this actually means. How does this truth make you feel? How does it resonate with you, and what does it call forth from your inner depths? Is it overwhelming or comforting, numbing or sensitizing? Whatever comes up is fine; any response, and even no discernible response, is a good place to begin.

"Open up for Me an opening like the eye of a needle, and in turn I will enlarge it to be an opening through which wagons can enter" (*Medrash Shir haShirim*, 5:2). Try to be as open as you can to say what you wish, with honesty and simplicity. If words come slowly or shyly at first, be patient. You can start small, and Hashem will assist you in increasing. Soon, you may become moved to praise or complain, to mention your needs, dreams or worries. Whether they are big issues or seemingly very insignificant, it does not matter. You can be content with whatever comes to you to say. If you can already give voice to all your fears, hopes, desires, yearnings, and dreams, then do so. If you feel the need to sing, sing; if an urge to cry comes up, let it happen. If all you can say right now is, 'My shoes are old, I need a new pair of shoes,' or 'Thank You for breakfast,' whatever comes up is fine; the main thing is to create an open and unpressured atmosphere for yourself. Flow does not come from force. Just mention whatever comes to your mind, and allow any pauses or silences to settle. Speak naturally, in your own voice and in your own language.

If you cannot find any issues to mention, or you feel empty of words and nothing is coming out, you can say just one word, and perhaps say that word over and over again, until it opens you up more. For example, you might be able to say the word 'Grateful,' or perhaps 'Worried,' 'Doubtful,' or 'Hopeful'. You could build on this intuitive word by beginning to repeat "I feel grateful," or "I feel worried...."

Since the objective of this openness and fluidity is to create a living relationship with Hashem and eventually to be able to express yourself fully to Him, if nothing comes to your mind to say, begin by repeating the phrase *Ribono Shel Olam* / "Master of the Universe," or whatever your 'reflex phrase' may be, such as "Oh my G-d." In Eastern Europe, in previous centuries, Jews reflexively referred to Hashem as *Ribono Shel Olam*, so it was natural to say in spontaneous prayer. Today, we most likely need to select a different familiar phrase or unpremeditated word that we use for Hashem. For example, if, G-d forbid, a person fell down the stairs, today, he might not cry out, *Ribono Shel Olam*, but rather "Oh my G-d!" Whatever the referent to G-d, you can build this word into a short prayer, such as, "Oh G-d, I am so worried."

You can take your most 'natural' word for G-d, and say it over and over again, until a connection, a sense of openness is achieved. If you find yourself repeating the same sentence for a long time, such as 'Thank you Hashem,' that too is fine. Don't worry, you cannot 'bore' G-d. You are speaking, expressing, connecting, and gradually you will open up and begin to express more and more feelings and thoughts.

Once you are free-flowing with your words, let everything pour out without restraint. Tell Hashem about everything that is on your mind, all your desires, worries, ambitions, insecurities, doubts, hopes, yearnings, your successes, failures and mistakes, anything that is troubling or inspiring you. Describe your feelings, emotions and ideas as they arise.

Tamim Tihyeh im Hashem... / "Be innocent and simple with Hashem...." If literally no words are coming or you feel uninspired and unable to open your mouth to say even one phrase, then render this very predicament as your prayer. Submit your sense of intelligence and maturity, and very simply ask the Creator to open your mouth to be able to speak. Ask to be able to ask. Pray to be able to pray.

If all that enters your mind is skepticism and an absence of Emunah in this process, you could just say, with childlike innocence, "I have no idea what I am doing. I would like to feel close to You Hashem, but I don't even know what that means. Who are You? I want to know You better."

If you feel doubtful that Hashem is really listening to you, tell that to Hashem. If you feel like you are talking to the wind, say that as well; 'Hashem I feel like I am speaking to a wall, it feels like I am speaking into the wind. I feel alone.' Even if you discover in yourself some doubt in Hashem's existence, give voice to that. Say, 'This feels insane. What am I doing, Hashem? If you are out there, please help me feel Your Presence. Help me know you exist.'

Let your *Temimus* / childlike simplicity guide you; if an urge naturally flows from inside you to dance, then dance; if you find your body trembling, or your hands gesticulating, be non-judgmentally present with this. It is all prayer. If it feels theatrical or self-conscious, do not push any emotion, expression or appearance. It does not have to look a certain way. You don't have to have a dramatic or intense or revelatory experience. You don't need to compose organized, intelligent sentences or paragraphs or follow a format. Let all judgments fall away.

You don't need to make yourself cry or emote; if you cry, you cry, if you laugh, you laugh. Just be natural, let go of distractions, and allow your feelings and thoughts to flow without manipulation or pretense. The more you practice this mode of relating to HaKadosh Baruch Hu, the more natural it will feel.

'Alone with the Alone...' Speaking intimately to Hashem as your closest friend, your loving parent, or as someone who knows you completely and only wants your best, this is the path to attain a deeper level of *Yichud* / conscious aloneness with HaKadosh Baruch Hu.

Of course, if spontaneous prayer emerges in public or in the middle of formal Davening, let it just flow quietly. For more expressive speech, you need to be alone, undistracted, and not causing a commotion that others can overhear, in order to open yourself in honesty and authenticity. Many people can find privacy in their car, and driving can be an opportune time to speak to HaKadosh Baruch Hu. Some people walk alone through city streets with a phone to their ear, pretending to speak with a person, but really speaking quietly to Hashem. Some arise early or remain awake while the rest of their household is asleep, and pace back and forth in their living room, whispering to their Creator.

Most people require being physically alone to speak to Hashem without self-consciousness or pretense. Some are able to be alone with Hashem even in a crowd. This type of inward aloneness is called בדידות בתוך בני-אדם / aloneness among other people (as the great Tzadik, Rebbe Shimshon Ostropoli teaches, טובה הפרישות עם הבריות, והבדידות בתוך בני-אדם / "It is good to be separate *with* people, and be alone among people": Rebbe Rayatz, *Likkutei Diburim*, 1, p. 288. Although this should be for periods of time and not a way of life": Ibid. *Sefer haSichos*, 5703, p. 191). Indeed, one can be amid a large crowd of people and yet be alone with and within himself, as if he was completely solitary, in a desert. Yet, most people, as they are climbing the ladder of spiritual empowerment and maturity, need some time in physical seclusion and external silence in order to feel totally alone with themselves and their Source, and open up in raw, honest, intimate prayer.

If you do use your car, for example, the familiarity of that space can be advantageous, if you find it relaxing. Also, if you repeatedly use such a space for Tefillah, you begin to associate it with spiritual openness, and this association facilitates an even deeper state of openness.

Once you feel opened, pour out your heart to Hashem with candidness and sincerity. Unburden yourself until you feel heard, relieved, elated and connected.

Once you have done so, declare, 'Hashem I give myself over to Your will and desire. With all my body, mind and heart, I surrender to Your will. I am Ayin, I empty myself into the Infinite possibilities that You have in store for me, my community, Klal Yisrael and the whole world.

This is one of the deepest modes of Tefillah, as we are both asking for what we need, and simultaneously surrendering our needs and will to Hashem, as explained above, and this is how to be a vessel for Hashem's infinite blessings.

Without taking away from the spontaneity, you might conclude with a prayer of thanks, praise and gratitude. And if it comes naturally, you might sing a Nigun. If you do, you might gradually allow the Nigun to fade into a silence. In this 'comfortable silence', perhaps you can sense the silence that is beyond all sound. You may have begun in a silence that did not allow for sound, a sense of stuckness prior to *Dibur* / speech, and then you moved into the free-flowing sound of Dibur, and now you are settling into a silence beyond Dibur.

This movement from stuck silence, to liberative sound, to revelatory silence, mirrors the process that Klal Yisrael traversed as they left Egypt. They began their exile with a loss of name and identity, and ultimately they lost their voice. They became so silenced by exile that they could not even complain about their condition of slavery. When they finally cried out, the process of the redemption of Dibur began.

Not only did they regain their voice as they went free, but they started using their voice to complain to Moshe and even voice their doubts in Moshe's mission. But Hashem had told Moshe that not only would they leave Egypt, they would become 'storytellers', experts in verbal transmission — they would live to tell their children of the miracles of the Exodus from Egypt. They even became singers, their voices channeling words of Divine prophecy, as they joined the *Shiras haYam* / Song of the Sea, after crossing through with Moshe.

Yet, before crossing through the sea, with the Egyptian army approaching from behind, having achieved a level of redeemed Dibur, Klal Yisrael called out in prayer for help. Hashem said to them, "Why are you crying out to Me?" Hashem was saying, 'Yes, your liberation began with a cry, then a word, then storytelling and you are ready now to become singers, but, right now,' Hashem says, 'I want silence, a silence so deep it includes and is beyond all sound.'

Similarly, in interpersonal relationships, first there is an awkward silence, then the relationship becomes more open and both partners feel comfortable to speak and share and become closer. When the intimacy of the relationship matures, the two can sit for periods of time together in a comfortable silence, not even needing to speak.

Our relationship with HaKadosh Baruch Hu can evolve in the same way. When you have spoken your entire Yesh and released it, you can just sit with Hashem in Ayin, enjoying the silent intimacy.

KAVANAH / MINDFUL INTENTION, 2:
FIRST 12 DAYS OF THE MONTH

As the first month of the lunar year, the first 12 days of Nisan correspond to the 12 subsequent months of the year. From a deeper perspective, every hour of the first 12 days of Nisan is like a full day of the coming year. In any case, this 12 day period is a very powerful time to positively influence the future.

Everything that will transpire during the upcoming 12 months is present on a seed level during these 12 days. As kernels of the blessings of the upcoming year are descending, we can widen our vessels to receive them. To do so, we can first of all be mindful of this inspiring time, and secondly make sure not to squander and waste it, by actively taking advantage of its powerful influence on our lives.

Practically, this means that we should take this 12-day period before Pesach to increase our Torah learning, spend a little more time in Tefillah each day, and give a little more in charity. Of course, increasing in holiness is a great benefit any day and moment of our lives, it does, however, come into greater focus in heightened times.

To begin, during each day of these first 12 days we can contemplate the qualities of the corresponding month of the year. For example, on day one of Nisan, think about the inner dynamics of Nisan, and on day two think about the inner dynamics of Iyyar, and so on. Some who are more spiritually attuned can meditate on each of these days and intuit what will occur in the corresponding month. However, our focus should be on how we can grow within the matrix of each month. Every month resonates with certain opportunities for growth, as explored in this series of books, so as you are thinking about the month that corresponds to the current day, resolve that you should avail yourself of these opportunities and grow in your capabilities.

Day One: Nisan, as has been explored here at great length, is a month of Geulah, redemption and liberation. During this first day, think about what in your life needs redemption. Think about the issues that you need to release in this coming year.

Day Two: Iyyar is all about healing and building the self. Think about your life issues that need healing, whether physical, mental, emotional or spiritual; healing between yourself and others, and healing within yourself.

Day Three: Sivan is all about the revelation of wisdom, of Torah. Think about your willingness to be open to receive Torah, to digest wisdom and apply it to growth.

Day Four: Tamuz is all about embracing destruction and brokenness. Think about how you would deal with any losses in the coming year. What can you do to ensure that you have the strength and stamina to overcome anything. Daven that you will have the *Koach* needed to persevere.

Day Five: Av is all about reconciliation. The building that comes after the destruction. Think about how you are going to deal with the hardships of life and how you will build and always get up.

Day Six: Elul is all about soul-searching and honest self-awareness. Think about being honest with yourself.

Day Seven: Tishrei is all about resolution and commitment. Think about the things in your life that need improvement and the resolutions or intentions you wish to take upon yourself for the coming year to implement these changes.

Day Eight: Cheshvan is all about transitions. Think about all the needed and healthy transitions that you hope will occur in the coming year.

Day Nine: Kislev is all about miracles. Think about what 'miracles' you wish to experience in the coming year and open yourself up to receiving or creating extraordinary, unexpected positive events.

Day Ten: Teves is focused on relationships. Think about the relationships you have, and those you wish to have or cultivate in the coming year.

Day Eleven: Shevat is a month connected with ingesting external stimuli and most importantly our relationship to food and eating. Think about your relationship to food. Is it healthy, obsessive, disciplined or 'neurotic'? How do you wish to grow in this area this year, and secure a healthy relationship with food?

Day Twelve: Adar embodies the qualities of joy, laughter and holy, productive 'doubt'. Think whether you are truly joyful. If yes, what can you do to grow in joy this year? If not, pray that Hashem will bless you with true reasons to be joyful and that you can cultivate an unconditional posture of joy throughout the coming year.

To heighten our awareness of these 12 days, there is also a custom to recite the account of the offerings that the corresponding *Nasi* / tribal leader made on that day in the Torah. When Klal Yisrael was in the Desert, the *Chanukas haMishkan* / inauguration of the Mishkan commenced on the first day of Nisan, and for the first 12 days of Nisan, each Nasi of the 12 Shevatim / tribes brought inaugural offerings as the representative of his Sheivet. Today, the custom is to recall the inauguration of the Mishkan by reading the *Pesukim* / verses in the Torah that describe the offering of each day's "Nasi." Besides evoking the merit of these offerings, this practice allows a person to become gratefully aware of the renewal, the 'inauguration', of the spring, the first month of the lunar year, representing the *Chidush* / renewal of the whole yearly cycle.

May we open ourselves to experience the newness and aliveness of every moment of life this Nisan and Pesach season. May this year be a year of creativity, generosity and new beginnings. May we become humble and kind leaders, who 'skip over' the apparent ego of others, and speak directly to their soul.

May we be always open to the gift of life and surrender to the Light of Hashem so that we become the vessels to receive miracles in our lives for the good of the world. May this be a month and year of truly new miraculous beginnings. And may we be blessed to witness the beginning of the miracle of all miracles, the Redemption of all Creation from all levels of slavery, speedily in our days.

TWO ESSAYS ON PESACH

ESSAY 1

THE STATE OF KLAL YISRAEL WHEN THEY LEFT EGYPT:
The 49th Level of Impurity or the 49th Level of Purity?

SIN & EXILE IS ROOTED IN A LACK OF DA'AS

GALUS / EXILE MEANS SEPARATION FROM ONE'S ROOT. An existential exile is estrangement and alienation from one's deepest self. This is an inner disconnect, a lack of proper *Da'as* / conscious awareness. The truth is, all exiles, external or internal, with Egypt being the prototype of all subsequent exiles, are essentially an exile of דעת / *Da'as*, of 'knowing' or conscious awareness (*Pri Eitz Chayim,* Sha'ar 21:1). As such, the prototype of all redemptions is the redemption and liberation of Da'as; a free mind is a free person.

Existential exile is rooted in the concept of *Aveirah* / sin, in which a person 'crosses over' (the root of *Aveirah* is *Avar* / cross), a certain fundamental, ethical, moral, or spiritual boundary and thus becomes estranged from their deepest self.

Cheit, also classically translated as 'sin', really means 'missing', as in 'missing the mark', or missing the point. When Adam and Chavah ate from the *Eitz haDa'as* / Tree of Knowing, they 'missed the point' of their relationship with life and with Hashem. This disconnect caused a separation, so-to-speak, between them and HaKadosh Baruch Hu, so much so that they felt they had to "hide" from the Divine Presence. The Cheit had dramatic effects on the entire cosmos, on Adam and Chava's relationship with the outer world, and on their personal relationship as well. Our sages tell us that after eating from the Tree of Knowledge Adam and Chavah 'divorced' each other for 130 years. The rift between themselves and the outside world resulted in a new biological configuration: now when they ate and drank, some of what they consumed was assimilated into the body, and some was ejected as waste. Ultimately, eating from the Tree of Knowledge caused a rift within themselves, dividing their own Da'as, blocking their self-knowledge and awareness. All this is clearly alluded to in the name of the tree itself: 'the Tree (reality) of the Da'as of (conflict between) Good and Evil'. Once internalized, this 'fruit' colored their awareness with conflict, separation and struggle.

When Hashem tells Avraham that his descendants will descend into exile, the Torah states, ידע תדע / *Yado'a Teida'* / "Know, you shall know" — know with certainty — "that your descendants will be strangers in a foreign land for 400 years" (*Bereishis*, 15:13). *Da'*, the root of *Da'as*, is repeated, as if to suggest that it will be an exile of *Da'as*. However, Hashem's words also suggest that 'Avraham' (as alive within his descendents) will 'know', will have some modicum of Da'as, even in exile. Although his descendants will lose the full Da'as of their true purpose, connection, and unity with Hashem, they will at least know that they do not truly know. And this Da'as, this knowing that they do not know, will become the very seed of their redemption.

מצרים / *Mitzrayim* alludes to the word מצר / narrow, meaning the 'narrowing' of Da'as. In the exile of Egypt there was a contracted state of spiritual awareness, and they descended into Egypt precisely because higher Da'as, an awareness of the revealed presence of Hashem, did not at this time penetrate the world and its inhabitants (*Sha'ar haKavanos*, Derush 9, Pesach). The occlusion of the infinite narrows one's perception of the world.

When Moshe conveys Hashem's message to Pharaoh, to let the Jewish people out of Egypt, Pharaoh declares, "Who is Hashem that I should heed his voice?" The spiritual archetype of Pharaoh is arguing that he does not sense Hashem's presence in this world and thus he can do as he pleases: his Da'as rules. Therefore, the words מלך מצרים / *Melech Mitzrayim* / king of Egypt equal numerically 470, and with the 4 letters of the name Pharaoh, the total is 474, the same value as the word דעת / *Da'as* (Rameh m'Pano, *Mayan Ganim*, 3, Seder Shel Pesach). The antidote to exile, as it was in Egypt and as it is today in our own constricted and narrow state, is to water the seeds of Da'as by becoming more and more aware of Hashem's Presence and deepening this awareness until we eventually achieve *Mochin d'Gadlus* / expanded awareness, total clarity and faith in Hashem, and by extension, faith in ourselves.

On the night of Pesach (writes the Rashash, *Nahar Shalom*, 37a), throughout the Seder, there is a Tikkun for the *Penimiyus* / internal dimension of the sin of Adam eating from the tree of *Da'as* / knowledge. (The Tikkun of Rosh Hashanah is for the external aspect of the Cheit). Pesach provides a fixing for Da'as three different levels — within oneself, with others, and with HaKadosh Baruch Hu.

Now let us go a little deeper into the world of Da'as in order to understand the significance of these rectifications.

**THE FRENZY OF IDOL WORSHIP &
THE FRENZY TO CONSTRUCT THE MISHKAN**

In the beginning of the Book of Shemos, the second book of the Torah, Klal Yisrael descends to Egypt and eventually becomes enslaved there. Later, as Klal Yisrael is released from Egypt (and all that it represents), the Torah tells us about the events of the Exodus, and of Klal Yisrael's ensuing journey to Mount Sinai to receive the Torah. Following Sinai and the transmission of many of the ethical laws of the Torah, Moshe is given the laws and details related to erecting the *Mishkan* / the temporary Temple in the Desert. Following this personal transmission and Moshe's return from the mountain, the Torah describes the tragic episode of the people fashioning and eventually serving the Golden Calf, sparing no detail about the devastating consequences of this idol worship. Toward the end of Shemos, Moshe informs Klal Yisrael of the Mishkan and of the Mitzvah to donate the materials needed to construct the Mishkan. The book then concludes with the construction of the Mishkan and the resting of the Divine Presence within it.

As Moshe is about to transmit the Mitzvah of donating and creating the Mishkan, the Torah narrates, ויקהל משה את־כל־עדת בני ישראל ויאמר אלהם אלה הדברים אשר־צוה ה' לעשת אתם / "And Moshe then gathered the whole community of Israel and said to them, 'These are the things that Hashem has commanded you to do'" (*Shemos*, 35:1).

Rashi (ad loc.) says the word ויקהל / *Vayakhel* does not literally mean "and he gathered," because "one does not actually 'gather' people with one's hand." It seems as if Klal Yisrael actually gathered on their own. Why then is the phrase *Vayakhel Moshe* used?

The Medrash (*Pesikta*, on the Pasuk) conceptually ties this use of *Vayakhel* to an earlier mention of the same term in the episode of the Golden Calf, when ויקהל העם על־אהרן ויאמרו אליו קום עשה־לנו אלהים אשר ילכו לפנינו כי־זה משה האיש אשר העלנו מארץ מצרים לא ידענו מה־היה לו / "*Vayakhel* / 'the People gathered' against Aaron and said to him, 'Come, make us a god who shall go before us, for that man Moshe, who brought us from the land of Egypt — we do not know what has happened to him'" (*Shemos*, 32:1). There, the Torah uses the same word to describe the people as 'gathering' on their own — no one gathered them. Our sages point out that these two gatherings are apparently spontaneous. The Arizal as well (*Likutei*

Torah on this Pasuk), ties the *Vayakhel* of the Mishkan to the *Vayakhel* of the Golden Calf.

Yet, there is a stark difference between these two gatherings: by the Mishkan the Torah says ויקהל כל־עדת בני ישראל / *Vayakhel Col Adas Bnei Yisrael* / "the whole community of Israel gathered," whereas by the Golden Calf the Torah says, ויקהל העם / *Vayakhel haAm* / "The nation gathered...." The difference is symbolized by the contrasting terms *Adas Bnei Yisrael* and *haAm*.

The word ויקהל comes from the word קהל / community, a gathering of people. *Col Adas Bnei Yisrael* literally means, "all the 'witnesses', the Children of Israel." עדת / *Adas* comes from the word עד / *Ayd* / witness, and it has the same three letters as the word דעת / *Da'as*. By the Golden Calf, Torah merely calls Klal Yisrael העם / "the nation." The question is, why is עדת used in reference to the gathering by the Mishkan, whereas by the Golden Calf it is simply העם?

Following the gathering by the Mishkan, Moshe tells them, אלה הדברים אשר־צוה ה' / "These are the things that Hashem has commanded." What are אלה / these things? Before he begins telling Klal Yisrael about the Mishkan, Moshe first tells them about the laws of Shabbos. In this context, Chazal tell us (*Shabbos*, 70a), the words אלה הדברים are an allusion to the 39 prohibited *Av Melachos* / 'father' or primary actions not allowed on Shabbos. The word אלה is numerically 36. דברים / "things" is plural, alluding to '2', raising the sum to 38, and finally the letter Hei / the, in "the things" counts as '1', bringing the total to 39.

This is the technical explanation, yet the question still remains: what is the Torah trying to convey to us? The relationship between the words אלה הדברים and the 39 main prohibited works we are not allowed to perform on Shabbos seems very tenuous.*

After gathering together and hearing from Moshe "these things Hashem has commanded," Moshe speaks to the people about Shabbos, that "Six days you shall do work and on the seventh day rest." He then continues, לא־תבערו אש בכל משבתיכם ביום השבת / "You shall kindle no fire throughout your settlements on the Shabbos day." Why does he single out the prohibition of kindling fire among all the 39 primary actions that are not allowed to be performed on Shabbos, such as, for example, writing or erasing, constructing or deconstructing?

Chazal deduce two reasons for the singling out of this prohibition. Perhaps it is to tell us that lighting a fire on Shabbos is ללאו יצאת / singled out as a prohibition to communicate that one who does it merely violates a prohibition and possibly receives a consequence of lashes, but nothing more. Or perhaps it is to tell us that lighting a fire on Shabbos is לחלק יצאת / singled out as a specific case in order to equate the other prohibited labors to it and to tell you, 'Just as kindling is one of the 39 primary categories of prohibited labor, and one is liable for performing it on its own, so

---

* In fact, there are other sources for the 39 Melachos. For example, corresponding to the 39 times the word *Melachah* / work appears in the Torah: *Shabbos*, 49b. Yerushalmi, *Shabbos*, 7:2. See Rabbeinu Chananel, *Shabbos* 49b. *Tosefos Yom Tov*, Shabbos, 7:2, regarding which (appearances of the word) *Melachah* are counted and which are not. Or corresponding to the 39 curses to Adam, Chava and the earth. *Tikkunei Zohar*, Tikkun 48. Corresponding to the harsh labors in Egypt: *Tosefos*, Pesachim 117b.

too, with regard to every primary category of prohibited labor, one is liable for each labor on their own' (*Shabbos*, Ibid). Yet, every word and letter of the Torah is precise and profound, so we need to ask, especially regarding the opinion that it is לחלק יצאת, why the Torah specifically chooses fire as the example to teach this law. Any one of the 39 actions would have taught the same idea.

A little further on, after the Torah describes how the people gathered and brought all the materials required to erect the Mishkan, the Torah tell us, ויבאו כל־החכמים העשים את כל־מלאכת הקדש איש־איש ממלאכתו אשר־המה עשים / "All the artisans who were engaged in the tasks of the sanctuary came, each from the task upon which he was engaged." In other words, Klal Yisrael was excited about this project, and enthusiastically left what they were previously doing and began giving all the materials required to fashion the Mishkan.

At some point, the artisans came to Moshe ויאמרו אל־משה לאמר מרבים העם להביא מדי העבדה למלאכה אשר־צוה ה' לעשת אתה / "And they said to Moshe, saying, 'The people are bringing more than is needed for the tasks entailed in the work that Hashem has commanded to be done.'" As such, ויצו משה ויעבירו קול במחנה לאמר איש ואשה אל־יעשו־עוד מלאכה לתרומת הקדש ויכלא העם מהביא / "Moshe thereupon had this proclamation made throughout the camp: 'Let no man or woman make further effort to bring gifts for the sanctuary!' So the people stopped bringing them" (*Shemos*, 36:4-6).

The obvious question is, what is the problem of bringing too much? מרבים העם להביא / "The people are bringing more than is needed." If they brought too many materials, maybe they could have stored them in case they needed them in reserve for when the first ones wore out. Apparently, it was so inappropriate to bring more, that it warranted a grand warning: ויעבירו קול במחנה / "And a proclamation was made throughout the camp." Ringing throughout the encampment was a grave "proclamation"; something terrible was occurring and had to be stopped — people were giving too much charity?

It is interesting that Chazal *Doresh* / tease out from this Pasuk the *Melachah* / prohibition of carrying from one domain to another domain on Shabbos, and this is how we know that carrying is a Melachah.*

The Mishnah says that a person is also not allowed to throw an object from one domain into another. Regarding this, the Gemara asks, "Consider: throwing is a derivative of carrying an item, and where is carrying itself prohibited?"

אמר רבי יוחנן דאמר קרא ויצו משה ויעבירו קול במחנה משה היכן הוה יתיב במחנה לויה ומחנה לויה רשות הרבים הואי וקאמר להו לישראל לא תפיקו ותיתו מרשות היחיד דידכו לרשות הרבים / "Said Rebbe Yochanan, the Pasuk says, 'And Moshe commanded, and they passed a proclamation throughout the camp "Let no man or woman do any more work for the offering for the Holy." So the people stopped bringing them.' Where was Moshe stationed? In the camp of the *Levi'im* / Levites, which was a public domain, and he said to them: 'Do not

---

* "Where is carrying out itself written?... As the verse says: 'And Moshe commanded, and they passed a proclamation throughout the camp'": *Shabbos*, 96b. From here we (also) learn that carrying is a Melachah: Rambam, *Hilchos Shabbos*, 12:8.

carry and bring objects from the private domain (your camp) to the public domain (the camp of the Levi'im)'" (*Shabbos,* 96b).

This is a very perplexing teaching of the Gemara. The simple reading of the Pasuk is that Moshe tells the people to stop bringing more material for the Mishkan; this has nothing to do with the prohibition of Shabbos, rather, as stated, it is because 'they had enough'. The issue at hand is that מרבים העם להביא, "the people are bringing *too much*," not that they are carrying objects, and therefore, ויעבירו קול במחנה איש ואשה אל-יעשו-עוד מלאכה לתרומת הקדש / "Let no man or woman make *further* effort toward gifts for the sanctuary." What compels Chazal to read into this that it was Shabbos, and to learn from it that we are not allowed to carry from one domain to another domain on Shabbos? Somehow, on a deeper level, this idea of 'ceasing to bring' — because they brought too much — is interconnected with the Melacha of carrying from one domain to another. How so?

The Arizal (*Likutei Torah,* Vayakhel) teaches (apparently based on the Medrash, Pesikta above) that since Klal Yisrael 'gathered' to create the Golden Calf, an act of frivolity, Moshe needed to 'gather them' and to reveal to them the light of Kedushah and intentionality, as a Tikkun for that gathering. As such, he gathers *Adas B'nei Yisrael* / עדת בני ישראל. *Adas* comes from the word *Da'as* / awareness, intentionality. And because they sinned, saying, אלה אלהיך ישראל / *Eileh Elo-hecha Yisrael* / "This (these) are the god(s) of Israel," their Tikkun came about when Moshe said to them and they listened, אלה הדברים / *Eileh haDevarim* / "These are the things…," which, as mentioned, alludes to the 39 Melachos of Shabbos.

Besides the etymological parallels, the Arizal is conveying something much more profound. Let us try to unpack and explain this concise, although perhaps abstruse, teaching.

MOSHE INJECTING DA'AS

As is already clear, there are two gatherings: one by the construction of the Mishkan, and one by the fashioning of the Golden Calf.

In both cases, these gatherings seem to 'gather on their own', almost a spontaneous assembling of the masses. Yet, at the Mishkan there is an addition: the idea of *Adas Yisrael*, meaning that Moshe is drawing down *Da'as* / intentionality into this mass gathering of people.

Moshe is the *Bechinah* / paradigm and embodiment of Da'as (*Pri Eitz Chayim*, Sha'ar Chag haMatzos, 1), the one who brings Torah, Divine wisdom and higher Da'as to Klal Yisrael. By the creation of the Mishkan, he is drawing down Da'as to the *Adas* of Klal Yisrael. Moshe is bringing healthy, productive, life-affirming awareness of Kedushah to a people who had gathered, only a short while before, without proper Da'as of themselves nor of their relationship with the Elokim Chayim. He is drawing down stabilizing Da'as to a community who had lost their minds, their Da'as, and in frenzied excitement and rapture followed the *Eirav Rav* / the mixed multitudes and submitted themselves to an idol.

The mixed multitudes who initiated the Golden Calf, represent the Da'as of *Kelipah* / spiritual blockage, and thus ערב רב / *Eirev Rav* equals *Da'as* numerically. Da'as is the place of connection, and the Torah uses Da'as as a euphemism for intimacy. Yet there is a 'dark' side of Da'as, as it were, a Da'as of Kelipah. Da'as of Kelipah involves an infatuation with and cleaving to objects, becoming obsessed with an idea or object, as an idol. The fact that the people gathered on their own to create the Golden Calf suggests a mass combustion of fervor. Such is the nature of mass hysteria, people flocking together in the heat of passion, without any sense of healthy, measured Da'as. Therefore, Moshe must bring to the people who have gathered to build the Mishkan, holy awareness, to counteract the Da'as of Kelipah injected into them by the Golden Calf.

How can a people, a few months after leaving Egypt and receiving the Torah, rush to create an idol with such a fever of enthusiasm? How could they in one moment forget their Da'as and everything that they had come to know as true and meaningful? The entire process of the Going Out of Egypt was "so you shall know (*Da'as*) that I am Hashem." Similarly was the Divine revelation at Sinai summed up: "You have been shown (this) to know (*Da'as*) that Hashem is Elokim, and there is nothing else." Klal Yisrael apparently had clear Da'as of HaKadosh Baruch Hu, and a Da'as of themselves in relationship with HaKadosh Baruch Hu. And yet, a mere 40 days later they are swept off their feet by idol worship. How is this possible?

Regarding the frenzy of the people as they ran to make the idol, the Pasuk says, ויתפרקו / *VaYisparku*... / "they stripped their gold rings from their ears" (*Shemos*, 32:3). The Zohar (*Zohar* 2, 192a), connects the word *Hisparku* to the word *Perikas Ol* / throwing off the yoke of Heaven. They threw off, stripped themselves, of the 'golden' yoke of Divine responsibility, mindfulness and intentionality. They went from Matan Torah, where they proclaimed with tremendous enthusiasm, "we will do and we will listen," to the manic excitement of worshiping an idol. And a few months later the pendulum swung back, and the people enthusiastically contributed to the building of the Mishkan to the extent that they threw all they had at the wise men, to the point that a proclamation had to be made throughout the camp: 'Let no man or woman make further efforts toward gifts for the sanctuary!'

How can their enthusiasm swing so effortlessly from one extreme to its opposite, and then back again? We need to examine more closely the state of Klal Yisrael during the Exodus which allowed such rapid and radical changes of spiritual status.

THE STATE OF KLAL YISRAEL AT THE EXODUS

There seems to be a very fundamental argument among many of the great sages and *Mekubalim* / mystics regarding the state of Klal Yisrael when they left Egypt.

On the one hand, the *Zohar Chadash* (Yisro) teaches us that Klal Yisrael had sunk to the 49th level of *Tumah* / impurity in Egypt, the next-to-lowest level, the lowest being the fiftieth. Yet, after a mere 49 days after leaving Egypt, on the fiftieth day, they received the Torah and reached a state of *Taharah* / purity, immortality and freedom from all negativity.

Forty-nine represents the world of opposites, which includes choice-making. The dimensions of this world are connected to the number seven, as in the Seven Days of Creation, and the fullest measurement of this world is 49, seven sublevels within each of the seven dimensions. In fact, the word *Midah* / measurement has a numerical value of 49 (*Sefer Rokeach*, Hilchos Pesach, 294. *Megaleh Amukos*, Parshas Behar). And since "Hashem created the world with opposites, one against the other," there are 49 positive, holy, pure states, parallelled by their opposite: 49 negative, unholy, impure states. The first rung of purity parallels the 49th rung of impurity, and the second rung of purity parallels the 48th rung of impurity, and so forth. Thus, the Torah itself is refracted into 49 possible ways of *Isur* / prohibition and 49 possible ways of *Heter* / permission (*Medrash Tehilim*, 12), as well as 49 levels of purity and 49 levels of impurity (*Yerushalmi*, *Sanhedrin*, 4:2. See also, *Eiruvin*, 13b; Ritva, ad loc.). This is, however, a 'sliding scale'; on every rung of one ladder, there is a potential to skip to the other ladder. On the 49th level of impurity, one can choose to jump onto the first rung of purity and begin to climb the ladder of 49 steps of purity.

At the time of the Exodus story, Klal Yisrael had descended to the 49th level of impurity, the lowest rung of negativity. They were almost swallowed eternally into the fiftieth, absolute level of darkness and negativity, a place of no return. Once one descends beyond the map of 49 levels, they no longer have the ability to choose.

Speaking about the condition of Klal Yisrael as they left Egypt, the prophet says, ואת ערם ועריה / "You were still naked and bare" (*Yechezkel*, 16:7). This means that we were "naked of Mitzvos" (*Medrash Rabbah*, Shemos, 1:35). And not only were we not on the rungs of purity and the Kedushah of Mitzvos, but the angels on high 'protested': "These people (the Egyptians) are idol worshipers, and these people (Klal Yisrael) are idol worshipers" (*Medrash Tehilim*, 1:20. *Zohar*

2, 170b. *Yalkut Reuveini*, Beshalach, 82). In other words, Klal Yisrael was so enmeshed in idol worship, and so deeply stuck in impurity, that they were almost at a point of no return.

"This Matzah that we eat is for what reason? Because the dough of our fathers did not have time to become leavened before the King of the kings of kings, the Holy One, blessed be He, revealed Himself to them and redeemed them." This passage that we recite during the Seder is from the Mishnah. It speaks about the great haste with which Klal Yisrael left Egypt; we left so quickly that even our bread was not able to rise. Many Mekubalim write, in the name of the Arizal, that the reason they could not be delayed is that they had sunk to the 49th level of Tumah, impurity, spiritual sickness and stuckness. If they were to stay for one more moment they would have sunk to the fiftieth level, and they would not have been able to leave Egypt (The Alshich, *Siddur Rebbe Shabtai*, Haggadah, and *Chayei Adam*, in their respective commentaries on this passage in the Haggadah. See also *Chesed l'Avraham*, 2:56. Ramdu, *Eis laChenina. Ohr haChayim*, Shemos, 3:8. *Beis haLevi*, Derush 2).

If Klal Yisrael had delayed their Exodus any longer, we would have fallen off the ladder into such a dark, traumatized state, that we would have not been able to be extricated, freed and redeemed. Just a few more moments, and we would have fallen into the fiftieth rung, and thus we needed to leave Egypt, the physical, mental, emotional and spiritual place of our enslavement, in great haste.

Indeed, everything about the Mitzvos of the night of Pesach, the night we left Egypt, is connected to 'haste'. Matza is baked in great haste, ensuring that it does not rise. Similarly, the other two

Torah-based Mitzvos of the night, eating the *Korban* / offering of the Pesach lamb and the Maror (during the times when we offered a Korban Pesach), are also connected to the idea of haste. The Torah instructs us that the offering needs to be roasted, not cooked or boiled. Cooking takes much longer than roasting, not including the time it takes to boil the water and slice the meat. Roasting is a much quicker process; the offering is placed on an open fire and it roasts. The *Maror* / bitter herbs are also connected to haste. The Mishnah (*Pesachim*, 2:6) mentions five types of herbs that are considered Maror. The first is *Chazeres* / lettuce. Today, the most common vegetables used as Maror are romaine lettuce and horseradish. While many vegetables need to be cooked before eating, Maror can be uprooted from the ground and eaten right away. Also, the manner in which the offering of Pesach was eaten in Egypt demonstrated haste: "This is how you shall eat it: your loins girded, your sandals on your feet and your staff in your hand; and you shall eat it hurriedly" (*Shemos*, 12:11). We needed to eat the offering in a posture of urgency, about to flee. Pesach is a night of haste.

As mentioned, 49 is the matrix of opposites. In this world, there is a possibility of sliding from one opposite to the other, from purity to impurity, from an ascending trajectory to a descending one, and the choice is always ours. On any of the 98 rungs between the 49 rungs of purity and the 49 rungs of impurity (corresponding to the 98 'curses' in the Torah), there is a binary system at play and we can always choose goodness and life, or their opposites. Wherever we may find ourselves, we can choose to live a higher life, a life of meaning and purpose, or, alternatively, to slide down the other ladder. However, the fiftieth level of each ladder is absolute, beyond the dichotomy and mobility of duality. The fiftieth level of Kedushah is absolute goodness, where a person transcends the world of free choice and enters the world of absolute goodness and life. Purity, goodness is, at this point, a מחויב המציאות / 'necessary existence'; there is no alternative and there is no falling from this rung. Purity, transcendence, holiness, connectivity, unity, on this level, are boundless and everlasting. Moshe himself only reached this level of total transparency, goodness, and Deveikus, as he ascended Mount Nevo (the word *Nevo* means 'Nun / 50 is *Bo* / in him') to pass from corporeal existence. Similarly, there is a fiftieth level of Tumah, of stuckness, of inward death, alienation, and the impurity of ego-based existence. (Note that the Gra writes that there is no actual fiftieth level of Tumah, only 49 of levels. כל פעל ה' למענהו וגם־רשע ליום רע (*Mishlei*, 16: 4). כל / *Col* / All, writes the Gra, is numerically 50, indicating a place beyond choice, and there in פעל ה, there is no possibility for Ra'. Yet, the word וגם / *V'gam* / and also, which equals 49, indicates a place where there is still the possibility of choice in Ra': וגם...רע).

The fiftieth level of Tumah is a space where one can become so removed from his *Yetzer Tov* / positive inclination, his inner purity and inner perfection, that there is no longer even a possibility of choosing to do good. Here *Ra* / negativity, evil, sin, is absolute and there are no alternatives; a person on this level is so stuck in their negativity that there is no way for them to make a decision to get out of the situation. Sometimes a person can be so stuck in an addictive negative behavior that they cannot even imagine an alternative; they have become the addiction.

Whatever the case, these Mekubalim are revealing that Klal Yisrael was so low, teetering at the bottom of the 49th level, and had they not immediately fled in haste, they would have sunk into the fiftieth level of absolute darkness. They would have become Egypt.

This is one version of the story.

On the other hand, Klal Yisrael seems to have been on a very high spiritual level during the exodus. The elapsed time between going out of Egypt and the pinnacle experience of receiving the Torah is only 50 days. Having left Egypt, Klal Yisrael actively counted down the time to Matan Torah. They counted 'day one', 'day two', until they arrived at day 49 and a total of seven weeks, all in tremendous anticipation of hearing the Divine Voice at Har Sinai (Ran, *Pesachim*, at the end in the name of the Medrash. *Sefer haChinuch*, Mitzvah 306. We too count the days from when the Omer is offered, the second day of Pesach, until Shavuos. Even though, in the year they left Egypt they did not bring the Omer (as the Omer offering was only brought once Klal Yisrael settled in the land of Israel), yet, the *Zohar* (3, 96b) teaches that Klal Yisrael nevertheless counted the Sefirah in anticipation of receiving of the Torah: *Ohr haChayim*, Emor, 23:15). And when they finally reached the fiftieth day, they reached the fiftieth and highest level of purity. When they received the Torah, they experienced a freedom from the effects of eating from the Tree of Knowledge Good and Evil (*Shabbos*, 156a), the Tree of Duality and Opposites, and they became free of all *Tumah* / impurity, and *Yetzer haRa* / negative inclination (*Zohar* 3, 97b). Moreover, they experienced total transcendence and freedom from the 'angel of death' itself (*Medrash Rabbah*, Shemos, 41), as death is a derivative of the Tree of Knowledge, of separation, regarding which Adam and Chava are told, "the day you will eat from it (Tree of Knowledge), you will die." Klal Yisrael was on the highest level at Matan Torah, and this suggests that if they were able to reach the fiftieth level of purity a mere 50 days after leaving Egypt, perhaps they were not so utterly stuck in the depths of Tumah when they were redeemed from Egypt.

Furthermore, it could be argued (as does the Leshem, *Sefer haDei'ah*, 2, Derush 5:2, 5), that after the display of all the wonders and miracles in Egypt, Klal Yisrael was on a very high level. The entire intention of the *Makos* / the plagues was that all people shall "know that I am Hashem," and certainly after several months of Makos they achieved their intended goal by the time of the Exodus. The intention of the Makos was for Klal Yisrael, and even the Egyptian oppressors, to come to realize the "existence," the "providence," and the "Unity" of Hashem; certainly this Divine intention attained its result. All this suggests that Klal Yisrael was perhaps even on a level close to the fiftieth level of Kedushah already during the Exodus.

Were they, then, on the lowest level or the highest level? Also, why is this even a question? It seems there should be no argument of whether Klal Yisrael was on the lowest level or was on the highest at the most defining moment of their history and destiny.

STATES OF IMMATURITY

Birth is an analogy that our sages use regarding Yetziyas Mitzrayim. The going out of Egypt is the birth of Klal Yisrael, as a newborn being drawn out of the mother's womb (*Medrash Tehilim*, 114:6). Pre-Exodus is the Ten *Makos* / Plagues, these, the Arizal teaches, are the birth pangs that occur during the release of a child, the blood, the croaking frogs, wild animals, the darkness, and so forth all represent the process of giving birth, and the passing through the birth canal (*Likutei Torah*, Shemos). The first action the people of Israel, who were still slaves, were asked to perform was to bring the Korban Pesach, the Paschal Lamb, which was then sacrificed immediately preceding their Exodus from Egypt. In order to eat of it, the offering needed to be roasted over a spit, "with its head upon its legs" (*Shemos*, 12:9). This posture, writes the Tzemach Tzedek (*Derech Mitzvosecha*, Korban Pesach. *Ta'amei haMitzvos*, Arizal, Parshas Bo), is similar to the fetal position of a child in the womb, ready to be born (*Niddah*, 30b). In Egypt we were in a condition of *Ibbur* / gestation (*Sha'ar haKavanos*, Derushei Pesach 1), as a fetus in the womb, and the Going Out of Egypt was our collective birth, the birth of Klal Yisrael.

If Yetziyas Mitzrayim is our birth, then our journey through the desert parallels the growth of a child into a mature adult. It is a forty year journey from the slavery of Egypt to the responsibility of the Promised Land. Forty is the age of *Binah* / understanding, and at forty, one reaches a fuller mental maturity (בן ארבעים לבינה: *Avos*, 5:21. אף משה רבינו לא רמזה להן לישראל אלא לאחר ארבעים שנה...אמר רבה ש״מ לא קאי איניש אדעתיה דרביה עד ארבעין שנין: *Avodah Zarah*, 5b. The word נשמה / soul has the letter of מ' שנה / forty years. The highest levels of Neshamah, connected to intelligence, do not enter a person's life until the age of forty).

By extension, this means that in the Desert we were like young children and adolescents. In one metaphor of Chazal, after Matan Torah, Klal Yisrael ran away quickly from Mount Sinai כתינוק הבורח מבית הספר / "like children running away from school." This image of Klal Yisrael being born as an infant at the Exodus, and then gradually becoming a child slowly maturing throughout the journey in the Desert, helps us understand the spiritual, mental, emotional condition of Klal Yisrael as they left Egypt.

Both opinions or perspectives are thus correct, and have verifiable textual and Medrashic sources. In truth, they are not contradictory. The people were not spiritually mature, nor did they need to be, in order to be present on the fiftieth plane of Kedushah. Neither were they so low that they could become stuck on a plane of total Tumah. Rather, their states fluctuated rapidly, from moment to moment. Because there was a lack of maturity, they were like children quickly moving in and out of higher and lower states. In one moment, a child is crying inconsolably because his toy broke, and in the next moment they are blissfully eating a cookie. In one moment they are speaking irrationally, and in the next they are wistfully proclaiming an idea that seems far beyond their level of development.

Klal Yisrael's pendulum swung rapidly from the highest highs to the lowest lows and back again in the blink of an eye. In one moment, they beheld the Presence of Hashem at the splitting of the sea and the Torah could declare, "They believed in Hashem and in Moshe his servant." Yet, in the very next moment, the next episode recorded in the Torah, they complained bitterly that they lacked fresh drinking water.

If they were like newborns coming out of Egypt, and young children at Sinai, in their journey through the Desert, they were like immature teenagers who are easily swayed by public opinion and open to be swept into a frenzy, to soar very high and fall very low. A person in such a stage of development can scream their head off at a meaningless ballgame or concert, and then, a few minutes later, sing a beautiful Nigun of Deveikus, of yearning to be closer to HaKadosh Baruch Hu.*

---

* Interestingly, this developmental metaphor also helps deepen our understanding of another important facet of the exodus story: the overwhelming presence of miracles. Throughout Jewish history, all other redemptions were 'natural' events. For instance, our return from the Babylonian exile after 70 years oc-

Intense enthusiasm, excitement and passion that has no real, internal, permanence is a sign of immaturity. The way an immature teenager expresses himself is dependent on the external situation at hand. In the narrative of the fashioning of the Golden Calf, and, *l'Havdil*, the contributions to the building of the Mishkan, Klal Yisrael moved very quickly from one state to its literal opposite. In one moment, they were so passionate about the Golden Calf, that they stripped their wives of their gold ornaments for the idol worship, threw off the Yoke of Heaven, and danced and revelled around the false idol, submitting to debauchery and a complete eradication of all morality, including the prohibition of murder, as evidenced in the killing of Chur. A short time later, they were passionately inspired by Moshe and in a frenzy began throwing everything they owned into the Mishkan, until a proclamation had to be made that it was "enough."

---

curred when the first Persian King Cyrus had the wisdom to allow the Jewish people to return to Israel and rebuild the Beis haMikdash. So, why was the first redemption from Egypt miraculous, why all the miracles?

The forty year journey of Klal Yisrael through the desert, from birth to mature adulthood, was a journey toward *Mochin* / mindfulness and independence of awareness. To arrive at the point of true maturity, in order to enter the land and make a life for themselves, Klal Yisrael first needed to pass through the stages of childhood and adolescence, as it were.

This explains the need for miracles and wonders as Klal Yisrael was extricated from Egypt. It was, in a spiritual sense, 'age appropriate.' We were children, we needed the excitement. Hashem took us out of Egypt in the way that we teach children, by giving them prizes and making the learning exciting. Then, with Moshe's guidance, we were weaned from this need for such 'treats', as we grew into mature, motivated, and experienced adults, capable of choosing to do the right thing without spiritual coercion.

GIVING WITHOUT DA'AS

At the end of Moshe's life, when he recounts and rebukes Klal Yisrael for the events that transpired in the Desert, he specifically mentions a place called ודי זהב / *v'Di Zahav* (*Devarim*, 1:1). Say Chazal (Sifrei, *Devarim*, 1:18. Berachos, 32a. Rashi, ad loc.), the name of the location literally means "Enough Gold." In singling out this location by name, Moshe reproved them on account of the Golden Calf, which they had made from their abundance of gold possessions.

Just as the gold they tried to contribute to the Mishkan was more than "enough," the amount of gold they attempted to give to the idol was more than "enough." How could they throw their gold into building an idol and then a mere few months later throw all their gold into building the Mishkan? The sages of the Medrash offer the following metaphor:

משל לבחור שנכנס למדינה ראה אותם גובין צדקה ואמרו לו תן, והיה נותן עד שאמרו לו דיך, הלך מעט וראה אותם גובין לתיטרון, אמרו לו תן, והיה נותן עד שאמרו לו דיך, כך ישראל נתנו זהב לעגל עד שאמר להם די, ונדבו זהב למשכן עד שאמר להם די / "This is similar to a young man who enters a city and sees that they are collecting charity, and they ask him to give, and he gives until they tell him 'enough!' Then he travels a bit and sees that others are collecting money for a theater. They ask him to give, and he gives, until they tell him 'enough!' Similarly, Klal Yisrael gave gold for the Golden Calf until they were told 'enough! and later on they gave to the Mishkan until they were told 'enough!'" (*Shemos Rabbah*, 51:8).

In the days of the Mishnah, a "theater" implied some form of idol worship and perhaps brutality, such as in gladiator games. In both moments of giving, the young man does not discriminate; he does not give mindfully, rather he just loves to feel inspired, no matter the cause, and throws money at anything which gives him that thrill. There is no Da'as that goes into his decision making, and therefore tending to the poor is equal in his eyes to people beating each other up in the ring.

Maturity is a state of *Da'as* / conscious awareness, mindful sensitivity, discernment and proper boundaries. Immaturity, a lack of Da'as, does not recognize or respect boundaries or consequences. In this state, 'yes' and 'no' have no meaning, and there is no sense of 'enough'. A child can stuff his mouth with ice cream until he feels nauseous. He can overindulge to an extreme, because he has not yet developed the Da'as to recognize and respond to limits in a moment of passion. His enthusiasm for the ice cream throws him completely off balance. This was the state of Klal Yisrael as they took their first steps into the Desert, brimming with enthusiasm and ready to commit to any seemingly inspiring project without taking the time to discern the quality or nature of the project.

Their spontaneous gatherings pulsated with a mob mentality and 'ecstatic' generosity, without conscious choice or any sense of proportion. And so, as they gather, Moshe infuses Da'as into Klal Yisrael by calling them *A-das* Yisrael. He tries to ensure that they are growing up and becoming a *Bar Da'as* / knowledgeable son — even though their Da'as would only be fully assimilated at the end of the forty year journey (ולא־נתן ה' לכם לב לדעת ועינים לראות ואזנים לשמע עד היום הזה: Devarim, 29:3. לא קאי איניש אדעתיה דרביה עד ארבעין שנין: *Avodah Zarah*, 5b).

Da'as creates the ability to discern, to not get swept off one's feet by intense emotions or ideas. "Without Da'as there is no *Havdalah / separation*" (Yerushalmi, *Berachos* 5). Da'as establishes boundaries, accountability and order, on all levels of our being. It allows us to separate ourselves from acting in ways that are not in our deepest integrity; it allows us to say, when necessary, 'no,' or 'enough.'

Klal Yisrael's journey from Egypt to the Land of Israel mirrors the process of human development from birth, to childhood, to mindful maturity. And both of these processes mirror the macrocosmic development of Creation as a whole. Much like a child or a young nation brims with passionate reactivity, yearning, and enthusiasm, with little Da'as or sense of borders and guidelines, the new universe, soon after the creation event, was in a state of immaturity, filled with "chaos and void."

A WORLD WITHOUT DA'AS (TIKKUN) EXPANDS INFINITELY

Originally, the universe was without Da'as, as it were. It kept expanding, enlarging, and rapidly unfolding with great 'enthusiasm', until the Creator said, 'Enough!' This is connected to the World of *Tohu / Chaos*. The Creator then set limits and gave the universe the definitions of finite existence. This limitation still allows the universe to expand, but within certain bounds and guidelines. This is the world we now exist within, the World of Tikkun, order and balance.

Chazal tell us, "At the time that the Holy One, blessed be He, created the world, it went on expanding like two balls of yarn (which lengthen as they unravel), until the Holy One, blessed be

He, rebuked it and brought it to a standstill… And that, too, is what Reish Lakish said: 'What is the meaning of the verse, I am G-d Sha-dai? [It means], I am He that said to the world: Enough'" (*Chagigah*, 12a).

In the first phase of the creation of the world, it was unstoppably unfolding, like the unravelling of two balls of yarn that are rolling away so fast in different directions there is no way to catch and stop them. The world kept on מתפשט ומרחיב / expanding and intensifying, without brakes. But then, the Creator declared, 'Enough,' and the boundaries of Da'as were set and the infantile universe began to mature. Similarly, when the proclamation was made throughout the camp, "Let no man or woman make further effort toward gifts for the sanctuary" and they stopped, they understood, at least for that moment, the idea of 'enough'. Moshe's effort to establish Da'as and civility was heeded and Klal Yisrael was able to stop.

This is the deeper reason that Chazal read the laws of 'carrying' from one domain to another on Shabbos from the Pasuk, "Let no man or woman do any more work." At the gathering of *Adas Yisrael* Moshe was transmitting Da'as, an awareness of boundaries and balance, the internal ability to not 'trespass' or overstep established borders, even in a state of great enthusiasm. Yes, we can and should be enthusiastic, passionate, filled with desire and yearning, but this needs to be supported by and grounded within emotionally and spiritually healthy borders. And so, from this unique gathering of Klal Yisrael to build the holy Mishkan, Chazal learn the laws of spiritual trespassing, of moving objects from the domain where they rest and 'belong' during the present Shabbos to another domain.

In this transmission, Moshe also tells Klal Yisrael the prohibition of kindling fire on Shabbos: לא־תבערו אש בכל משבתיכם / "Do not kindle fire in all your dwellings" (*Shemos*, 35:3). Besides telling them about the prohibition of literally lighting fires on Shabbos, in the context of the gathering, Moshe is also hinting to them – yes, you can and should have the "fire" of passion and desire, yet, passion needs borders and limitations; you need to know how to stop, let go, be still, and experience life as already 'enough'. By imparting a sense of order, rest and maturity within the chaos of their exuberance, Moshe creates a Tikkun for Klal Yisrael.

THE YOUNG ARCHITECT OF THE MISHKAN: UNITING THE PASSION OF IMMATURITY WITH THE MINDFULNESS OF MATURITY

For the fashioning of the Mishkan, the chief architect was Betzalel. Why was Betzalel chosen for this role?

Speaking about the delicate dexterity required for building the Mishkan, the Ramban (*Shemos*, 31: 2) writes that the entire Nation of Israel was crushed under the burdens of mortar and brick labor, and thus no one had acquired the refined art of manipulating gold and silver. Indeed, it was a *Peleh* / wonder that there was a person like Betzalel who was able to craft such materials (כי ישראל במצרים פרוכים בעבודת חומר ולבנים, לא למדו מלאכת כסף וזהב וחרושת אבנים טובות ולא ראו אותם כלל. והנה הוא פלא שימצא בהם אדם חכם גדול בכסף ובזהב ובחרושת אבן ועץ וחושב ורוקם ואורג, כי אף בלומדים לפני חכמים לא ימצא בקי בכל האומניות כלם, והיודעים בהם בבא ידיהם תמיד בטיט ורפש לא יוכלו לעשות בהן אומנות דקה ויפה. ועוד, שהוא חכם גדול בחכמה בתבונה ובדעת להבין סוד המשכן וכל כליו למה צוו ואל מה ירמוזו). The Ramban is telling us that it was a miracle of sorts that Hashem had invested within him the wisdom of how to craft the materials of the Mishkan. This is one answer to the question; Betzalel was the only one who had the skill.

On the other hand, Chazal tell us (*Sanhedrin*, 69b) that Betzalel was only 13 years old when he was chosen as the chief architect of the Mishkan. If the whole issue is immaturity and lack of Da'as, as described above, why have a young child who had just become a *Bar Da'as*, or Bar Mitzvah, be the chief architect of the Mishkan? In contemporary terms, most people would hesitate to allow a 13 year old to drive the family for a trip in their new car — how much more so to construct the dwelling place of the Creator within this world?

The answer is that he was chosen specifically because he had just become Bar Mitzvah, and just entered the world of Da'as. His inner maturity was new, but it was vivid and undiluted.

HEAVEN IS 'BEING', EARTH IS 'BECOMING'

Regarding Betzalel, it is said that "he knew how to לצרף / *l'Tztaref* / to combine the letters through which שמים וארץ / *Shamayim vaAretz* / Heaven and Earth were created" (*Berachos*, 55a).

Shamayim and Aretz are opposites. שמים / Heaven comes from the words שם מים / there is water there (*Chagigah*, 12a). Heaven is a 'place' of "there is", of already being present — it is a 'being' state. *Aretz* is connected to the word *Ratza* / running, as the Medrash (*Bereishis Rabbah*, 5:8) says, למה נקרא שמה ארץ שרצתה לעשות רצון קונה /

"Why is the earth called *Aretz*? Because it 'runs' to perform the will of her Creator." Earth is in a constant state of becoming. We live our journey on earth, and eventually we get to Heaven. Heaven is a goal, an end, a destination. It is fixed and unmoving; being. Earth is a place of desire and journeying; becoming.

In terms of our discussion, Aretz represents the immature state, never being satisfied, wanting more and more, a place of infinite yearning, longing, aspiring and wanting — running in search of water. Whereas Shamayim is a place where "there is," the place of maturity and restfulness, the place where we can say, *Dai* / enough, or *Dayeinu* / we have enough. There is already sufficient water there, and there's no need to run after anything. *Shamayim* can be called a 'mind space', consciousness at rest, or Shabbos, whereas *Aretz* can be referred to as a heart space, representing the starving of the six days of the week.

Betzalel is someone that stands in the liminal space between the two, in the crossroads between Shamayim and Aretz, immaturity and maturity, heart and mind, desire and 'enough'. And thus he knows how to לצרף / *l'Tztaref* / to combine Heaven and Earth, and unify the construct of what they each represent.

Betzalel had just left his childhood and immaturity, the place where nothing ever seems enough, and one is always moving and becoming, 'carrying' things from one domain to another and constantly lighting fires. He has now entered into a mature, settled mind space, he has a more expansive sense of proportion and is able to just be. He knows when to continue building and when to stop building.

Hashem wants us to dedicate ourselves to living inspired lives, with overflowing enthusiasm and youthful excitement, abundant zeal, alacrity and a fiery heart. It is, in fact, good for us to be so inspired that we *want* to give everything away, and to ride the power and newness of the world of *Tohu* / chaos, and to break through into redemption. However, Hashem also wants for us to restrain ourselves at times, and to maintain this unbridled power of Tohu within the *Kelim* / vessels of Tikkun, of Da'as, of presence of mind.*

---

* A similar idea is expressed by the life of Sarah. The verse says ויהיו חיי שרה מאה שנה ועשרים שנה ושבע שנים / "this is the life of Sarah, one hundred year, and twenty year, and seven years" (*Bereishis*, 23:1). Why is each unit of time signaled out? Says the Medrash (*Bereishis Rabbah*, 58:1 as Rashi quotes) לכך נכתב שנה בכל כלל וכלל לומר לך שכל אחד נדרש לעצמו בת מאה כבת עשרים לחטא ובת עשרים כבת שבע ליופי / "The reason the word שנה is written at every term is to tell you that each term must be explained by itself as a complete number: at the age of 100 she was as a woman of 20 with regard to sin — for just as at the age of 20 one may regard her as having never sinned, since she had not then reached the age when she was subject to punishment, so, too, when she was 100 years old she was sinless — and when she was 20 she was as beautiful as when she was seven."

An alternative Medrash writes, אלא בת מאה שנה היתה כבת עשרים לנוי. ובת עשרים כבת ז' לחטא / "At one hundred years she was like a 20 year old in beauty, and at 20 she was like seven, with no sin" (*Medrash Lekach Tov*, 23:1-2). Clearly whether 20 or seven is beauty, depends on the type of beauty. The beauty of seven is a type of innocence, whereas 20 is more of external beauty.

There are three periods or ages in our lives: the age of innocence, the age of ambition, and the age of maturity. Normally, we think of time as progressing linearly; we leave the age of innocence and enter the world of drive, ambition, desire, the age of *Shir haShirim* and passionate love — and then we enter midlife and beyond, become wiser and more settled, in our maturity. Sadly, however, as we get older, we may become less innocent and less ambitious. Often, people give up on their dreams, their youthful desires, and as they become more level headed and 'realistic', they lose their innocence and their trust in the inherent goodness of humanity and Hashem's Creation. Yet, this Medrash is teaching us that at every stage of life we need to be able to include the beneficial aspects of the other stages. Being wise and mature should not come at the expense of our

The ultimate objective is to combine Aretz with Shamayim, tie and bind Earth to Heaven and draw Heaven down to Earth. This requires combining the movement and fire of passion with the stillness of the waters of pure being.

ויקהל / *Vayakhel* / gathering occurred at both the casting of the idol and the building of the Mishkan. And that is indeed the Divine desire, that Klal Yisrael gather with intense excitement to build the Mishkan, and that they yearn to give everything away and reach for Infinity. And Hashem also wanted for Moshe to instill Da'as into Klal Yisrael and show them that they are always already more than enough.

This is the *Chidush* / novelty of the project of the Mishkan, and in fact, of all of life; harnessing the unrestrained, wild, child-like 'heart' of Tohu, by circulating it within the vessels of Tikun, the orderly, clear space of 'mind'. We should be, in this way, like a young person on the border between adulthood and childhood; we should have mature Da'as and also the enthusiasm of a child. This is why the chief architect of the Mishkan is a 13 year old boy.

This idea can also help us better understand some deeper teachings on the foundation of the Mishkan.

THE AMUDIM / PLANKS OF THE MISHKAN STAND FOREVER

We are told that the Mishkan is an eternal edifice and was never destroyed. The Mishkan that was erected through Moshe is eternal,

---

ambition and our innate innocence.
We need to learn how to be like Betzalel and to unify the Light of Tohu, of youthful dynamism, with the vessels of Tikkun, maturity and Da'as.

and when the Beis haMikdash was built the Mishkan was buried (*Sotah*, 13a).

An eternal aspect of the Mishkan is the *Amudim* / pillars or planks supporting the walls and overall structure of the Mishkan. The Torah tells us that the Amudim need to be עצי שטים עמדים / "Upright acacia wooden planks" (*Shemos*, 26:15). The word עמדים / upright, say Chazal, means שעומדין לעולם ולעולמים / "they stand upright forever and ever" (*Yuma*, 72a). The planks of the Mishkan seem to lend eternity to the structure of the Mishkan.

Acacia wood in Hebrew is called שטים / *Shittim*. Why is Shittim used above all other woods? Says the Medrash, it is to create a Tikkun and bring a healing for an earlier experience with שטים. As the Pasuk says, וישב ישראל בשטים ויחל העם לזנות אל־בנות מואב / "While Israel was staying at Shittim, the people profaned themselves by whoring with the Moabite women" (*Bamidbar*, 25:1). In a geographical location called Shittim, Klal Yisrael sinned with licentiousness and sensual debauchery, i.e., *Tohu* / untamed, unfocused self-expression. Their Tikkun then needed to come through holy Shittim — bringing Shittim to create the Mishkan (*Tanchumah*, Terumah, 9. עצי שטים עומדים כמה מיני ארזים הן ומכלם לא בחר אלא בזה ששמו שטים לפי שישראל חטאו בשטים לקו בשטים ונתרפאו בשטים: Rabbeinu Bachya, *Shemos*, 26:15).

As a location, the name *Shittim* comes from the word *Sotah* / going astray (*Bamidbar*, 5:12), and from the word *Sh'tus* / foolishness, nonsense, as in שנתעסקו בדברי שטות / "They were engaged in matters of nonsense" (*Sanhedrin*, 106a. *Medrash Rabbah*, Bamidbar, 2:22). This is related to a general principle: "A person sins only if a spirit of *Sh'tus* / folly first enters him" (*Sotah*, 3a).

To replace the negative, destructive type of foolishness (Sh'tus, Shittim), Klal Yisrael is asked to construct the Mishkan with a positive, constructive kind of Shittim. This is referred to as שטות דקדושה / *Sh'tus d'Kedushah* / holy silliness or craziness (a major theme in the Torah of the Rebbe זצוק"ל זיע"א).

'Sh'tus of Kelipah', of negativity, involves descending to a place below the mind, as it were, opening oneself to indulge desires of the flesh, for example, despite knowing intellectually that one should not. Allowing temptations for instant gratification to rule over one's better judgement is negative Sh'tus. Positive, holy Sh'tus is to transcend the mind, to have faith in positive outcomes, despite not seeing a logical way out. It means to go beyond the letter of the law in Mitzvos and acts of kindness, beyond what you normally think is your capacity. Whereas Sh'tus of Kelipah is sub-rational, letting go of your mind and free choice, submitting to animal instincts, Sh'tus of Kedushah is super-rational, beyond mind.

Where did Klal Yisrael find Shittim wood in the desert? Says the Medrash (*Tanchuma*, Terumah, 9), Yaakov planted these trees hundreds of years earlier when he first descended into Egypt, telling his children, 'Eventually you will leave Egypt and you will need these planks to build a Mishkan.' Hundreds of years prior to their redemption from Egypt, and even before they were actually even enslaved, Yaakov prepared the wood that they would only need after they had been redeemed. Therefore, for hundreds of years, Klal Yisrael in their most harsh moments of enslavement were able to look at those majestic trees growing and attain a measure of hope.

Faith is what sustained Klal Yisrael in Egypt: faith in a brighter future, faith that one day, despite being oppressed and broken by the supreme power of the ancient world, they (certainly the women) had faith that despite all odds, redemption would come. This supra-rational faith is the Sh'tus of Kedushah, which is mystically the Shittim, the very walls and supports of the Mishkan.

Our Sh'tus of Kedushah counters our Sh'tus of Kelipah. Holy 'foolishness' defies all logic, transcends all predictions, and thus also literally becomes eternal, transcending the ravages of time, thereby becoming the essential foundation of the Mishkan, the eternal dwelling place of HaKadosh Baruch Hu in this world.

FROM DA'AS TO BEYOND DA'AS: THE NIGHT OF THE SEDER

On one hand, the entire process of Seder Night, this sublime celebration, reenacting and re-living our redemption, is all about assimilating Da'as into our consciousness. The inner constriction of Egypt was a constriction of Da'as and redemption occurs when all of Klal Yisrael and even the Egyptian oppressors "know that I am Hashem." The medium through which Hashem's Presence is revealed is Moshe, the *Bechinah* / aspect of Da'as.

On the night of the Seder, we drink wine together as a Mitzvah, and as we do so we create a Tikkun for the original drinking of wine, which was the eating of the grapes of the Tree of Knowledge that caused death and separation. And we also eat Matzah, which is also connected to the rectification of the Tree of Knowledge (according to another opinion that the Tree was actually stalks of grain). The grain of the Matzah is also connected to Da'as, as our sages tell us, "A child does not יודע / know how to call out 'father,' or 'mother,' until he tastes grain" (*Sanhedrin*, 70b). This implies that the consumption of wheat is associated, in some way, with our intellectual development, specifically, Da'as. Matzah brings Tikkun and maturity into our spiritual constitution. Yet, on the other hand, at the end of the Seder, we reach a point of *Atik* / Cosmic Transcendence (such as the level Klal Yisrael reached at the Splitting of the Sea), an aspect of the Sephirah of Keser / Crown, a place higher than all knowing, beyond Da'as.*

Da'as is the world of order, Tikkun, definition; where everything is distinct and marked and orderly. Indeed, the whole structure of Pesach night is called the *Seder* / Order, and everything is set up on the Seder plate in a very orderly fashion. As we move through the Seder, drinking more and more wine, slowly the orderly quality unravels and we attain a level beyond Seder.

We end the night singing praises to HaKadosh Baruch Hu, almost in the image of a 'drunken' lover, singing love songs to his Beloved One.

---

* Keser is *Ratzon* and *Ta'avah*, beyond Mochin. And within Keser itself there is the level of *Radla / Reisha d'Lo Isyada*, beyond knowing, even knowing itself, as it were. Radlah is the level of *Reisha D'lo Isyada* / 'the Unknowable Head' or 'the head that does not know'. This is the highest of the three levels within Keser. 'Below' Radla there is a level called *Galgalta* / skull, which is the meta-source of all defined masculine qualities. Below that, there is Mochin Stima'a / hidden 'brains' or mind, which is the meta-source of all defined feminine qualities. The level of Radla is so transcendent, it cannot be known by any living being or angel, nor even by itself, so-to-speak. Radla is beyond all Da'as.

Indeed, ultimately we are seeking a total Yichud of love, a Yichud between Da'as and the Crown beyond Da'as, between mind and heart, between maturity and child-like passion, the unbridled desire of Tohu and the vessels of Tikkun. This Yichud allows us to harness the *Ohr* / Light of Tohu within the *Kelim* / vessels, context and container of Tikkun.

ESSAY 2:

STAGES OF FREEDOM:
Redeeming our Name, Voice, Speech, Song, and Silence

*Y*ETZIYAS MITZRAYIM / THE GOING OUT OF EGYPT IS MENTIONED in the Torah fifty times (*Zohar* 2, 85b, and 3, 262a. *Tikkunei Zohar*, Tikkun 32. Rabbeinu Bachya, *Devarim*, 2:23. *Pardes Rimonim*, Sha'ar 13:1), telling us time and again to "remember" this most formative experience of our freedom. The fifty references to Yetziyas Mitzrayim correspond to the fifty weeks and the fifty Shabbosim in every year (*Pirush haGra*, Tikunei Zohar, p. 84). We remember Yetziyas Mitzrayim throughout the entire year, and in fact every day, for on each day there is a Mitzvah of the Torah to remember Yetziyas Mitzrayim. (Perhaps even women are obligated, and not just on the night of the Seder. *Sefer haChinuch*, Mitzvah, 21. Although, see *Minchas Chinuch* and *Sha'agas Aryeh*, 12.)

A Mitzvah to 'remember' implies that there is a possibility of forgetting, and by repeatedly urging us to remember Yetziyas Mitzrayim, the Torah is clearly warning us against this possibility. What type of 'remembering' or 'memory' is the Torah demanding of us? What does it mean to remember Yetziyas Mitzrayim? Surely the Torah is not commanding us to merely have a nostalgic rumination about the past. Is the Torah interested in us memorializing a historical event to help us remain aware of where we came from as a people, and where we are heading? Is the point of 'remembering' to learn from the past for the sake of improving the present? What does the Torah want from us in the act of remembering, and what is the intended result?

GOING OUT OF EGYPT:
HISTORICAL, PRESENT COLLECTIVE, PRESENT PERSONAL

Our sages say, "In every generation a person must regard himself as if he himself had gone out of Egypt" (*Pesachim*, 116b). Simply this means that when recalling the Exodus from Egypt thousands of years ago, we should envision our own lives as if *HaKadosh Baruch Hu* / the Holy One, has taken us, in our generation, out of Egypt. Indeed we were there, because our ancestors' redemption is ours as well, and if not for their being redeemed in the past, we would not even be here, in the present. This remembrance thus relates to the historical past as it resonates in the present.

On a collective level, remembering Yetziyas Mitzrayim encapsulates all the minor redemptions of Klal Yisrael from their constant exiles and *Gezeiros Ra'os* / negative decrees throughout time. On the night of Pesach we sing, "And it is this (referring to the Torah, the Shechinah, and/or our resolute faith) that has stood by our ancestors and for us. For not only one (enemy) has risen up against us to destroy us, but in *every* generation they rise up to destroy us. But HaKadosh Baruch Hu, delivers us from their hands."

On a more inward level, *Mitzrayim* / Egypt represents any and all *Meitzarim* / constrictions and limitations that paralyze or silence the human spirit. Enslavement, in this context, represents a state of ambiguity, doubt, lack of clarity and focus, in which a person lives inauthentically, without direction, purpose or aim. The notion that each generation is taken out of Egypt by HaKadosh Baruch Hu implies that we must experience our own redemption, as if the Exodus is happening to us right now. Every generation has their own *Meitzar* / constriction, the principal Kelipah of that generation, be it secularism or communism, materialism or universalism, nationalism or globalism, or any other -ism. Every generation has its own challenges and unique struggles, and yet, if we would merely open our eyes and reclaim what is innately ours, we would recognize that Hashem is always giving us the power and the means to be lifted out of these exiles and constricted states of mind and spirit.

"Every generation" means not only every era, rather, each *day* a person must regard himself as if he had come out of Mitzrayim (*Tanya*, 47); on each day it should be as if you had personally left Egypt that very day (Rashi, Shemos, 13:4, as explained by the Chasam Sofer, *Derashos l'Pesach*, p, 521). Ultimately, Hashem is taking us out of our inner Egypt each and every *moment* (as the Rebbe would often add; see for example *Sefer haSichos*, 5751, Shemos).

Yetzias Mitzrayim is a continuous, ever-unfolding process. Ever since we left Egypt at the great Exodus, every generation has had its own exiles and redemptions, expulsions and revivals. Individually as well, every person throughout their life goes through stages of feeling small, constricted, empty, lifeless or aimless — only to later experience breakthroughs, redemptions, and expansions, leading to greater openness, clarity and spiritual confidence. We all fall, and then Hashem gives us the strength to stand back up again.

To inwardly be in exile, in Egypt, means to live in-authentically, lacking direction, clarity and focus. On a collective and personal level, in a consciousness called *Mitzrayim*, we forget who we are and what we stand for, whether as a people, or as an individual. In order to go out of Mitzrayim, or at least make the vessels to receive the gift of redemption that comes from Above, we need the clarity that begins to percolate into our consciousness through 'remembering' and 'understanding' such truths.

We begin to facilitate redemption when we 'remember' and become a channel for a flow of deeper understanding of ultimate reality. This flow of understanding is described as the *Mei Binah*, the waters of *Binah* / understanding (The numerical value of Mei-Mem (40) Yud (10) = 50. These are the 50 gates of Binah: *Ta'alos Yaakov*, p. 102, corresponding to the 50 times the Torah mentions Yetziyas Mitzrayim). מצרים / Egypt is comprised of two words, מצר ים / 'constriction of water'. Egypt is a place where the Mei Binah, the waters of understanding and expansiveness, are restricted. In fact, in the paradigm of Mitzrayim, everything is stuck, and thus there is no flow at all. In Egypt, even the literal natural water was turned, for a period, into blood and death, which represents the great depth of the exile in Egypt.

As we leave our inner Mitzrayim, there is a breaking open of the waters, like the splitting of the waters of the sea, and we achieve clarity and perfect faith. As the Torah declares, Klal Yisrael's state of mind at that moment was such that "they believed in Hashem and in Moshe his servant." They had steadfast faith in the Creator and Source of all Life and Living, in Moshe, and by extension (see *Tanya*, 42), faith in themselves.

THE WORLD OF FORGETFULNESS

There are 50 'gates' or levels of understanding, and the fiftieth gate is Binah itself, absolute clarity and thus absolute openness and freedom. The Torah mentions the idea of remembering Yetziyas Mitzrayim exactly 50 times, as 50 is the level of total freedom. In fact, when one has attained freedom on this level there is no possibility for its opposite. Forgetfulness is connected to a type of brokenness in our perception of time. The world of *Pirud* / separation is where the past is considered separate from the present, and is thus forgotten. In the place of integration and unity, the world of Yichud, there is no forgetfulness, as the past is present in every moment. כל / *Col* / everything, is numerically 50. *Col* is the place of total recall, as in the world of all, the eternal now in which 'everything' is present.

'Exile' means separation, whether it is a geographical exile, separated from one's land, or an inner exile, in which one is alienated from his essential, authentic self. It is one thing to be in a literal and existential exile and still remember and thus long for home and authenticity. When one holds strong to the memory of where he came from or who he really is, he is still connected. Sadly, over time, if and when deeper levels of exile set in, one begins to no longer even recall that there is another place to go and a deeper self to reveal. Forgetfulness is a deeper, more traumatic state of stuckness and exile, in which one no longer even remembers that their life could be better. The situation is so dark, that one mistakes the darkness for light, goodness and life.

Egypt was one such place, where Klal Yisrael was steeped in deep exile to the point of almost utter forgetfulness of its past and destiny. Pharaoh, the king, and master of Egypt was the personification of the world of forgetfulness. The beginning of the descent of Klal Yisrael into slavery starts with ויקם מלך־חדש על־מצרים אשר לא־ידע את־יוסף / "A new king arose over Egypt who did not know Yoseph (who was the savior of Egypt)" (*Shemos*, 1:8). What does it mean "who did not know?" It means דהוה דמי כמאן דלא ידע ליה כלל / "He comported himself as though he did not know him at all" (*Sotah*, 11a). Pharaoh manages to *pretend* to forget what Yoseph had done for the Egyptians and for the king himself, and begins to enslave Yoseph's family. Pharaoh is the paragon of forgetfulness. Even the name Pharaoh is connected to forgetfulness, as it is connected to Hebrew word *Oreph* / neck, the back of the head. The back of the head is the place where things are forgotten*, while the front is the place of memory.

---

* The back side is connected to forgetfulness: See *Tanya*, Kuntres Acharon, 6. The Ten *Makos* / plagues undo this existential forgetfulness. For example, the Baal Shem Tov teaches that the first plague is דם / *Dam* / blood (numerically 44), which is the Sacred Name *Mah* / 45 (also אדם) missing an Aleph. The missing and 'forgotten' Aleph, Aleph being 'the One'. Through the water turning to blood, the Oneness of Hashem is remembered. The second plague is צפרדע / *Tzfardeah* / frogs. In Hebrew the word can be divided into צפר / *Tzafar* / a revealing of, דע / *De'ah* / awareness, which is the opposite of forgetfulness: *Toldos Yaakov Yoseph*, Beshalach. p. 53. The fact that *Tzfardea* is connected to the word *De'ah* is already found in the Medrash: *Pesikta Zutrasa*, Shemos, 7:29. See also *Pirushei haTorah l'Ba'alei Tosefos*, Shemos, 7:29.

כל / *Col* / everything, the fiftieth Gate, which is perfect Binah, is the world of ever-present clarity, openness and transparency, and thus total freedom of mind. As it is a place of perfect transparency, it is thus a world of freedom from physical mortality, which is a symptom of disunity and separation. The fiftieth Gate is also free of any *Yetzer haRa* / negative inclination: on the fiftieth day after leaving Egypt we received the Torah and were temporarily freed from death and from our *Yetzer haRa*.

RELATIVE VS. ABSOLUTE FREEDOM: FREEDOM OF ACTION OR OF THOUGHT

In addition to the fiftieth Gate of Understanding, the number 50 reflects 'the fiftieth year', what the Torah calls the *Yovel*, the Jubilee year. During the Yovel, slaves went free, debts were cancelled, and land returned to its original owner. In other words, in the fiftieth year, all people and things clearly 'remembered' and understood their own inner truth, their original source, and were thereby redeemed, returning to their origin, as explained earlier.

Within the Name Hashem (the Yud-Hei-Vav-Hei) there are two 'active' or 'masculine', assertive letters: the Yud, a point, and the Vav, a line. There are also two 'passive' or 'feminine', receptive letters: the two Heis. Hei is the sound similar to an 'H'. It can be used as a soft consonant, and can also be a 'silent letter', often at the end of a word. Sometimes the silent Hei is there to indicate a vowel, and sometimes it is just for syllabic or etymological emphasis. When Hei is sounded as a consonant, it mimics a person sighing from tiredness or relaxation, releasing a deep exhale: *Hhhh...* (*Amud haAvodah*, R. Baruch of Kasuv, Kuntreisim l'Chochmas Emes, p. 328). In any case, Hei represents rest and release.

Every seventh year in the Land of Israel is a *Shemitah* / Sabbatical year. The six days, and more broadly the six years of work and toil, are connected with the active letters within the name of Hashem (and more specifically to the letter Vav, the number six), whereas the seventh day and the seventh year are connected with the lower Hei within Hashem's Name.

The lower Hei of Hashem's Name symbolizes the resting of the earth that manifests with each Shemitah year. The earth corresponds to the *Sefirah* of *Malchus* / the Attribute of Sovereignty which is also the lower Hei. Within ourselves, the 'resting of the earth' means resting in the world of action — it is a state of non-doing.

Shemitah is a 'lower freedom'; a freedom to stop working, to recognize that the earth belongs to Hashem (*Sanhedrin*, 39a. *Sefer haChinuch*, Mitzvah, 84), and to focus more on spiritual work. In terms of "remembering", we remember that the earth and all it represents belongs to Hashem.

There is yet a greater cycle: seven times seven years; after seven cycles of seven years there is a fiftieth year, the year of *Yovel*. Yovel is a manifestation of the higher Hei of Hashem's Name (the complete freedom of Yovel corresponds to the upper Hei in the Name of Hashem: *Zohar* 3:108a). Hei numerically equals five, however, the upper Hei is called the 'full Hei' — the full or expanded five, which is 50. In the fiftieth year, not only does the land (earth, Malchus, lower Hei) rest, but also "slaves go free." In ancient times, when most of the

Jewish People lived in the Land of Israel, each in their designated tribal territories, "slaves" and those who needed to commit themselves to indentured service*, were set free. This represents a higher form of "rest" — a rest not just of earth and actions, but of thought, of consciousness, and identity.

As the upper Hei of Hashem's Name is *Binah* / understanding, this higher form of rest includes releasing our mind from all distracting thoughts and limited understandings. It is a state of existential rest, redemption and freedom from all forms of slavery, especially the worst form of slavery, the inner slavery of dependency, addiction, despondency and constricted consciousness.

When on the *Shemitah* year the land is allowed to rest, the lower Hei of the Divine Name experiences a lower, temporary degree of redemption. After the land rests from being planted and worked, it returns to its 'labors' and burdens.

In our own lives, this lower, relative type of freedom manifests as freedom from reactive behavior. If someone insults you, and you choose not to react but remain silent, you are refraining from 'planting new seeds' of conflict. Although you did not act in retribution, your mind and heart might still be upset. This is only a 'one-dimensional' form of freedom; it is a 'rest' from action alone. You have merely silenced your reaction, but you have not yet transformed your reactivity at its root — at the level of will and desire. Your mind and your heart may still 'want' to react and you have only temporarily controlled your outward actions, your level of Malchus. You did not yet redeem yourself on the level of Binah, of consciousness.

Yovel, however, brings transformational freedom for the entire human being — in 'thought' or consciousness, as well as in action. Binah contains seven permutations of each emotional attribute. This 'multi-dimensionality' has a balancing effect, freeing one from unconscious reactivity. In a state of clear understanding, our emotions are contained and balanced by a higher perspective sometimes called *Mochin* / intellect or mind. For example, if you are experiencing the expansive emotion of *Chesed* / loving-kindness and generosity from a higher perspective, you can be simultaneously in touch with the contractive emotion of *Gevurah* / strength and withholding. You are 'thinking out of the box' of your emotions, and are therefore free to respond with awareness, rather than merely reacting or stuffing your reaction.

This is the deeper freedom that is spiritually available through the 50 times that the Torah speaks of Yetziyas Mitzrayim. It is a remembering of not only what we, as a collective, should or should not be doing, but, deeper, who we are as a people. To 'remember' in this sense is to free our minds and live freely and consciously.

When we as a people remember who we are, including our collective past and our purpose and destiny, we also remember ourselves individually, who we truly are, and can thus begin to live authentically. We are free from the choke-hold of Pharaoh, the force of forgetfulness. Mitzrayim, and everything it represents, falls away.

On the night of Pesach, on the night of our collective and individual release from bondage, the more we 'remember' Yetziyas Mitzrayim, the more we internalize the upper Hei of complete freedom of consciousness and Binah. On this cosmic night when

HaKadosh Baruch Hu takes us out from all *Metzarim* / constrictions and limitations, the more we recite the Haggadah and re-live the meta-narrative of the Going Out of Egypt, the more we become saturated with the *Koach* / power and *Shefa* / flow of Yetziyas Mitzrayim.

HAGGADAH: THE BIRTHING OF SELF

As mentioned, in Egypt we were like fetuses within our mother's womb, without the freedom to be individuals. We were 'confined' to being an extension of someone else's agenda, owned by the state and simply defined as "slaves to Pharaoh in Egypt". We were a 'nameless' people — with no self-understanding. Certainly, as a fetus, we had no voice. Our going out of Egypt was our birth. Binah is sometimes called *Eim haBanim Semeicha*, 'the Mother that gives birth to joy' (*Tehilim*, 113:9), referring to the joy of birth and redemption. By attaining Binah and self-understanding, we can joyfully leave our inner exiles and experience life as if for the first time.

Throughout the Seder and the recitation and exploration of the Haggadah, we experience a reenactment and a re-living of the Exodus and thus the birth of selfhood. This is our birth as a people, and the birth of ourselves as distinct, authentic, conscious individual selves.

Haggadah means 'telling'. Through telling the story of the Exodus, we remember that we too are going out of Egypt. Yet, the deeper meaning of the word Haggadah is, as the word *Agadah*, 'drawing out': "Words of *Agadah* draw out" (וכל משען מים אלו בעלי אגדה)

שמושכין לבו של אדם כמים באגדה / "And every support of water"; these are the masters of Agadah, who draw people's hearts like water by means of Agada": *Chagigah* 14a. The Mordechai writes that indeed *The Haggadah* should be called the *Agadah*, beginning with an Aleph, not a Hei: Mordechai, *Pesachim*, 117a). By reciting the Haggadah with intention, passion and fervor, we relive the Exodus and draw down the waters of higher intelligence and expansive awareness, from the inner world of Binah and beyond.

Therefore, *L'Saper* / to tell the story is essential on Pesach Night, not simply 'remembering' and 'revealing,' but relishing and reveling. Every day and night of the year we need to remember Yetziyas Mitzrayim by mentioning that Hashem took us out of Egypt in our daily prayers and recitations. While this is a Mitzvah to do every day, on Pesach Night the Mitzvah is more than simply stating the fact; it is to tell the story (*Ma'aseh Nisim*, Pesicha. *Shevach Pesach*, Magid, 1. *Siddur MaHaRid*, Inyan Mitzvah. *Malbim*, Bo, 13:8).

On Pesach night we are storytellers. To be a storyteller, one needs to be proficient in crafting language and nuances of expression and tonality. An ability to tell stories shows the mastery of language, as well as the skill to "draw out" the process of revelation and expression. The deeper we go inwards and into our collective narrative, and the more we draw out and reveal the "waters" of understanding, the more there is a psychosomatic effect on us. The more we connect with our deeper self and reveal it through consciousness, the more exile fades and redemption becomes real to us.

In this way, telling the story of the Exodus from Egypt, and then turning it inward and speaking about our own inner exiles, challenges, tribulations, and hardships — and then giving thanks for all the miracles Hashem has shown us — all of this helps us rediscover our true collective and individual identities. We reclaim ourselves, becoming essentially free and spiritually open beings.

This process of redemption-through-storytelling is part of the very mechanism which empowered us to leave Egypt many centuries ago, as well as now on this powerful night. In order to hone our storytelling abilities, let us review the story of our Exodus, as transmitted to us in the Torah, and deepen our understanding of all the above discussions.

FROM A PROUD, 'NAMED' PEOPLE TO A NAMELESS PEOPLE

The Hebrew title of the *Book of Exodus* is *Shemos* / Names, suggesting that it is a book all about names. Indeed, *The Book of Shemos* begins when the members of the household of Yaakov are still free people, and it lists the names of each family who came down to Egypt: ואלה שמות בני ישראל הבאים מצרימה... / ראובן שמעון לוי... / "These are the Names of the children of Israel who came to Egypt...Reuvein, Shimon, Levi..." naming all the twelve tribes. They enter Egypt a proud people, with distinct names and identities. However, as they descend into the Egyptian exile, the Torah begins to refer to the children of Yaakov without names, but rather with pronouns. Immediately after naming them, the Torah continues, "*They* multiplied; *they* increased; the land was full of *them*..." (*Shemos*, 1:7). It does not say, 'And Reuvein became a huge tribe, and Shimon multiplied,' rather "...*they* multiplied."

/ ובני ישראל פרו וישרצו וירבו ויעצמו במאד מאד ותמלא הארץ אתם

"But the children of Yisrael were fertile and prolific; they multiplied and increased very greatly, so that the land was filled with them." The root of the phrase וישרצו, translated as 'prolific,' is שרץ / swarmed, like insects. The analogy of insects suggests a proliferation, multiplying and giving birth as animals do, which is typically in abundance and as many six offspring per birth. (In fact, according to the deeper teachings of the Torah [*Galei Raza*, see *Yalkut Reuveini* on the Pasuk] the souls of the Jews in Egypt were transmigrated souls from the sheep of Lavan, who in turn were the souls of the 974 generations before Creation: *Chagigah*, 13b. They are also the souls whom Yaakov brought to Egypt).

Seforno gives us an alternative meaning of "swarmed": נטו לדרכי שרצים / "(The People) veered to the ways of *Sheratzim* / creeping insects." While the Torah is certainly hinting at their multiplying like insects, the term וישרצו can also be understood to mean that the People first reduced themselves, acting and feeling like lowly insects, and then they were reduced by their oppressors to being nameless, expendable creatures, disgusting creepy crawly things that swarmed the terrain. They first diminished themselves from being a proud, distinct, named people, to being a group that acted like roaches and pests. This self-degradation opened them up to being further diminished by their overlords as unworthy creatures, insects upon which to trample.

People may name their cats or dogs, but no one names the roaches that swarm their basement. To be viewed as a roach is to be reduced to nothing, with not even the respect given to a dog.

They begin as proud people, with distinct, holy names and a strong sense of identity. Their names reminded them of their past, of the patriarchs of each tribe. These names empower them in their present mission, and signify their glorious future (*Medrash Rabbah, Shemos*, 1:3-5). First, they descend by their own commission and then by external forces, into a mental and spiritual condition of slavery, a state of stuckness, *Tumah* / impurity. Finally, they reach the low point of losing their names and sense of identity, and live as debased, crushed, lowly forms of existence.

There is a total eclipse of their humanity and selfhood. Nameless people with no access to authentic or meaningful expression. Exiled in a place of deep paralysis and silence, they say nothing.

Yet, as 'insects,' they proliferate, arousing Pharaoh to devise a plan to exterminate every newborn boy. ויאמר מלך מצרים למילדת העבריות אשר שם האחת שפרה ושם השנית פועה / "The king of Egypt spoke to the Hebrew midwives, one of whom was named Shifrah and the other Puah" (*Shemos*, 1:15), and informed them of his diabolical decree. Here it seems that the two Hebrew midwives were clearly named, one Shifa the other Puah. Chazal, however, reveal that these were not their actual names, rather descriptions of their work: שפרה שמשפרת את הולד.... פועה שהיתה פועה ומוציאה את הולד / "(Why is she called) 'Shifrah'? Because she would prepare (*Shaferes*) the newborn (for birth). And (why) 'Puah'? Because she would make a comforting, cooing sound [*Pu-ah*] as she would remove the child" (*Sotah*, 11b). In fact, Chazal go on to reveal that they were actually either Yocheved and Miriam or Yocheved and Elisheva (the wife of Aharon). Just at the very moment the Torah is seeming to give us the names of the two Jewish midwives, Chazal reveal to us that these were not their real names.

In another view, these *are* their proper names, but they were not Jewish women, rather Egyptians, as the Abarbanel writes: מילדת העבריח means they were "midwives *to* the Hebrews" not "Hebrew midwives." This further supports the idea that Klal Yisrael are not named in Egypt; Shifrah and Pu'ah are not names of Jewish women, nor are they even pseudonym names based on their jobs (ולא היו עבריות כי איך יבטח לבו בנשים העבריות שימיתו ולדיהן אבל היו מצריות מילדות את העבריות: Abarbanel, *Shemos*, 1:1).

How do Chazal know that these are not literal names? The Torah says clearly, "The name of one was Shifrah and the name of the other was Puah." Perhaps it is because in the very next episode, which talks about the birth of Moshe, the most important figure in the Torah, the Torah refers to his parents namelessly, and Moshe himself is not given a clear name. Unlike all the other very important characters of the Torah, Yitzchak, Yaakov and the Shevatim, for example, who are all named right at birth — Moshe is not given a name at birth.

When the Torah begins the story of the birth of Moshe, it says (*Shemos* 2:1), "A man from the house of Levi married a daughter from Levi." No name is given; he is just "a man from the house of Levi," who marries a likewise nameless woman. When Moshe is born, the Torah only says, "The woman conceived and bore a son; and when she saw how beautiful he was, she hid him for three months." A nameless couple has a nameless child (Chazal, in *Sotah*, 12a, tell us that his name was Tov or Tuvia, but he is not named clearly in the Torah). Only later is he named by his adoptive (albeit converted, *ibid*, 12b) step mother, Pharaoh's daughter.

Up until this point in the Torah, every time it speaks of the birth of a child, it tells us right away what the mother or father names the child. Now, in stark contrast, the greatest prophet and leader of Klal Yisrael is born in anonymity.

This is a deeper reason that Moshe, at the Burning Bush, asks Hashem, "What is Your Name?" Moshe says, הנה אנכי בא אל־בני ישראל ואמרתי להם אלקי אבותיכם שלחני אליכם ואמרו־לי מה־שמו מה אמר אלהם / "When I come to Bnei Yisrael and say to them, 'The G-d of your fathers has sent me to you,' and they ask me, 'What is His Name?' what shall I say to them?" (*Shemos*, 3:13). This is because enslavement is the reduction of named individuals into statistics, but redemption begins with a consciousness of the power of the name. Moshe needs a "name" for Hashem in order to be able to transmit the vision of freedom to the as yet nameless people, who seemingly do not even have names for their children, much less their Creator.

TO NAME / DEFINE / FRAME / CONTEXTUALIZE IS A BASIC HUMAN FUNCTION

Naming things is essential to the basic human project of survival and determining one's place in the world. One of the first acts Adam performs in the Garden is to name and define the animals: ויבא אל־האדם לראות מה־יקרא־לו וכל אשר יקרא־לו האדם נפש חיה הוא שמו / "And (Hashem) brought them (the animals) to the man to see what he would call them; and whatever the man called each living creature, that would be its name" (*Bereishis*, 2:19).

Naming things makes distinctions and contextualizes our reality. By naming the world around us, like Adam, we are able to navigate relationships, describe our experiences, and define our space. Without the ability to name and be named one is trapped, perceptually cut-off from the world, from human reality and all communication.

Personal interactions are based on having a personal name. Only free people have names, and having a name allows one to give names to others. A slave is a nameless statistic with no independent personal identity or existence, no power to speak, communicate, contextualize or define. The exile of Klal Yisrael was so deep that they could not even name themselves.

FROM NAMELESS TO NAMED

The transition from namelessness to possessing a name, representing the process of redemption, occurs with the emergence of the adult Moshe. He now appears as a named person, although his name Moshe was not given by his parents. Moshe gradually identifies with his people and begins to feel concerned about their plight.

Once Klal Yisrael has a leader who is one of them, and who sees them as individuals — as real people with honor and pride, not just as statistics or nameless slaves — the process of their redemption can begin. For this reason, in the *Book of Shemos* (6:14), amid describing the hardships of slavery, the Torah begins reviewing the names of the households of the people of Israel. It is thus revealed that they had always kept their own names, at least among themselves: "The following are the heads of their respective clans. The sons of Reuvein, Israel's first-born: Enoch and Pallu, Hezron and Carmi; those are the families of Reuvein…" These verses seem totally out of context. In the middle of speaking about how Moshe and Aharon are going to Pharaoh, and while the plagues have already begun, the Torah suddenly begins to name the tribes, their children and lineages.

For a redemption to occur, there needs to be 'someone' who can be redeemed. A person or people who feel like *Sheratzim* / creepy crawly things, who are broken and reduced to the point of not having a sense of self or *Tzuras Adam* / human form, cannot be redeemed. Klal Yisrael could not at first be lifted out of their situation, as there was 'no one' to uplift. And such, their process of redemption from this exile began with Moshe seeing them as real people. After experiencing that small but significant recognition, they were able to remember their names and tribal identities, as the Torah's narrative reveals. Once they had reclaimed their names, they could gradually regain their voice.

EXILE OF SPEECH

Naming is a function of speech, the ability to inwardly define and then outwardly express an idea. In the depth of slavery, Klal Yisrael lost its capacity to name and be named, because, as the Zohar teaches, in Egypt, *Dibbur* / speech itself was in exile (*Zohar*, 2:25b). The exile of speech, and the inability to voice, even to oneself, one's needs and desires is the deepest exile possible. To be human is to be a *Medaber* / a 'speaking being'. When we cannot express ourselves inwardly, never mind articulate to others what we are thinking or feeling, we are exiled from our own humanity. To take away someone's ability to speak robs them not only of their humanity but of their capacity for meaningful relationship to other humans.

A person who is in a personal exile speaks in a mode of broadcasting, like speaking about sports, the weather or any other trivial matter. They are just filling the void with empty noise. This is not real speech, nor an expression of human consciousness, it is like being a *Sheretz* / a swarming creature, like a cricket, producing sound. In a deeper level of exile, one loses their voice altogether. In Egypt Klal Yisrael lost their voice and self-expression.

Speech implies choice, for through language we define our reality. We contextualize and navigate life linguistically. A slave does not have the choice to articulate or reveal who he really is, for his reality is imposed upon him. Nor can a slave listen to another; their ability to hear the possibility that their circumstances may change is completely absent. Even Moshe, who was essentially above slavery, born into the free Sheivet of Levi and raised as an Egyptian prince, could not easily speak.

At the Burning Bush, Moshe says of himself, לא איש דברים אנכי / I am not a man of words" ..., כי כבד־פה וכבד לשון אנכי / for I have a כבד / hard (or heavy) mouth and a hard tongue" (*Shemos*, 4:10), and says, "the people will not listen to my voice" (*Shemos*, 4:1). These two statements are intricately related: Moshe 'did not have the choice' to speak because the people were not yet open to listen. At the same time, the people were unable to listen because there was no one to speak for them. There was no opening, no self-perception, no speech and no conscious choice making.

A slave has no story to tell. As the devastation of their humanity robs them of their inner life, their dreams, aspirations, desires and longings, a slave has nothing to say, nothing meaningful to talk about or share. A slave is subjugated not only physically, but emotionally, intellectually and spiritually.

When, G-d forbid, a human being is reduced to a statistic, such as a prisoner under a dark regime, they are forced to think and dream of nothing but surviving the demands of the moment. They end up devoid of an inner life. They stop speaking because there is nothing inside to describe. Even if they can speak physically, there is no insightfulness, no warmth, no appreciation of life, in their words. And this is what occurred, on some level, to Klal Yisrael in Egypt; their voice was silenced until they lost their inner life. Physically, at least some of them could speak, but their words were shallow, superficial words and *Lashon haRa* / negative speech.

Reflecting on the predicament of Klal Yisrael, Moshe says, שהייתי תמה עליו, מה חטאו ישראל מכל שבעים אומות להיות נרדים בעבודת פרך, אבל רואה אני שהם ראויים לכך / "The matter I was wondering about, why Klal Yisrael are considered more sinful than all the seventy nations to be subjugated with back-breaking labor, has become known to me. Indeed, I see that they deserve it (because they speak *Lashon haRa*) (Rashi, 2:14, from *Medrash Rabbah*, Shemos, 1:30).

Klal Yisrael was silent until quite late in the exile, according to the Torah's account. We do not hear in the narrative that they complained or demanded to be treated better, nor that they rebelled or fought. Perhaps they were too overwhelmed to feel anything, or perhaps they had become so accustomed to their harsh subservience, that they no longer noticed it or felt that it was foreign to who they truly were. They embraced their identity as slaves. Usually, when a community is oppressed, at least a couple courageous individuals arise to challenge the status quo and decry their internalized oppression. Before Moshe there was no one who stood up.

Not only did they not speak about the possibility of becoming free, not only did they cease to recall their glorious past, they stopped speaking altogether; their Dibbur was completely in exile.

Their descent into silence and loss of choice was gradual, yet, at the end, there was a deeply devastating level of trauma, a total eclipse of their voices and self-recognition. They did not even dream or yearn for their freedom. In fact, they were so completely stuck and paralyzed that not even a cry or groan of conscious pain or sadness could escape their lips.

THE BEGINNINGS OF REDEMPTION

"Now it came to pass in those many days that the king of Egypt died, and the children of Israel sighed from the labor, and they cried out, and their cry ascended to Hashem from the labor" (*Shemos*, 2:23). The Chizkuni writes that when the King of Egypt finally died, the Jewish people realized that they might get an opportunity to rest briefly from their labors. Only when this thought crossed their minds, did they become aware of their exhaustion and trauma, and when it did not happen, and the slavery continued, a "sigh," a groan finally emitted from their throats (כל זמן שאותו מלך חי היו מצפין שמא כשימות זה יתבטלו גזרותיו... וכשמת זה לא נתבטלו גזרותיו אמרו מעתה אין לדבר סוף לפיכך ויאנחו / "As long as the old king had been alive, they had hoped that with his death the harsh decrees against them would 'die' also. When they found out that they had hoped in vain, they groaned").

Perhaps when the king died all the Egyptians were busy with the funeral and it was the first day, in many years, that there was a day off, as surely the Egyptian slave taskmasters did not show up to work (*Imrei Shefer*, Vanitzak). Or, perhaps they were even intentionally given a day off (*HaEmek Davar*, Shemos, 2: 23). In any case, now that they had a moment of rest and a break from incessant labor, they now realized that there could be another way. They had the faintest glimmer of an insight that slavery was not their 'ontological' and permanent condition. As they rested, a buried memory arose; there is something called freedom, they were human beings and slavery had been imposed upon them from the outside — and so they sighed and cried out in grief.

People who are really stuck, physically, mentally or emotionally, can be so enmeshed in their condition that they stop remembering that there is even a possibility for an alternative. Even grief can be suppressed from awareness. Yet, once there is even an externally imposed pause in the oppressive conditions, the person can abruptly wake up and shake out of their stupor.

With just a glimmer of understanding of where they were, and perhaps who they truly were — with just a hint of the possibility of freedom — a convulsive wave of grief arose. In its wake, a yearning to be free became palpable and real. The Torah says, "and they groaned…and Hashem heard their groan…" (*Shemos*, 2:23-24). The Ohr haChayim on this verse notes that the "groan" was not an utterance of prayer, nor a cry to Hashem for help, a directed groan, rather it was a visceral, elemental cry of pain. Similarly, when Hashem tells Moshe at the Burning Bush, "I have seen their plight," ואת־צעקתם שמעתי מפני נגשיו / "and I have heard their cries because of their taskmasters" (*Shemos*, 3:7), the verse is saying clearly that their cries were not a form of prayer, rather a reaction to their being beaten, a visceral, instinctual scream of the pain of being abused. This is a very primal kind of cry, a cry coming 'from' pain, not a cry 'to' Hashem. It was simply a shout of "Ouch!" Yet because they were softened and opened enough for their voices to vibrate in some way, Hashem heard and received their groan as a prayer. Hashem welcomed their groaning as a prayer, interpreted it as a reaching out, a yearning 'to', and a longing 'for'.

There is a distinction between *Kol* / sound and *Dibbur* / speech. Sure every Dibbur is rooted in Kol, yet, Dibbur is articulate. They cried out on the level of Kol, an inarticulate sound of recognition of the hurt they were experiencing. Nonetheless, their Kol was heard on High as a Kol directed toward Hashem, a Dibbur, a communicative expression, a prayer for help.

As they softened and opened, so in a manner of speaking, did Hashem 'soften and open', and responsively began to open the way for their Redemption. Hashem listened and 'felt compassion', so-to-speak, because they cried. There was an unshackling of rigidity and stuckness *Keviyachol* / as it were, in Hashem's Presence, as well as in the people.

ה' צלך / "Hashem is your *Tzel* / shadow" (*Tehilim*, 121:5). The simple meaning of this verse is that Hashem protects us, but a deeper reading reveals that Hashem's Presence is literally like our shadow; moving and responding according to our actions, thoughts and words, much like a shadow mimics our movements (*Keser Shem Tov*, Hos'fos, 60. *Shaloh*, Sha'ar haGadol, 22a). Whereas Hashem, Infinite Timeless Beingness, does not move or change (כי אני י-ה-ו-ה לא שניתי:)

Malachi, 3:6), the emanation of Hashem's Divine Presence manifests in relation to us and our movements and changes.

When we are open and there is some positive movement on our part, even a simple cry, a corresponding openness and movement manifests 'Above'; there is a 'shadowing' or mirroring of our activity in the 'activity' of the Divine Presence. When we, 'below' in this world, cried out in Egypt, when we became open and softened enough to recognize where and who we really were, there was a corresponding opening and softening, Above, a recognition of who we really were, a Divine 'capacity' for listening: "And Hashem heard...."

In Egypt, the process of redemption, of a movement away from slavery into freedom, does not begin until there is some percolation of movement, of vibration, a stirring of aliveness and human consciousness, on the part of Klal Yisael. So long as we were stuck in the posture of slavery, without even a recognition of our own pain or a desire to cry out, there was a mirrored response Above of stuckness, as if the One Above did not recognize them or desire to redeem them.

We, too, need a break in the monotony of day in day out work, a time to stop, just to let go of doing and to consciously 'be'. This is why Pesach, *Zeman Cheruseinu* / the season of our release into freedom, is called *Shabbos*. To be free, we need Shabbos, a day of returning to ourselves, softening and expanding our consciousness. We also need a day of national mourning such as Tisha b'Av, when we can pause and feel, and open to the pain of exile. In Mitzrayim, Klal Yisrael needed a break from *Avodah Kashah* so that they could expand even slightly from the consciousness-narrowing effect of their *Meitzarim* / dire straits and stresses of exile. When we do so, we can entertain the thought of freedom. This is why Tisha b'Av is also known as the birth of Redemption. When the darkness of exile is seen for what it is, the opposite, the light of Redemption, is paradoxically apprehended as well. Then we can realize, even minimally that we are not essentially slaves, but Hashem's People. And from this realization, when we are able to cry out to Hashem for help, Hashem manifests His Presence as עוזר דלים ועונה לעמו ישראל / "Helper of the destitute, Who answers His People, Yisrael" (*Siddur*).

In Egypt, once Hashem heard the cries of 'His People' and received them as prayer, this receptivity rippled back downward and now their sound and voice raised their vibration and further opened their consciousness, allowing them to sense a relationship with something greater than themselves, something beyond and outside their predicament of slavery. Eventually, they were able to reclaim their true names, to speak, and to dream of freedom.

PHARAOH: THE PERSONIFICATION OF STUCKNESS

There are three partners, as it were, in the Exodus story: Hashem, the People of Israel, and the *Mitzrim* / Egyptians. Once they groaned, the protective shell around Klal Yisrael softened, and they became open to change. Pharaoh, the antagonist of the narrative, is a self-absorbed, stubborn ruler, and he himself is the ultimate archetype of a stuck person, even to the point of self-destruction. Naturally, in the wider context, his state needs to be shifted as well in order for change to occur on behalf of all the characters in the story.

Regarding the first five plagues in Egypt, the Torah states the Pharaoh 'hardened his heart' and refused to let Klal Yisrael go. However, referring to the next series of plagues, Hashem tells Moshe, כי־אני הכבדתי את־לבו / " I have hardened his heart" (10:1). Hashem is telling Moshe that Pharaoh has shut down his heart and closed himself off emotionally to the plight of his slaves to the extent that now it is as if the Creator created him with a hardened, sealed heart in place of self-directed will.

A person may be born, for example, with the free choice to drink or not drink alcohol, but sadly, once a person becomes habituated to having a drink every few hours, the force of addiction becomes all the more difficult to let go. This is not only true for obvious addictions; any type of behavior repeated over time becomes "second nature," and almost impossible to stop. It may seem to the person that although they have free choice in other areas of life, regarding this issue in life, it is 'beyond' their capacity of free choice to do or not do. Once a person becomes stuck in this way, it feels to him as if he was simply born an addict, this is the way the Creator created him, and thus has no free choice at all.

Indeed, feeling sunken, paralyzed and without choice or power, is itself part of the 'punishment' of willfully closing one's own heart. As the Rambam writes, if a person closes his heart down completely, whether through committing grave sins or through many smaller acts repeated many times, and refuses to make *Teshuvah* / a return to spiritual sanity, part of the punishment is that the gates of Teshuvah are 'closed' before him (ואפשר שיחטא אדם חטא גדול או חטאים רבים עד שיתן הדין לפני דין האמת שיהא הפרעון מזה החוטא על חטאים אלו שעשה ברצונו ומדעתו שמונעין ממנו התשובה ואין מניחין לו רשות לשוב מרשעו: Rambam, *Hilchos Teshuvah*, 6:3).

As Hashem is our shadow, and our actions below are mirrored by actions Above, if we close ourselves to Teshuvah, *Chas veShalom*, Hashem closes Teshuvah to us. Now, it is true that the path of Teshuvah is always available, and even when the door of Teshuvah is seemingly closed, one can always bang down the door if one chooses. ("The doors of *Teshuvah* are forever open": *Psikta d'Rebbe Kahana*, Parsha 45:8. Even when it says the doors of Teshuvah are closed, they are not completely sealed and if one really tries the doors can be opened: Rav Chasdai Cresces, *Ohr Hashem*, Ma'amar 3, Klal 2:2. Meiri, *Chibur haTeshuvah*, Meishiv Nefesh, Ma'amar 1:3. *Tanya*, Igeres haTeshuvah, 11.) However, as long as one were to deliberately obstruct oneself from any desire for Teshuvah or acts of Teshuvah, that blockade will stand, and it will certainly appear to him as if the doors of Teshuvah are shut closed; meaning, it will appear to him as if he had no further choice in the matter.

Pharaoh did not think that Teshuvah or a change of heart was possible. He was utterly mired in a harmful hierarchy of lords and slaves, and that was the only way, he believed, that the world could and should function. He believed in a hierarchy in the pantheon of gods in the cosmos, and as a result that was his experience of the social and economic world. Not only did he believe in an absolute structure of higher and lower castes within society, he believed that he was a god himself. Thus he ruled his people as if from above them. Aloof and immune to criticism, Pharaoh's heart and mind was bolted shut, paralyzed within his psychotic self-deification, and cemented within a belief in his divine right to enslave any human being.

Pharaoh was so stuck in his rigid mode of thinking, that it penetrated his entire body. He proclaimed that as a 'god', he consumed food but never needed to relieve himself (*Medrash Rabbah,* Shemos, 9:8). On the one hand, this supposed feat represents a form of self-control and self-sufficiency. On the other hand, it represents an absence of all natural movement from intake to output. There was no flow within his body, as if there were no 'openings' in his body. This is the epitome of systemic exile. Both the slave and the slave owner are tied to being enslaved; they are both stuck in their narrow perspectives and their dependency upon each other. Up until the point at which the slave groans or the enslaver falls, neither is flexible enough to change the pattern or make a different choice.

THEY HAVE BECOME SOFT, HARDEN THEM!

Once the Pharaoh dies, whether this is literal or metaphorical, and once Klal Yisrael cries out, Hashem hears their cry and a new kind of leader arises for and from the people. As Hashem beckons Moshe to leadership, he complains that he has a "hard/heavy mouth" and cannot speak and express himself correctly. Yet he is commanded to go challenge and speak to Pharaoh, the most powerful earthly ruler in the world at that time, and tell him to let the slaves free.

Moshe, with the help of Aaron, then begins to overcome his own speech impediment and to convey Hashem's words and message to Pharaoh. When Moshe's declarations and advancements towards freedom begin to have an effect upon the inner mindset of the slaves, Pharaoh reacts by telling his task masters, תכבד העבדה / *Tichbed haAvodah* / (from the word *Kaveid* / hard or heavy) "*Harden* upon them the work" (*Shemos,* 5:9). He snaps, "Make them work 'harder', because they are נרפים / *Nirpim* / lazy" (5:17). The word נרפים / *Nirpim* comes from the word *Rofha*, 'soft'.

In other words, Pharaoh senses that the slaves have 'softened', they are listening to and internalizing Moshe's words, they are being stirred to the possibility for freedom. Pharaoh, who is himself still very stuck in and functioning from the place of a hardened heart, cannot tolerate this soulful softening. In order to prevent any redemptive 'opening' Pharaoh shouts at his taskmasters to make it even 'harder' on them. In contrast to *Nirpim*, he uses the term *Tichbad* — '*Harden* their hearts, which are getting too *soft*!"

A similar linguistic contrast is employed in Pharaoh's decree to use 'straw' for the 'bricks'. After Moshe and Aaron come to Pharaoh and demand that he let Klal Yisrael go, Pharaoh becomes agitated and decrees to the slave task enforcers: לא תאספון לתת תבן לעם ללבן הלבנים / "You shall no longer provide the people with straw for making bricks" (*Shemos*, 5:7). From now on, the slaves themselves have to gather the straw to form the bricks, all without reducing their productivity.

Straw is relatively soft and flexible, while bricks are hard and fixed. Pharaoh is saying to his enforcers, 'Stop letting the slaves become malleable and susceptible to change! Through my new decree

---

* Chazal tell us (*Shemos Rabba* on the Pasuk) that Klal Yisrael had scrolls which they would read on Shabbos, telling them that HaKadosh Baruch Hu would one day redeem them, thus Pharaoh says, *Tichbad haAvodah*, let them no longer read these scrolls. What are these scrolls? the *Shalsheles HaKabalah* and the *Malbim* (Hakdama to Iyov) bring down that it was the book of Iyov/Job (see *Bava Basra*, 15a, משה כתב ספרו ופרשת בלעם ואיוב). A book that demonstrates that despite the harific present condition, there is hope, and salvation will eventually and certainly come.

I am going to תכבד / harden them. And I am going to demonstrate this to them in a tangible way: take soft straw and mix it with a solution that hardens it into inflexible bricks. I want you to take the softness of their heart and make it as hard as a brick.'

Softness and hardness of the heart are primarily psychological qualities — openness versus stuckness, the ability to speak and emote versus paralyzing self-censorship. Straw and bricks are those same qualities manifest in physical objects. Pharaoh is telling them, 'This is how reality is; your hardening will not be a mere subjective psychological quality, it will be as objective as the bricks you will be making.'

For all Pharaoh's stubbornness, once the people cried out, the redemption of speech and thus their eventual redemption from enslavement was already an inevitability. The snare had been broken, the rigidity had been softened, and Klal Yisrael had begun to listen to Moshe's words about their imminent redemption and to regain their own voice.

The nameless, voiceless, stuck slaves, began to be redeemed the very moment they cried out. The moment Hashem heard their prayers was the moment they began to regain their real voice and to articulate what they truly needed.

MOUTH THAT SPEAKS VS. NEGATIVE MOUTH

On Pesach we reenact and 'relive' the Exodus and the redemption of speech. The word פסח / *Pesach* can be split into two words פה סח / *Peh Sach*, a mouth that speaks.* This stands in stark contrast

---

* Although *Sach* / 'speaks' is with a Shin שׂ, not a Samach as in סח, (and *Pesach* is spelled פה סח) yet, in the language of the Gemara, Chazal refer to pleas-

to the word *Pharaoh*. פרעה / Pharaoh can also be broken into two words: פה רע / *Peh Ra*, meaning 'negative mouth' (Arizal, *Sefer ha-Likutim*, Shemos 2). Pharaoh embodies and symbolizes the force of negative speech, a reactive, rigid form of expression that is meant to keep others stuck, hardened, deaf and mute. On the holy day of 'Peh-Sach', the Torah wants us to demonstrate our freedom by opening our mouths and speaking, raising our voices in retelling the story of the Exodus. Reciting the Haggadah allows us to accept and own our history, our enslavement, as well as our future, redemption, in the present moment.

In Egypt, the slaves were forced to do עבודת פרך / *Avodas Perach* / harsh labor. The word פרך / *Perach* can be broken down into the two words, פה רך / *Peh Rach*, 'weak mouth' (*Sotah*, 11b). This refers to the exile's diminishment of Kla Yisrael's power and potential to authentically speak; even when the yearning for freedom was awakened, the People of Israel were not able to articulate their thoughts, dreams, and yearnings. Their mouth was in a weak condition. The *Ra* / Negative, harsh, enslaving mouth of Pharaoh imposed this condition of a weakened mouth.

Klal Yisrael, as slaves, were tasked to build the cities of פתם and רעמסס / Pisom and Ramses (*Shemos*, 1:11). The names of these two cities are also indicative of this enslavement: פתם can be split into two, as in פי תום / *Pi Tom*, closed or sealed mouth (or פי תהום / the mouth of the abyss: *Sotah*, 11a), and Ramses can be split into רע מסס

---

ant speech as סיחה נאה, with a Samach: *Bava Basra*, 78b. Also, the word *Peh* / mouth within the word *Pesach* is missing the final Hei, (פסח instead of פה-סח). The missing Hei represents the five places of articulation in the mouth, which need to be revealed through actual speech, and were thus 'missing' from Klal Yisrael's experience while enslaved.

/ *Ra Moses* (ילד משמעו כצורתה זו תיבה מצרי דבלשון, 'Moses,' or *Mezes* / son in the Egyptian language is Moshe: *HaAmek Davar*, Shemos, 2:10.). *Ra Moses* means 'negative Moshe', indicating a constriction of the person and idea of Moshe, who would eventually become the great 'speaker' on behalf of both Hashem and Klal Yisrael.

Parenthetically, it should be noted, there is the possibility that רע מסס is also actually the name of the Egyptian ruler at the time of the Exodus, Ramesses or רעמסס, and the city is called by his name. *Ra* is also the name of the 'sun deity', the idol that the Egyptians worshipped. The ruler of Egypt claimed to be the son of a god, and thus was called *Ra Meses* / the Son of Ra.

Essentially, there are three levels of speech discussed here: פה רע / *Peh Ra* / negative mouth, פה רך / *Peh Rach* / weak mouth, and פה סח / *Peh Sach* / a mouth that speaks (*Zohar Chai*, Tazria). The Peh Ra caused a Peh Rach. The Lashon haRa of the *Mitzrim* / Egyptians contracted and weakened the capacity of the people to speak, until they descended into a place of utter voicelessness. In contrast, their Geulah comes through Peh Sach, thus פסח, speaking and storytelling about the miracles and wonders of the Going Out of Egypt.

Despite the benefits of speaking and storytelling, sometimes the best form of speech is transcend control and mastery and actually remain silent. The middle letters of the מצרים / Egypt is יצר / inclination, generally referring to our negative inclination. The first letter is an open Mem, מ, representing an open mouth, whereas the final letter is a closed Mem, ם, representing a closed mouth, a mouth that is silent. (A closed Mem is similar to a closed womb: *Sha'ar haPesukim*, Tehillim, 18. See also *Sefer haBahir*, 84. Whereas an open Mem represents giving birth: *Sefer haBahir*, 85. An open Mem represents a state of 'giving' and expressing: *Pardes Rimonim*, Sha'ar haOsyos, Mem. Tzemach Tzedek, *Sefer haLikutim*, Mikvah, p. 1,458.) A spiritually, emotionally, mentally healthy *Peh* / mouth (פ is numerically 80) is one that knows the balance of when to open their mouth and when to keep the it closed (two Mems also equal 80). The exile in Egypt represents a separation, a divide, a disunity between the two possibilities of the mouth. There *Peh Rah*, negative speech, which would be best unspoken, was expressed, and this led to a weak and powerless mouth. Pesach and redemption brings about a healthy, balanced Peh Sach.

In Egypt, our mental, emotional, physical and spiritual state of פה רך / weakened mouth, eventually devolved into פה רע / a negative, lifeless, hopeless mouth. In this hopeless state we submissively went along with Pharaoh's agenda, and occupied ourselves with building the city of פי תום / *Pi Tom* / Closed Mouth, which was a פי תהום / Pi Tehom / opening of the abyss, a gateway into a bottomless spiritual void known as the 49th gate of impurity. Surrounded by such self-reinforcing structures of רע / negativity and brokenness, we did not even have the will to return to ourselves and leave this gate, which stands before the eternal abyss of impurity, despair and enslavement.

At some point after we groaned, a miracle occurred, and the space that was once Pi Tom, was transformed — the buildings they constructed sunk, one by one, into the mouth of the earth (*Sotah*, 11a). In fact, once we set off to leave Egypt, we immediately chanced upon a place called פי החירת (*Shemos*, 14:2). Says Rashi, הוא פיתום, ועכשיו נקרא פי החירות על שם שנעשו בני חורין / "This place was actually *Pi Tehom* but now it was called פי החירת / the Mouth of Freedom, as they had now become a free people." Pi Tehom, the energy of chaos, had been transformed into Pi HaCheirus, the song of freedom. Our closed and misdirected mouth was opened, and that same mouth became one of freedom, a redeemed mouth.

From Mitzrayim we were liberated forever to use constructive, positive, holy language, words of freedom, aspiration, hope, possibility and positive movement. There were, of course, subsequent exiles, oppressions and censorships, but after Yetziyas Mitzrayim, our Peh Sach, our liberative ability to speak, will never fully leave us; we became free people *b'Etzem* / in our essence, and "Etzem is unchangeable" (כל עצם בלתי משתנה See, *Ma'amorei Admur HaZaken,* Shemos 2, p. 474. *Toras Chayim,* Vaera 1, 78b). This is why we will inevitably leave behind our current exile, as well, already armed with holy, authentic, positive speech, song, and words of Torah and *Tefillah* / prayer.

FREE SPEECH IS NOT ONLY WHAT WE SAY, BUT HOW WE SAY IT

A truly free person is not only redeemed physically, but in speech as well. There is a difference in speech between an inwardly enslaved person, chained to his whims and instincts, and someone who has control and mastery over his consciousness and behavior.

Redeemed speech is more than being able to express yourself when needed. It is more than an ability to express your deepest desires and yearnings. It is even more than having the refined awareness to honestly express who you really are. Redeemed speech also has a certain quality, tone and vocabulary.

You can hear in someone's voice if he is inwardly free or enslaved, in control of himself or bound tightly to his whims, rigidities, and instinctual behaviors. The wise Shlomo haMelech / King Solomon says, דברי חכמים בנחת נשמעים מזעקת מושל בכסילים / "Words spoken softly by wise men are heeded sooner than those shouted by a ruler in folly" (*Koheles*, 9:17). Not only are words spoken softly more effective, as in the simple reading of this verse, but in general, a wise person naturally speaks softly, without screaming (Rambam, *Hilchos De'os*, 2:5), and you can tell a wise, inwardly free person by the gentleness of their speech (*Otzar Medrashim*).

Beyond the tonality of the voice, is also the refinement of their voice. A free and truly empowered individual, speaks בלשון נקיה / clean language. Whereas an unredeemed, unrefined individual speaks in coarse and foul language. This is the deeper reason why Chazal's teaching about speaking בלשון נקיה is recorded in the beginning of Tractate Pesachim (3a), the tractate dedicated to the laws of Pesach — it is a mark of a truly free and empowered person.

Furthermore, a 'redeemed' person consciously chooses words that frame the Divine goodness in a given situation, or which have a relatively positive effect on the consciousness of others as well as themselves. For instance, instead of 'This publication has a deadline,' the Rebbe would say, 'This publication has a due date.' In this way, even the slight negativity of a (non-literal) reference to death is replaced by the positivity of a (non-literal) reference to birth. The positive effects of such elegant word choices could be subliminal or obvious, depending on the situation.

REDEMPTION OF SPEECH & THE HIDDEN EIGHTH PLAGUE

Recall that Moshe began his journey as an individual with a "heavy" or "hard" mouth. Much like all of Klal Yisrael, Moshe too had a compromised capacity for speech. Whereas the actual slaves were laboring under the harsh, 'hard' conditions of *Peh Ra* / negative speech and *Peh Rach* / weak speech, Moshe, who was not enslaved, could still speak, but his mouth was heavy. Words did not come easy to him and it was difficult for him to emote or speak assertively in front of Pharaoh.

Redemption, as explained, began when the people finally cried out, and it continued to unfold when Klal Yisrael was able to really hear Moshe. Prior to the initiation of this process, Moshe was 'unable' to speak because the people were not yet open to hear; speaking and listening are interdependent. As such, the more the people and Pharaoh listen to Moshe speaking, the fuller and clearer Moshe's expression becomes. The more open and receptive the listener, the more eloquent and articulate is the speaker. In place of a heavy mouth, with the opening of Klal Yisrael's hearts and ears, Moshe gains a fluent mouth and an ease with language and direct communication.

This phenomenon of Moshe's metamorphosis helps us explain a perplexing event within the story of *Yetziyas Mitzrayim* / the Going Out of Egypt.

In the beginning of the Torah portion Bo, before the eighth plague, the portion opens, ויאמר ה' אל־משה בא אל־פרעה כי־אני הכבדתי את־לבו ואת־לב עבדיו / "Then Hashem said to Moshe, בֹּא / *Bo* / Come to Pharaoh. For I have hardened his heart and the hearts of his courtiers.... ולמען תספר באזני בנך ובן־בנך את אשר התעללתי במצרים / "So that you tell over, to the ears of your sons and of your sons' sons how I made a mockery of the Egyptians..."(*Shemos*, 10:1-2). Unlike the other nine plagues, Moshe is not told what exactly the next plague will be, yet, when he comes before Pharaoh he says, "Thus says Hashem…'How long will you refuse to humble yourself before Me? Let My people go that they may worship Me. For if you refuse to let My people go, tomorrow I will bring ארבה / locusts on your territory'" (10:3-4).

Moshe is never told that the eighth plague will be locusts, all he is told is בא אל־פרעה / *Bo El Paroh* / Come to Pharaoh." How does he know that the next plague will be ארבה / locusts? There are deeper reasons why this plague was not overtly and clearly articulated to Moshe (ארבה בגי׳ יצחק סוד הדין...כדי שלא יתעורר הקטרוג והגבורה והדין...לא דברו הקב״ה בפירוש רק ברמז: *Agra D'Pirka*, 273), but the question remains, how does Moshe know what the plague will be?

It is possible, as the Chasam Sofer suggests (*Toras Moshe*, Bo), that Hashem allows Moshe to freely choose what he desires or thinks the next plague should be, and in that case a great swarm of locusts was Moshe's choice. We also know from the teachings of the Arizal that the Ten Plagues correspond to the Ten Utterances of Creation and express the Ten Sefiros, but in an imbalanced way. Counting from the bottom up, the eighth plague is connected to unbalanced *Binah* / understanding, which is manifest in the idea of locusts. Indeed Moshe took these correspondences into account when proclaiming locust as the next plague.

The Medrash (*Shemos Rabbah*, 13) answers that Moshe knew that the next plague would be locusts from Hashem's description: the next plague will inspire people to "tell the story to their children and grandchildren." As the Maharal (*Gevuras Hashem*, 34) explains, only a 'natural' event, but one that is extreme, like a plague of locusts, would be told generation after generation. Every time in the future locusts would swarm, and this occurs frequently in Egypt, they would remember that there was once a locust plague of extreme proportions. A 'supernatural' event, such as blood or the death of the firstborn, would not be told for generations, as there would be no constant reminders, whereas every locust swarm would remind Egypt of this event. (The Ramban, *Shemos*, 10:14, writes that never has a locust swarm, and such are frequent, destroyed all the crops in Egypt, and regarding this it is said, "Sing praises to Him; speak of all His wondrous acts." *Tehilim*, 105:2. וכתב רבינו חננאל בפירוש התורה שלו מעת עתרת משה רבינו ועד עכשיו אין ארבה מפסיד בכל מצרים, ואם יפול בארץ ישראל ויבא ויכנס בגבול מצרים אינו אוכל מכל יבול הארץ כלום עד עכשיו, ואומרים כי זה כבר ידוע הוא לכל...ועל זה נאמר שיחו בכל נפלאותיו.) In this way, Moshe intuited from Hashem's description of the effects of the plague what type of plague it would be.

In addition to the above answers, there is a cryptic teaching by the saintly student of the Megaleh Amukos, Rav Shimshon of Ostropoli, the great *Mekubal* / Kabbalist who was massacred together with his community in the devastating Cossack uprising in the year 1648. Rav Shimshon teaches (*Likutei Rav Shimshon Ostropoli*. See also, *Ohev Yisrael*, Bo), that in the words בא אל־פרעה / *Bo El Paroh* Hashem is hinting to Moshe what the next plague will be.

Based on a hyper-literal read of the words "*Bo el Paroh* / Go to Pharaoh," one can take the letters Beis-Aleph from the word בא / *Bo*, and put them into the word פרעה / *Pharaoh*, spelling ארבה / *Arbeh* / locust. This is accomplished by employing the art of interchanging letters. In both the word פרעה and the word ארבה there are two similar letters, the ר ה. In the word פרעה there is a Pei/פ and Ayin/ע, and in the word ארבה there is an Aleph/א and Beis/ב.

There are five places of articulation in the mouth: the lips, tongue, throat, teeth, and palate. The letters Beis and Pei both come from the lips, and for this reason they are considered interchangeable. The letters Aleph and Ayin both come from the throat, making them interchangeable, as well. Hashem thus tells Moshe, בא אל-פרעה: 'Take the letters Beis and Aleph, and put them into the name *Pharaoh*; the Pei will be replaced by Beis, and the Ayin will be replaced by Aleph, and then instead of פרעה it will be ארבה.'

Superficially, this seems to be merely a sophisticated linguistic trapeze act. This teaching is nevertheless hinting at something very profound, and that is the transformation which is occurring within Moshe throughout this process. It means that Moshe is becoming a great linguist, a master of words and letters, and this represents a metamorphosis of his capacity to speak. Moshe who, like all of Klal Yisrael, began with a *Kaveid Peh*, is now able to manipulate language in a lucid, creative way. This is a sign of redemption, which must begin with the redemption of speech and language. From a stutterer, he becomes a great orator, and eventually his speech impediment is totally healed (at Matan Torah: *Medrash Rabbah*, Devarim, 1. *Zohar* 2, 25a. *Agra d'Pirka*, 166).

In fact, while the letters of *Pharaoh* can be transformed into those of ארבה / *Arbeh*, the letters of the word ארבה can spell the phrase ברא-ה / create five. Moshe is able to create new words using the five places of articulation in the mouth, and thus was able to intimate and tell Pharaoh that the next plague would be locusts.

Finally, at the eighth plague, an unprecedented fluency of speech appears within Moshe. Eight represents going beyond the natural cycle of sevens, beyond nature as it were, as Moshe is in this moment breaking free of his personal constriction of speech. In the process of his own personal redemption Moshe miraculously becomes a master of language, and communicator par excellence. Hashem never clearly instructed Moshe to announce the plague of locusts, yet Divine speech spontaneously flowed through him and he was able to deduce the word 'locust' out of the coded information Hashem had given over to him.

Indeed, this eighth plague inspired Klal Yisrael למען תספר / "so that you will tell over," to become storytellers, and to relate the story of exile and redemption "to the ears of your children and grandchildren."

Klal Yisrael, who descended into a condition of enslavement and lost their names, identities and voices, have now regained their voice to the extent that they have become storytellers, masters of voice and language.

NEED TO SPEAK AND TELL THE STORY OF THE MITZVOS OF THE NIGHT

On the night of Pesach, as we sit down to remember and tell over the story of the Exodus, we mirror the process of Klal Yisrael going from a nameless, voiceless people to a people possessing a clear, confident voice. Therefore, we must conduct our Seder with a full, empowered voice, as well.

Yet, before we begin to recite the Haggadah in a proud, passionate voice, we break the middle Matzah, the poor man's broken bread, representing a pre-verbal state of brokenness. Even before this, we wash our hands before the Seder without making a blessings; this too represents, among other things, our inability to speak at this early stage of the Seder. Then we take a bitter or bland vegetable, an onion or potato for example, dip it in salt water and bite off a piece. This reflects the state of exile and enslavement, with all its bitterness, brokenness and voicelessness. Only after tasting of this salty bitterness do we begin to recite the Haggadah and redeem ourselves through holy, vital speech.

The Mishnah in *Pesachim* (116a-b) teaches, "Rabban Gamliel would say, 'Anyone who did not mention these three matters on Pesach night, has not fulfilled his obligation (fully, Ran, *ad loc.*): *Pesach, Matzah* and *Maror*... the Pesach is brought because the Omnipresent Passed Over the houses of our forefathers in Egypt, as it is stated: 'That you shall *say*: It is the sacrifice of Pesach to Hashem, for He passed over the houses of the Children of Israel in Egypt, when he smote the Egyptians, and delivered our houses'" (*Shemos*, 12:27). The source of this *Halacha* / law of *saying* the words Pesach, Matzah and Maror, and mentioning at least briefly what they are referring to, is based on the above verse: "That you shall *say*: It is the sacrifice of Hashem." From this verse about the Pesach sacrifice, the Paschal Lamb offering, we learn that we need to "say" something not only about our larger story, but specifically about Matzah and Maror as well (as Tosefos, *Pesachim*, 116a, explains. ואמרתם זבח פסח הוא פי' באמירה, שצריך לומר פסח זה שאנו אוכלין, ואיתקש מצה ומרור לפסח, וצריך לומר נמי - מצה זו מרור זה).

This teaching of Rabban Gamliel is recorded in the Haggadah: "This *Pesach* / Passover sacrifice that we are eating is for the sake of what? To commemorate that the Omnipresent *passed over* the homes of our ancestors in Egypt… (One lifts the Matzah and says,) This Matzah that we are eating is for the sake of what? To commemorate that the dough of our ancestors did not have enough time to become leavened before the Holy One, blessed be He, revealed Himself and redeemed them immediately…' (Then he lifts the *Maror* / bitter herbs and says,) These bitter herbs that we are eating are for the sake of what? To commemorate that the Egyptians embittered the lives of our ancestors in Egypt."

Why do we need to "say" *Pesach*, *Matzah* and *Maror* and mention what they are about? Beside the fact that the Pasuk commands us, "you shall *say*," what is the 'technical' reason for this command, as it were? When we put on Tefillin, for example, there is no Mitzvah to *say*, 'These are Tefillin and we put them on because of such and such.' Additionally, why do we "say" these things in a question and answer format, asking "…for the sake of what?" Why not just simply say, for example, 'We eat the Pesach because our homes were passed over.'

We are told to answer that we eat the Pesach offering because Hashem "passed over" our doors, we eat the Matzah because we left in haste, and we eat the Maror to be reminded of the bitter exile in Egypt. These are actually puzzling responses to our three questions. The reason we ate the Pesach offering during the time period that we offered it, is that it is a Mitzvah to *eat* a Korban Pesach. This was a Mitzvah that Klal Yisrael received even before the night that HaKadosh Baruch Hu passed over their homes. Similarly, we eat Matzah today, just as we ate it on the night of the Exodus, because there is a Mitzvah to "Eat Matzah in the evening." Again, this Mitzvah was given days before we left in haste Egypt. And the reason we eat Maror is because there is a Mitzvah to eat Maror together with the Korban Pesach. In this way, it seems we do not in fact eat the Pesach offering because "Hashem passed over us," not Matzah because "we did not have enough time," nor Maror because "they made our life bitter"?

Yes, again, the simple answer given by the sages for this question is because the Pasuk says, "That you shall *say*: It is the (Pesach) sacrifice of Hashem who passed over the houses of the Israelites in Egypt..." The Torah is saying that we *eat* the Pesach sacrifice because Hashem passed over the houses. But what does the Torah mean when it makes it a Mitzvah to "say", when in fact, the Torah clearly states that it is simply a Mitzvah to eat the Pesach?

Every Mitzvah contains both the element of *Chok* / a decree that is transcendent of human reasoning and *Mishpat* / a decree that relates to human reason. Each has dimensions of *Na'aseh* / doing and *Nishmah* / listening, obedience and inspiration, 'prose' and 'poetry', the letters and the musical notes.

We relate to the Creator as servants to a King; Hashem commands and we obey. But we also relate to HaKadosh Baruch Hu as a child to a Parent. Hashem gives us the means to connect to Him as our Beloved Parent, and we lovingly 'participate' in Mitzvos by decoding and understanding their deeper 'reasons'.

On the night of the Seder, as we ourselves are experiencing a departure from our inner Egypt and becoming a holy people, we are asked to fully participate and fully engage our full selves in this process. Similar to Klal Yisrael, we are beckoned to become storytellers. לְמַעַן תְּסַפֵּר. The Mitzvah of this night is *Sipur* / to tell the Exodus as a story — not just to *mention* Yetziyas Mitzrayim as we do all the days and nights of the year.

There is a primary element of *Chok* / mysterious command in the Mitzvos of Pesach, Matzah and Maror: we do them simply because we are commanded. The core of the Mitzvos and the 'real' reason why we do them is that they are the absolute will of HaKadosh Baruch Hu. Hashem commands and we do; there is no 'poetry' in this, and in a sense, no questions to be asked. Yet, on the night of Pesach we also need to think about these Mitzvos in terms of their historical unfolding and their inner significance. In this way, not only do we eat the Pesach, Matzah and Maror because we were so commanded, but we also need to immerse, embody, and participate in the stories related to them. Hashem also wants us to be storytellers on this night; passionate, poetic transmitters of the narrative. Hashem wants us to get involved, to ask provocative questions and offer evocative answers, to excavate the deeper meanings of the Mitzvos, to sing, to use *our* voice. Thus, as we are personally and collectively going out of Egypt on this night, we "*say*" the stories of Pesach, Matzah and Maror. And we do not merely pronounce that tonight we eat these items because of the given reasons, but we verbally flesh out the history, the narratives, and the spiritual implications for our own lives.

On this night we activate the *Geulah* / redemption of our authentic voices. Through poetically intermingling our people's history with our own personal stories and inner life, expressing it all vocally, Yetzias Mitzrayim becomes real to us in the present. We *participate* in it. We are no longer slaves with muted self-awareness. We have a voice, and Hashem hears us.

Stories are sometimes the only medium through which we can fully express ourselves. The more relaxed mode of expression makes us feel more comfortable, warm and open. If we had only dealt with 'cold', detached ideas and facts on this night, we would never be able to open ourselves and identify with the narratives and experience ourselves as if *we* were actually leaving Mitzrayim on this very night. Stories take us beyond where ideas can reach.

FROM STORYTELLERS TO SINGERS

When we *feel* the story of our Exodus unfolding within us, we naturally burst out in song; on this night we go beyond even from the level of storytellers — to become singers.

Our voice, language, self-understanding and identity have been regained and forged on a higher level. In fact, even while we were still in Egypt, when the Mitzvos of eating Pesach, Matzah and Maror, were revealed to us, we were raised to the level of a future Matan Torah — the revelation of Divine speech and an outpouring of Divine commandments and communications.

We were 'first-hand witnesses' of the miracles and wonders displayed in Egypt and are empowered to tell these stories and miracles in vivid detail to our children, spouses, friends and communities, for all of history. Finally, having left Egypt and having miraculously crossed the Sea of Reeds, together with Moshe himself, we break out in songs of praise and sing the Great Song, the *Shiras haYam* / Song of the Sea.

When we look back upon the night, we see how far we have come in just a few hours. Mirroring the birth of Klal Yisrael from the 'Land of Constrictions', we began with a broken Matzah, with salty water and humble acknowledgments of our state as slaves. As we gradually moved through the Haggadah, we felt and expressed the bitterness of our past, and realized that Hashem hears our voice and story, and sees our afflictions. More and more, our voice, name and true identity emerged. We miraculously left behind our inner enslavement and reactive behavior; we became independent, free. We became empowered to articulate ourselves, and to actively *create* the story of our lives, to the point that Divine speech began resonating to us and through us, revealing our purpose and reason for existence.

A REDEEMED VOICE SINGS PRAISE

At the end of Maggid, the bulk of the 'speaking' part of the Haggadah, we begin singing the first part of Halel, which speaks about the miracles and wonders that occurred at the Exodus from Egypt. Then we lift up a cup of wine and declare, "*Therefore, it is our duty to thank, laud, praise, glorify, exalt, adore, bless, elevate, and honor the One who did all these miracles for our ancestors and for us!*" Our speech is fully redeemed, we speak openly and clearly, with a refined, confident voice, and we begin to sing Hashem's praises.

Praise and thanksgiving are the highest form of speech and expression, and they are the very reason our mouths were created. In the words of the Arizal and later Poskim, הפה נברא להודות לה / "The mouth was created to offer thanks and praise Hashem" (*Kaf haChayim*, *Shulchan Aruch*, Orach Chayim, 60:4, in the name of the Arizal. Chida, *Midbar Kedeimos*, Zayin).

We sing praises not only for all the miracles that occurred during Yetziyas Mitzrayim, but also for all the miracles that continue to occur throughout our history. Not only do we sing for all the specific miracles within our glorious, albeit often tragic history, but for the greatest miracle of all, the survival of our people. We also offer thanks for our own lives, for the gifts and miracles in each of our individual stories. On the night of the Seder we are moved to speak "about all the kindness and miracles Hashem has done for us, both collectively and individually — and one who does so fulfils a Mitzvah" (*Peleh Yoetz*, "Erech Dibbur").

Seder Layl Pesach / 'The Order of the Night of Passing Over' is a template for 'passing over' to the exalted level of giving thanks to HaKadosh Baruch Hu for all the miracles and kindnesses that Hashem shown us, in such a way that we open ourselves up to receiving even greater wonders and goodness. With this powerful, initiatory template, we can begin to fill all the other nights and days of our lives with thanks and praise. The *Kli* / vessel to receive Hashem's infinite kindness, blessings and miracles beyond imagination, is humble gratitude. Continually thanking Hashem, and joyfully singing about all the *Chasadim* / kindnesses and miracles that HaKadosh Baruch Hu does for us every moment — this is what forms the vessel that draws down and receives even more Divine kindness, miracles and salvations.

After singing the first part of *Halel* / Praises at the end of the Magid section of the Seder, we eat and physically internalize the Mitzvos, and then proceed to enjoy a royal meal. After reciting the *Bentching* / Blessings and Thanks After the Meal, we continue with the second part of Halel, which speaks of the future Ultimate Redemption. As the Haggadah crescendos with the final praises of Halel, there begins an almost spontaneous, free-flowing singing up until the final stage of the Haggadah, *Nirtzah* / Acceptance. We have reached a sense of clarity and mastery over our articulation, our speech is thus elevated to the level of joyful song. We are now a liberated nation singing at the Splitting of the Sea of Reeds, celebrating our birth into Redemption, and pouring out our hearts in overwhelming praise and gratitude. We have evolved from slaves to storytellers to singers, and a cascade of beautiful, enlightened tunes comes tumbling out of our mouths.

FROM SINGERS TO TRANSCENDENT SILENCE

At the peak of the Exodus, as Klal Yisrael is standing at the banks of the Sea, with the Egyptian army in hot pursuit, Hashem asks Moshe, "Why do you cry out to Me? Speak to the people of Israel and they shall journey forward!" (*Shemos*, 14:15). After the long process of the redemption of their speech and dignity, from dark silence to brilliant stories and praises, now, at the climax of redemption, the people are told to remain silent. This seems counterintuitive. The Zohar remarks on this verse, that this event expresses the Divine mystery of *Atik Yomin* / Ancient of Days, also known as simply *Atik* / the Primordial, the place of Pure Transcendence (בעתיקא תלייא מלתא. *Zohar* 2, 48a).

Experientially, the level of Atik corresponds to the 'silence beyond sound'. This is in profound diametric contrast to the 'silence before sound', the silence that mutes all sound, which was the condition of Klal Yisrael as slaves in Egypt. Now we have attained a level that is *beyond* all expression. When words fail, we sing, and where even song fails, we fall into ecstatic silence.

This is a rich inner quietness, like the warm blanket of silence that descends upon us after riding the final crescendo of a magnificent symphony, when all the music, and noise, emotion and movement, suddenly cease. Beyond sound, beyond expression, this silence is pure *Deveikus* / unity. It is a sense of effortless expiration within the Infinite One.

Much like Klal Yisrael in the historical Exodus from Egypt, we began the night of the Seder in a place of 'silence' before sound. That silence came from an exile of speech, an inability to express ourselves. In fact, even when one is able to physically speak, but all that comes out are empty words, weather, politics, sports, emptiness — this too is a form of silence, 'noisy silence', which fills one's inner void with meaningless static.

Now, at the end of the Seder, almost miraculously, we find ourselves at the other end of the spectrum, the pinnacle of meaningful self-expression. Having drunk three cups of wine, having songs, melodies and infinite light flow from our mouths, now a happy exhaustion envelopes us, and we sink into the world of Atik, silent transcendence. This is the stage of *Nirtzah* / Acceptance. Suddenly there is nothing to do and nothing needs to be said. All is complete and accepted. We are home.

We have spoken and sung until there is nothing else that can be said or sung. We have reached a point of silence beyond words, song beyond sound, this is the level of Atik Yomin, the same silence that Klal Yisrael reached at the Sea.

Indeed, מצווה לספר ביציאת מצרים / the Mitzvah to tell over and speak about Yetziyas Mitzrayim is to do so until שתחטפנו שינה / *Shetichatfenu Sheina* / sleep takes hold of you, even after the Seder is complete (Tosefta, *Pesachim*, 10:8. Rosh, Pesachim 10:33. Tur and *Shulchan Aruch*, Orach Chayim, 481:2). The obligation on this night includes continuing to speak of the wonders and miracles of Yetziyas Mitzrayim until we fall asleep. (Note that the obligation is לספר ביציאת מצרים / "to tell over the story of the Exodus from Egypt" all night, even after the Seder, but if you fall asleep after the Seder you become absolved of the obligation because you simply cannot continue. The obligation is 'up until the point' of falling asleep; as such, if you doze off and wake up again, you can go to bed and return to sleep, and you do not need to continue with speaking about Yetziyas Mitzrayim.)

Sleep is somehow the crescendo of telling over the Going Out of Egypt. This total surrender is not simply a demarcation, the point at which we can stop telling the story. "Until sleep overtakes you" means that we need to tell the story until we reach the level of sleep.

The root letters of שינה *Sheina* / sleep are the same letters as ישן / *Yashan* / old, hinting at the level of *Atik* / ancient. Through sleep you take leave of 'this world' as it were, and enter into more inner worlds. In sleep, you let go of the world of noise, commerce and activity, and enter a world of subtlety, silence and potentially, self-transcendence.

On the night of Pesach, at the culmination of the Seder, the apex of leaving all forms of Mitzrayim, all shackles of limitation, restriction and constriction, we move from the place of sound, activity, and even praise, into the utter Transcendence of Atik Yomin. We slip into a consciousness of unity with HaKadosh Baruch Hu, 'the Ancient One', a subtle, quiet Deveikus in having arrived. At this point we simply let go and give ourselves over to Hashem.

COMFORTABLE SILENCE, BEYOND SOUND, BEYOND SEDER

Experientially, this transcendent silence is experienced as the melding of two into one, like the comfortable silence that comes about when you are so intimate with another person that you can walk for twenty minutes with them and not say a word. Walking side by side in silence with someone you are less comfortable with can be awkward and unsettling; you are not 'at one' with them or sharing a space 'beyond words'.

Ultimately, the whole point of the *Seder* / order of the night is to arrive at this place 'beyond Seder'. It is essentially an 'order that transcends order'. After all the steps, all the work and words, all the *Haggadah* / storytelling, all the Mitzvos we have done and the praises we have sung, we have reached a pinnacle 'beyond' all effort or activity, beyond all Avodah /spiritual work. All of it vanishes into the repose of *Nirtzah* / complete acceptance. In this loving embrace of silence, we become aware of a perennial Divine reverberation that constantly calls to us saying, "I want you for 'you', not for what you do, say, think, feel or sing. I love you just for who you are, My child."

We have come full circle, from silence to sound and back to silence. But now, we are suspended in the blissful silence of two lovers in a deep embrace. There are no more questions. There is only silence. And that silence is itself the answer, it is Redemption, the eternal acceptance of Nirtzah.

**EVEN HIGHER:
SONGS BIRTHED IN SILENCE & SOUNDS THAT INCLUDE SILENCE**

For many, the Seder concludes with the drinking of the fourth cup of wine, the joy-filled declaration, "Next year in Jerusalem", the final step of Nirtzah, and then, sleep. Yet, many have the custom to continue the night with a post-Seder recitation of *Shir haShirim* / Song of Songs, and various other *Piyutim* / symbolic hymns and poems.

In a semi-drunk, semi-asleep state, late at night, after four cups of wine, those with *Koach* / strength keep singing what on the surface might sound like (*leHavdil*) 'bar tunes': "Who knows one? I know one… Who knows two, I know two!" and the like (although, of course there is tremendous hidden depth in these Piyutim). Yet, in truth, these frivolous seeming songs are rooted in a deep place of quietness, *Sheinah* / sleep, and Atik. Poems and songs such as these give voice to the innocence that emerges from within stillness — they are the childlike sounds of mature silence. The songs sung in this hypnagogic Atik state are songs of such depth and mystery that they remain deep and mysterious despite being expressed and exposed.

There are plain words, the world of noise and sound, and there is the higher expression of sound, the world of poetry and song. And yet, interestingly, songs produced on this level are still birthed within the world of noise. They are higher vibrations that are created out of a lower context of noise. Thus, in a way, they are just another form of noise, albeit a more subtle, more harmonious manipulation of noise.

Such tunes are indeed a more beautiful sound emanating from within the external world of sound, yet there is also a deeper sound of and from the inner world of silence.* There is a type of Shirah that emanates from the deepest recesses of the soul, from the place of utter transcendence, a place of silence beyond noise, beyond words, and from that deep quiet place, a song effortlessly flows. A song that, even while emanating from the deepest depths, always remains deep.

The great singer of Israel, Dovid HaMelech, says in Tehilim, למען יזמרך כבוד ולא ידם / "For my whole soul will sing to You and not remain silent" (30:13). He is referring to a level of song that emerges from the place of utter *Dom* / silence, inwardness and stillness, and from there pours forth into the world.

---

* After Klal Yisrael reached the level of Atik, there was the Shira at the splitting of the sea, and six weeks later the revealing of Matan Torah, Anochi Hashem / I am Hashem. Anochi is the level of Keser (Keser - Ani / I). Chazal tell us (*Medrash Rabbah*, Shir HaShirim, 1; 2,4) that when Klal Yisrael heard Anochi Hashem, נתקע תלמוד תורה בלבם, והיו לומדים ולא היו משכחין / "the Torah was imprinted upon their hearts so that they would learn and not forget." נתקע / imprinted comes from the root תקע, the same letters (with the Yud) as עתיק. The Torah is a revelation of the Ten *Dibros* / words that are rooted within Keser, the utter Transcendence of HaKadosh Baruch Hu.

Re-enacting the cosmic, historical Exodus narrative, we hear the Divine challenge: "Why do you cry out to Me? Speak to the People of Israel and they shall journey forward!" The response to this mandate is the key to attaining the Transcendent level of Atik. When Klal Yisrael emerged on the other side of the split Sea of Reeds, they all, together with Moshe, sang the great *Shirah* / song, the Song of the Sea. On the night of Pesach, we do the same.

This *Shirah* is a song that emanates from within the depths of a profound inner quietude. In that redemptive moment on the other side of the sea, Klal Yisrael sang out from their deepest *Penimiyus* / interiority. Their highest song was an echo of their deepest silence. The Shirah is thus a song that emerges from a place deep within, a place beyond "crying out to Me," beyond all noise and even beyond all prayer.

In the world of duality, sound contradicts or cancels silence, yet, on the deepest level, such opposites are not mutually exclusive. The songs that emerge from the depths of Atik at the end of the Seder are so deep that nothing holds them back or eclipses their interiority, even outward expression. This is the level we all, G-d willing, reach on the night of Pesach, a measure of the level that Klal Yisrael attained at *Kriyas Yam Suf* / the Splitting of the Sea, when they burst into spontaneous song from the deepest point of inner stillness. This is the song of redemption.

☾

Other Books by the Author

RECLAIMING THE SELF
The Way of Teshuvah

Teshuvah is one of the great gifts of life. It speaks of a hope for a better today and empowers us to choose a brighter tomorrow. But what exactly is Teshuvah? How does it work? How can we undo our past and how do we deal with guilt? And what is healthy regret without eroding our self-esteem? In this fascinating and empowering book, the path for genuine transformation and a way to include all of our past in the powerful moment of the now, is explored and demonstrated.

THE MYSTERY OF KADDISH
Understanding the Mourner's Kaddish

The Mystery of Kaddish is an in-depth exploration into the Mourner's Prayer. Throughout Jewish history, there have been many rites and rituals associated with loss and mourning, yet none have prevailed quite like the Mourner's Kaddish Prayer, which has become the definitive ritual of mourning. The book explores the source of this prayer and deconstructs the meaning to better understand the grieving process and how the Kaddish prayer supports and uplifts the bereaved through their own personal journey to healing.

UPSHERNISH: The First Haircut
Exploring the Laws, Customs & Meanings of a Boy's First Haircut

What is the meaning of Upsherin, the traditional celebration of a boy's first haircut at the age of three? Why is a boy's hair allowed to grow freely for his first three years? What is the deeper import of hair in all its lengths and varieties? What is the meaning of hair coverings? Includes a guide to conducting an Upsherin ceremony.

A BOND FOR ETERNITY
Understanding the Bris Milah

What is the Bris Milah – the covenant of circumcision? What does it represent, symbolize and signify? This book provides an in depth and sensitive review of this fundamental Mitzvah. In this little masterpiece of wisdom – profound yet accessible —the deeper meaning of this essential rite of passage and its eternal link to the Jewish people, is revealed and explored.

REINCARNATION AND JUDAISM
The Journey of the Soul

A fascinating analysis of the concept of Gilgul / Reincarnation. Dipping into the fountain of ancient wisdom and modern understanding, this book addresses and answers such basic questions as: What is reincarnation? Why does it occur? And how does it affect us personally?

INNER RHYTHMS
The Kabbalah of MUSIC

Exploring the inner dimension of sound and music, and particularly, how music permeates all aspects of life. The topics range from Deveikus/Unity and Yichudim/Unifications, to the more personal issues, such as Simcha/Happiness and Marirus/ sadness.

MEDITATION AND JUDAISM
Exploring the Jewish Meditative Paths

A comprehensive work encompassing the entire spectrum of Jewish thought, from the sages of the Talmud and the early Kabbalists to the modern philosophers and Chassidic masters. This book is both a scholarly, in-depth study of meditative practices, and a practical, easy to follow guide for any person interested in meditating the Jewish way.

TOWARD THE INFINITE

A book focusing exclusively on the Chassidic approach to meditation known as Hisbonenus. Encompassing the entire meditative experience, it takes the reader on a comprehensive and engaging journey through this unique practice. The book explores the various states of consciousness that a person encounters in the course of the meditation, beginning at a level of extreme self-awareness and concluding with a state of total non-awareness.

THIRTY - TWO GATES OF WISDOM
into the Heart of Kabbalah & Chassidus

What is Kabbalah? And what are the differences between the theoretical, meditative, magical and personal Kabbalistic teachings? What are the four paths of interpreting the teachings of the ARIzal? What did Chassidus teach? These are some of the fundamental issues expanded upon in this text. And then, more specifically, why are there so many names of G-d and what do they represent? What are the key concepts of these deeper teachings?

The book explores the grand narrative of the great chain of reality, how there was and is a movement from the Infinite Oneness of Hashem to a world of (apparent) duality and multiplicity.

THE PURIM READER
The Holiday of Purim Explored

With a Persian name, a masquerade dress code and a woman as the heroine, Purim is certainly unusual amongst the Jewish holidays. Most people are very familiar with the costumes, Megilah and revelry, but are mystified by their significance. This book offers a glimpse into the hidden world of Purim, uncovering these mysteries and offering a deeper understanding of this unique holiday.

EIGHT LIGHTS
8 Meditations for Chanukah

What is the meaning and message of Chanukah? What is the spiritual significance of the Lights of the Menorah? What are the Lights telling us? What is the deeper dimension of the Dreidel? Rav Pinson, with his trademark deep learning and spiritual sensitivity guides us through eight meditations relating to the Lights of the Menorah, the eight days of Chanukah, and a fascinating exploration of the symbolism and structure of the Dreidel. Includes a detailed how-to guide for lighting the Chanukah Menorah.

THE IYYUN HAGADAH
An Introduction to the Haggadah

In this beautifully written introduction to Passover and the Haggadah, we are guided through the major themes of Passover and the Seder night. This slim text, addresses the important questions, such as: What is the big deal of Chametz? What are we trying to achieve through conducting a Seder? What's with all that stuff on the Seder Plate? And most importantly, how is this all related to freedom?

PASSPORT TO KABBALAH
A Journey of Inner Transformation

Life is a journey full of ups and downs, inside-outs, and unexpected detours. There are times when we think we know exactly where we want to be headed, and other times when we are so lost we don't even know where we are. This slim book provides readers with a passport of sorts to help them through any obstacles along their path of self-refinement, reflection, and self-transformation.

THE FOUR SPECIES
The Symbolism of the Lulav & Esrog

The Four Species have inspired countless commentaries and traditions and intrigued scholars and mystics alike. In this little masterpiece of wisdom both profound and practical - the deep symbolic roots and nature of the Four Species are explored. The Na'anuim, or ritual of the Lulav movement, is meticulously detailed and Kavanos,, are offered for use with the practice. Includes an illustrated guide to the Lulav Movements.

THE BOOK OF LIFE AFTER LIFE

What is a soul? What happens to us after we physically die?

What is consciousness, and can it survive without a physical brain?

Can we remember our past lives?

Do near-death experiences prove immortality?

What is Gan Eden? Resurrection?

Exploring the possibility of surviving death, the near-death experience and a glimpse into what awaits us after this life.

(This book is an updated and expanded version of the book; Jewish Wisdom of the Afterlife)

THE GARDEN OF PARADOX:
The Essence of Non - Dual Kabbalah

This book is a Primer on the Essential Philosophy of Kabbalah presented as a series of 3 conversations, revealing the mysteries of Creator, Creation and Consciousness. With three representational students, embodying respectively, the philosopher, the activist and the mystic, the book, tackles the larger questions of life. Who is G-d? Who am I? Why do I exist? What is my purpose in this life? Written in clear and concise prose, the text, gently guides the reader towards making sense of life's paradoxes and living meaningfully.

BREATHING & QUIETING THE MIND

Achieving a sense of self-mastery and inner freedom demands that we gain a measure of hegemony over our thoughts. We learn to choose out thoughts so that we are not at the mercy of whatever belches up to the mind. Through quieting the mind and conscious breathing we can slow the onrush of anxious, scattered thinking and come to a deeper awareness of the interconnectedness of all of life.

Source texts are included in translation, with how-to-guides for the various practices.

VISUALIZATION AND IMAGERY:
Harnessing the Power of our Mind's Eye

We assume that what we see with our eyes is absolute. Yet, beyond our ability to choose what we see, we have the ability to choose how we see. This directly translates into how we experience life. In a world saturated with visual imagery, our senses are continuously assaulted with Kelipa/empty/fantasy imagery that we would not necessarily choose. These images can negatively affect our relationship with ourselves, with the world around us, and with the Divine. This volume seeks to show us how we can alter that which we observe through harnessing the power of our mind's eye, the inner sanctum of our imagination. We thus create a new way to see and experience the world. This book teaches us how to utilize visualization and imagery as a way to develop our spiritual sensitivity and higher intuition, and ultimately achieve Deveikus/Unity with Hashem.

SOUND AND VIBRATION:
Tuning into the Echoes of Creation

Through our perception of sound and vibration we internalize the world around us. What we hear, and how we process that hearing, has a profound impact on how we experience life. What we hear can empower us or harm us. A defining human capacity is to harness the power sound -- through speech, dialogue, and song, and through listening to others. Hearing is primary dimension of our existence. In fact, as a fetus our ears were the first fully operating sensory organs to develop.

This book will guide you in methods of utilizing the power of sound and vibration to heal and maintain mental, emotional and spiritual health, to fine-tune your Midos and even to guide you into deeper levels of Deveikus / conscious unity with Hashem. The vibratory patterns of the Aleph-Beis are particularly useful portals into our deeper conscious selves. Through chanting and deep listening, we can use the letters and sounds to shift our very mindset, to induce us into a state of presence and spiritual elevation.

THE POWER OF CHOICE:
A Practical Guide to Conscious Living

It is the essential premise of this book that we hold the key to unlock many of the gates that seem closed to us and keep us from living our fullest life. That key we all hold is the power to choose. The Power of Choice is the primary tool that we have at our disposal to impact the world and effect change within our own lives. We often give up this power to outside forces such as the market, media, politicians or peer pressure; or to internal forces that often function beyond our conscious control such as ego, anger, lust, greed or jealousy. Making conscious, compassionate and creative decisions is the cornerstone of living a mature and meaningful life.

MYSTIC TALES FROM THE EMEK HAMELECH

Mystic Tales of the Emek HaMelech, is a wondrous and inspiring collection of stories culled from the Emek HaMelech. Emek HaMelech, from which these stories have been taken, (as well as its author) is a bit of a mystery. But like all good mysteries, it is one worth investigating. In this spirit the present volume is being offered to the general public in the merit and memory of its saintly author, as well as in the hopes of introducing a vital voice of deeper Torah teaching and tradition to a contemporary English speaking audience

INNER WORLDS OF JEWISH PRAYER
A Guide to Develop and Deepen the Prayer Experience

While much attention has been paid to the poetry, history, theology and contextual meaning of the prayers, the intention of this work is to provide a guide to finding meaning and effecting transformation through the prayer experience itself.

Explore: *What happens when we pray? *How do we enter the mind-state of prayer? *Learning to incorporate the body into the prayers. *Discover techniques to enhance and deepen prayer and make it a transformative experience.

This empowering and inspiring text, demonstrates how through proper mindset, preparation and dedication, the experience of prayer can be deeply transformative and ultimately, life-altering.

WRAPPED IN MAJESTY
Tefillin - Exploring the Mystery

Tefillin, the black boxes and leather straps that are worn during prayer, are curiously powerful and mysterious. Within the inky black boxes lie untold secrets. In this profound, passionate and thought-provoking text, the multi-dimensional perspectives of Tefillin are explored and revealed. Magically weaving together all levels of Torah including the Peshat (literal observation), to Remez (allegorical), to Derush, (homiletic), to Sod (hidden) into one beautiful tapestry. Inspirational and instructive, Wrapped in Majesty: Tefillin, will make putting on the Tefillin more meaningful and inspiring.

SECRETS OF THE MIKVAH:
Waters of Transformation

A Mikvah is a pool of water used for the purpose of ritual immersion; a place where one moves from a state of Tumah; impurity, blockage and death— to a place of Teharah; purity, fluidity and life.

In SECRETS OF THE MIKVAH, Rav Pinson delves into the transformative powers of the Mikvah with his trademark all-encompassing perspective that ranges from the literal, Pshat observation and Halachic implications of the texts, to the allegorical, the philosophical, and finally, to the deep secrets of the

Mikvah as revealed by Kabbalah and Chassidus.

This insightful and inspirational text demonstrates how immersion in a Mikvah can be a transformative and life-altering practice, and includes various Kavanos—deep intentions—for all people, through various stages of life, that empower and enrich the immersion experience.

THE SPIRAL OF TIME:
A 12 Part Series on the Months of the Year.
The following titles from the series are now available!

THE SPIRAL OF TIME:
Unraveling the Yearly Cycle

Many centuries ago, the Sages of Israel were the foremost authority in the fields of both astronomical calculation and astrological wisdom, including the deeper interpretations of the cycles and seasons. Over time, this wisdom became hidden within the esoteric teachings of the Torah, and as a result was known only to students and scholars of the deepest depths of the tradition. More recently, the great teachers, from R.Yitzchak Luria (the Arizal) to the Baal Shem Tov, taught that as the world approaches the Era of Redemption, it is a Mitzvah / spiritual obligation to broadly reveal this wisdom.

"The Spiral of Time" is volume 1 is a series of 12 books, and serves as an introductory book to the basic concepts and nature of the Hebrew calendar and explores the special day of Rosh Chodesh.

THE MONTH OF IYYAR: EVOLVING THE SELF
& The Holiday of LAG B'OMER

The month of IYYAR is the second month of the spring, a month that connects the Redemption from Egypt in Nissan with the Revelation of Torah in Sivan. The Chai/ Eighteenth day of the Month is the day we celebrate the Rashbi (Rabbi Shimon Bar Yochai) and the revealing of the hidden aspects of the Torah. This is the 'Holiday' of Lag b'Omer. The book explores the unique quality of this special month, a month that has a Mitzvah of counting the Omer every day. In addition, the book explores the roots and significance of the mystical 'holiday' of Lag b'Omer. Including the customs & Practices of Lag b'Omer, such as, bonfires, bows & arrows, parades, Upsherin, and more.

THE MONTH OF SIVAN:
The Art of Receiving: Shavuos and Matan Torah

Sivan is the third month of the lunar cycle. One is a singularity. Two is division. Three is harmony, a unity that synthesizes individuality and multiplicity, Heaven and Earth, Spirituality and Physicality. During this month we celebrate Shavuos and the giving of the Torah, the ultimate expression of the unity of the Above and Below and we aspire to connect with the Keser/Crown of Torah that Transcends and yet includes all Worlds. Learning how to truly receive Higher wisdom in our Lower faculties is the mental, emotional, and spiritual exercise of the month.

THE MONTHS OF TAMUZ AND AV:
Embracing Brokenness -
17th of Tamuz, Tisha B'Av, & Tu B'Av

Each month and season of the year, radiates with distinct Divine qualities and unique opportunities for growth and Tikkun.

The summer month of Tamuz and Av contain the longest and hottest days of the year. The raised temperature is indicative of a corresponding spiritual heat, a time of harsher judgement and potential destruction, such as the destructions of the first and second Beis HaMikdash, which began on the 17th of Tamuz and culminated on the 9th and 10th of Av.

A few days later, on Tu b'Av, the darkness is transformed and reveals the greatest light and possibility for new life. During these summer months of Tamuz and Av we embrace our brokenness so that we can heal and transform darkness into light.

THE MONTH OF ELUL:
Days of Introspection and Transformation

Each month of the year radiates with a distinct quality and provides unique opportunities for growth and personal transformation. Elul, as the final month of the spring/summer season is connected to endings. Elul gives us the strength to be able to finish strong, to end well. Elul also serves as a month of preparation for the New Year/Rosh Hashanah.

We inhale our past year, ending with wisdom and then we also gain the wisdom to begin anew and exhale a positive year into being. The mental, emotional, and spiritual objective of this month is introspection and the reclaiming of our inner purity and wholeness.

THE MONTH OF TISHREI:
A Time of Rebirth & Upward Movement

Each month of the year radiates with distinct Divine qualities and unique opportunities for growth and spiritual illumination. As Tishrei begins the new yearly cycle, it is an appropriate month to introspect, reflect and resolve to move forward and preserve moving forward into the more inward months of the winter. This month creates the space to unburden ourselves from our negativities, and enter a more sacred, grounded sacred space. In Tishrei we are given the gift of forgiveness and then the ability to truly regain our space and inner joy.

THE MONTH OF CHESHVAN:
Navigating Transitions, Elevating the Fall

Directly on the heels of the inspiring and holiday-filled month of Tishrei, Cheshvan is a month that is quiet and devoid of holidays. In the month of Cheshvan we use the stored up energies of the previous months to self-generate our inspiration and creativity and provide ourselves with the strength to rise up after a fall. In Cheshvan we are entering into a stormier, wetter and colder season. It is a month of transition. The mental, emotional and spiritual objective of this month is to weather the transitions, learn to self-generate and stand tall. And if we do fall, we use the quality of this month to get back up and do so with more conviction, strength, wisdom and clarity.

THE MONTH OF KISLEV:
Rekindling Hope, Dreams and Trust

Kislev is the final month of the fall. Throughout this month, daylight progressively shortens, and the temperatures drop. Towards the end of the month, at the darkest hour, the winter solstice arrives and we begin the celebration of Chanukah. We commemorate the miracle of a small jug of oil that burned for eight nights, and as we celebrate, daylight expands. In the month of Kislev-despite the darkness, or perhaps because of it-we have the ability to tap into the Ohr HaGanuz, the hidden light of hope that rekindles our dreams and aspirations.

THE MONTH OF TEVES:
Refining Relationships, Elevating the Body

The quality of Teves is generally harsh—much like its counterpart Tamuz in the summer, thus the tendency for many is to hunker down, retract, curl up and wait for the month to pass by, only to reemerge when the harshness has dissipated. Think for a moment about the 'easier' months of the year, which, like gentle waves in the ocean, carry us where we want to go. We can ride these energies easily and they can propel us forward effortlessly, we just need to go with the overall flow, so to speak. The harsher months, on the other hand, can be compared to the more powerful waves that emanate from the belly of the ocean, which come forcefully crashing down and can easily drown a person before they even realize what has happened. However, those who want to utilize the momentum of the powerful energy that is available during such times can, with caution and creativity, harness these intense waves and ride them higher and farther than other, more gentle circumstances may allow. However, harnessing the power of Tohu, the raw energy of the body, does in fact need to be approached with great care and attention.

THE MONTH OF SHEVAT: ELEVATING EATING
& The Holiday of Tu b'Shevat

Each month of the year radiates with a distinct Divine energy and thus unique opportunities for growth, *Tikkun* and illumination. According to the deeper teachings of the Torah, all of these distinct qualities, opportunities and natural phenomena correspond to a certain data set. That is, the nature of each month is elucidated by a specific letter of the Aleph Beis, a tribe, verse, human sense, and so forth. The month of Shevat is particularly connected to food and our relationship to bodily intake. During this month we celebrate Tu b'Shevat, the New Year of the Tree, and aspire to create a proper and physically/emotionally/spiritually healthy relationship with food.

THE MONTH OF ADAR:
Transformation Through Laughter & Holy Doubt

Each month of the year radiates with distinct Divine qualities and unique opportunities for growth and spiritual illumination. As Adar concludes the monthly cycle of the year, as well as the solar phenomena of the winter, it is an appropriate month to think about our essential identity, before moving out to meet the world come spring. This month we strive to create a healthy relationship with holy humor, unbounded joy, and a general sense of lightness of being. Through the work of Adar we transform negative, crippling doubt and uncertainties into radical wonderment and openness.

New Book!
THE MYSTERY OF SHABBOS
Shabbat Rediscovered

Delving into the transformative power of Shabbos. With an all-encompassing perspective that ranges from the literal, Pshat observation and Halachic implications of the texts, to the allegorical, the philosophical, and finally, to the deeper secrets as revealed by Kabbalah and Chassidus, creating an elegant tapestry of thought and experience. THE MYSTERY OF SHABBOS is a profound meditation on the meaning of Shabbos and demonstrates the physical, emotional, mental and spiritual possibilities available and given to us with the gift of Shabbos. Studying and contemplating this inspired text on the depths of Shabbos will unveil a redemptive light in your experience of the Seventh Day -- and by extension, every day of your life.

www.ingramcontent.com/pod-product-compliance
Lightning Source LLC
Chambersburg PA
CBHW060755100426
42813CB00004B/829